Inside Tax Law

What Matters and Why

Inside Tax Law

What Matters and Why

Stephen Utz

Professor of Law
University of Connecticut School of Law

Wolters Kluwer
Law & Business

Copyright © 2011 CCH Incorporated.

Published by Wolters Kluwer Law & Business in New York.

Wolters Kluwer Law & Business serves customers worldwide with CCH, Aspen Publishers, and Kluwer Law International products. (www.wolterskluwerlb.com)

No part of this publication may be reproduced or transmitted in any form or by any means, electronic or mechanical, including photocopy, recording, or utilized by any information storage or retrieval system, without written permission from the publisher. For information about permissions or to request permissions online, visit us at www.wolterskluwerlb.com, or a written request may be faxed to our permissions department at 212-771-0803.

To contact Customer Service, e-mail customer.service@wolterskluwer.com, call 1-800-234-1660, fax 1-800-901-9075, or mail correspondence to:

Wolters Kluwer Law & Business
Attn: Order Department
PO Box 990
Frederick, MD 21705

Printed in the United States of America.

1 2 3 4 5 6 7 8 9 0

ISBN 978-0-7355-9440-1

Library of Congress Cataloging-in-Publication Data

Utz, Stephen, 1947-
  Inside tax law : what matters and why / Stephen Utz.
    p. cm.
  Includes index.
  ISBN 978-0-7355-9440-1
  1. Taxation—Law and legislation—United States.   I. Title.
  KF6289.U89 2011
  345.7304—dc23
                        2011025639

SUSTAINABLE FORESTRY INITIATIVE

Certified Chain of Custody
Promoting Sustainable Forestry
www.sfiprogram.org
SFI 00754

About Wolters Kluwer Law & Business

Wolters Kluwer Law & Business is a leading global provider of intelligent information and digital solutions for legal and business professionals in key specialty areas, and respected educational resources for professors and law students. Wolters Kluwer Law & Business connects legal and business professionals as well as those in the education market with timely, specialized authoritative content and information-enabled solutions to support success through productivity, accuracy and mobility.

Serving customers worldwide, Wolters Kluwer Law & Business products include those under the Aspen Publishers, CCH, Kluwer Law International, Loislaw, Best Case, ftwilliam.com and MediRegs family of products.

CCH products have been a trusted resource since 1913, and are highly regarded resources for legal, securities, antitrust and trade regulation, government contracting, banking, pension, payroll, employment and labor, and healthcare reimbursement and compliance professionals.

Aspen Publishers products provide essential information to attorneys, business professionals and law students. Written by preeminent authorities, the product line offers analytical and practical information in a range of specialty practice areas from securities law and intellectual property to mergers and acquisitions and pension/benefits. Aspen's trusted legal education resources provide professors and students with high-quality, up-to-date and effective resources for successful instruction and study in all areas of the law.

Kluwer Law International products provide the global business community with reliable international legal information in English. Legal practitioners, corporate counsel and business executives around the world rely on Kluwer Law journals, looseleafs, books, and electronic products for comprehensive information in many areas of international legal practice.

Loislaw is a comprehensive online legal research product providing legal content to law firm practitioners of various specializations. Loislaw provides attorneys with the ability to quickly and efficiently find the necessary legal information they need, when and where they need it, by facilitating access to primary law as well as state-specific law, records, forms and treatises.

Best Case Solutions is the leading bankruptcy software product to the bankruptcy industry. It provides software and workflow tools to flawlessly streamline petition preparation and the electronic filing process, while timely incorporating ever-changing court requirements.

ftwilliam.com offers employee benefits professionals the highest quality plan documents (retirement, welfare and non-qualified) and government forms (5500/PBGC, 1099 and IRS) software at highly competitive prices.

MediRegs products provide integrated health care compliance content and software solutions for professionals in healthcare, higher education and life sciences, including professionals in accounting, law and consulting.

Wolters Kluwer Law & Business, a division of Wolters Kluwer, is headquartered in New York. Wolters Kluwer is a market-leading global information services company focused on professionals.

For Emily, Clara, and Annabel

Summary of Contents

Contents

Chapter 15. Capitalization and Cost Recovery

Chapter 16. Assignment of Income

Preface

Today, most law students take a tax course, as indeed they should. It is a basic part of legal training, affecting a lawyer's practice in many areas that may not seem tax-sensitive. Fortunately, the subject does not live up to widespread fears that it will be dry or involve difficult math.

Tax is in fact a skeleton key to many financial and everyday relationships. The reason is simple. To measure income and other taxable aspects of our lives, a knowledge of motives, behavior patterns, and especially arm's-length relations is essential. For those who knew little about the real world before law school, tax points a straight path to the practical side of life.

Lawyers, moreover, should not find the subject foreign. Legislatures, courts, and the bar had to invent income taxation on the go, without much help from economists and accountants, because the public at a crucial moment wanted radical tax reform and wanted it right away. People with legal training were up to the task, because they were used to fitting rules to fact patterns. They learned to do this just as the economy and our lives as consumers and investors were emerging in modern form. The result has been a continuing dialogue between lawyerly skills and the country's evolving economic life.

Inevitably, tax offers an effective introduction to the study of public policy. Most governments need taxes to survive. The process of filing returns, paying taxes, and enduring audits puts people in closer contact with the government than any other interface. Refinements in tax law therefore face an intensely democratic testing ground, which is the foreground of tax policy, both at a general level and in the specifics that populate an introductory tax course. This book draws attention to the one-on-one input of the taxpaying public.

Any tax course must also include a healthy portion of administrative law. We must understand what works and what is too far-fetched, sometimes to the dismay of theorists. But theory becomes all the more compelling when it does offer good solutions to tax challenges.

One enjoyable feature of the subject, which this book tries to keep at the forefront, is the delicate interplay of tax rules that ultimately achieve a close harmony, a more coherent result than is either possible or necessary in other legal areas. Getting there, however, requires a certain openness on the reader's part, an ability to go forward with incomplete familiarity, and to make retrospective connections. In the end, most students find the subject satisfying precisely because it circles back on itself in this way.

This book explains the basics. It selects topics that are common to most introductory courses and offers simple explanations with related problems. The level of detail is tailored to standard course books. There are a few exceptions: there may be more here, for example, on depreciation and interest imputation than your professor will cover, but approaches vary and it is worthwhile to be inclusive.

Each chapter begins with an Overview and includes Sidebar comments and FAQs set apart from the main text. Each chapter ends with a Summary and Connections that link the content learned in this chapter with what readers have learned or will learn in other chapters. The table of cases and Code sections will help you to link your course with explanations in this book. Most of these features are common to the Inside series, but they are particularly well suited to a book on income tax because of its recursive nature, the circling back referred to above. They will also help you navigate, if your course follows a slightly different path through the material. The book includes frequent detailed examples as well. This combination of elements will make it easier for you to conduct your own dialogue with the subject.

In summary, this book is about an engrossing subject, central to the lawyer's calling. It identifies and stresses what is peculiar to the student's first encounter with its subject, always intent on dispelling the clouds that sometimes cling to the landmarks.

I thank Lew Kurlantzick, Ruth Mason, Sachin Pandya, Michelle Querijero, and Peter Siegelman for conversations that improved the book's substance; Lynn Churchill for the chance to write it for Aspen; Carmen Corral-Reid for her editorial support; and anonymous reviewers for their valuable suggestions.

Stephen Utz
June 2011

Inside Tax Law

What Matters and Why

Getting Started: Basic Facts, Concepts, and Techniques

1

Tax is more like other law school subjects than you might expect. The reasoning of courts and government officials in deciding tax cases is

OVERVIEW

specialized but not exotic. Tax concepts have fuzzy edges like those in tort or contract law, and the lawyer's tasks in these fields are closely akin. Above all, tax law is partly common law, and broad principles that go beyond the statutory source are pervasively present. In this chapter, we first notice some special features of the legal environment, among them the sources of U.S. tax law — the Internal Revenue Code, case law, and administrative pronouncements. Then we focus on basic terms used in a wide range of U.S. tax rules. Along the way, we pause to notice a robust body of partly popular, partly theoretical thinking that inspired the income tax and to which the law remains responsive.

A. THE LAWYERLY APPROACH TO TAX CONCEPTS

B. LEGAL MATERIALS

1. Interpreting the Code
2. Common-Law Principles
3. Regulatory Process
4. Tax Reform Issues
5. Legislative History
6. Judicial and Administrative Rulings
7. Constitutional Issues
8. Filling in Forms?

A. The Lawyerly Approach to Tax Concepts

The introductory tax course is mostly about the conceptual scheme of the income tax, with only incidental concern for its mechanical side. Most law students find this perspective more interesting than they anticipated. It is also challenging. You learn to live with clusters of concepts that do not always fit into neat boxes. Fundamental concepts and the network of rules that articulate them cannot resolve all issues that arise in novel fact situations — in tax as in other areas of law.

Even where broad tax principles are concerned, a sophisticated approach has to be broken down into well-focused frames. The purpose of this book is to guide you through the basic frames and give you a way of piecing them together. Sometimes frames overlap, because large parts of income tax law exhibit an underlying unity. The areas of overlap will be highlighted. For example, you will have no trouble understanding the rule that classifies stolen money as income that may be taxed; how this fits into the broader set of rules about control over disputed gains will not be obvious at first, but we will learn how the courts harmonized these matters. Again, pay for work done is a paradigmatic type of income, and it is usually no problem to distinguish such pay from other benefits, but not always — the corner office given to a key employee may look like additional compensation to her coworkers, but it is never considered income. Conceptual relationships among superficially disparate rules are of utmost concern to us.

B. Legal Materials

(1) Interpreting the Code

We can be grateful that there is indeed an income tax statute, more familiarly known as the Internal Revenue Code. Long and detailed, the Code's basic framework has remained constant for more than half a century. We will concentrate only on those of its provisions that are legally puzzling and that will challenge your interpretative skills. But reading the statute is only part of the job.

(2) Common-Law Principles

Yes, there is precedent in tax law. Tax lawyers and judges use the methods of common law, which means that they are concerned at times with rules that do not have a straightforward legislative source. These rules emerge from and reflect the purposes and practicality of taxing income. The first-year law school curriculum should stand you in good stead in dealing with them. Statute and precedent interact, however, and you have to pay close attention to the interaction to learn this subject matter.

(3) Regulatory Process

The IRS not only collects taxes, of course; it also interprets the Code. You will learn something of how the agency works and how it shapes the law. Congress and the courts have the last word, but they defer to the expertise of the IRS in many respects; when the courts have not spoken, and often even when they have, regulations are the government's front line in encounters with the taxpayer. If you are new to administrative law, introductory tax offers a prime example of this halfway house between legislation and adjudication.

(4) Tax Reform Issues

The tax law is not perfect. Sometimes we need to know how it could be improved to see why courts and tax officials interpret it as they do. The government's reading of the law, however, exhibits a mix of idealism and cunning. It may dedicate resources to selective enforcement—going after apparent abuse to prevent compliant taxpayers from rebelling—even though the abuse is economic folly that would soon go away by itself. It may also *not* challenge dubious tax strategies to which the political party in power is well disposed. On the whole, however, the diverse sources of tax wisdom within the government perform creditably.

It is useful to keep in mind who are the main tax interpreters in the legislative and executive branches: Congress has tax experts spread among the tax staff of the Senate Finance Committee and the House Ways and Means Committee, as well as the staff of the Joint Committee on Taxation. On the executive side, the Tax Legislative Counsel's Office, a group in the Treasury Department that is not part of the IRS, formulates broad tax legislative strategy and has a hand in writing regulations; the Tax Division of the Justice Department represents the government in all tax litigation except that before the Tax Court, which entails formulating many of the government positions that we study in appellate decisions; the IRS itself announces interpretative positions that originate in the Chief Counsel's Office, which is responsible for Tax Court litigation, and in the Rulings Branch, which rules on private and administrative requests for tax determinations of narrowly drawn taxpayer issues.

When you put these voices together, the result is not always harmonious, but important themes win out. It is the tax lawyer's job to tell the difference between trial balloons and more assured initiatives, and a grasp of the merits at least helps. In Chapter 2, we examine some prominent nongovernmental sources of income tax theory and possible reform.

F   A   Q

Q: Given the division of tax authority and the difficulty of interpreting the Code, is the law in the area open to easy manipulation by the unscrupulous?

A: No. Much of our income tax law is straightforward. For example, the statutory definition of "dependent," on which a deduction called dependents' allowances turns,[1] is extremely detailed and seems to answer all questions that could arise. On the other hand, Congress

---

[1] See Chapter 10.B.2.

chose, for an apparently strategic reason, not to define "income" explicitly in the Code. The courts and the IRS have since answered most but not all questions about this basic concept. What little uncertainty remains does not encourage abuse or noncompliance.

(5) Legislative History

Legislative history can of course shed light on the meaning and purpose of particular Code sections. It can also expose their shortcomings. Given that not all legislators are at home with tax issues, their work is predictably uneven, as is that of the executive branch when it has an active hand in the process. For example, Congress reacted sharply to a Supreme Court decision approving tax regulations under which a landlord could have been taxed immediately on the value of tenant-created leasehold improvements if the tenant defaulted on the lease. The Code provisions that Congress inserted are short and simple but display a technical awareness of the interplay between tax-free acquisition of property and later tax consequences. Someone with expertise must have been involved in the process. The result is reasonably trouble-free.[2] On the other hand, Congress has been known to muff it. When the House and Senate disagreed on how severely to restrict the deductibility of business meals, the language of the Code section they agreed upon was at best ambiguous about how directly a meal must serve business purposes to be deductible. We must recognize that the restriction is halfhearted in order to apply it. It has been suggested that Washington, D.C.'s K Street, home of expense-account restaurants and the lobbyists who eat there, got what it wanted.[3]

(6) Judicial and Administrative Rulings

Two main bodies of precedent — judicial decisions and IRS determinations — shape and make substantive contributions to U.S. income tax law. Moreover, the IRS sometimes talks to itself and publishes the soliloquy. The internal monologue is to be found in the publication of "procedures," "notices," and "announcements" that do not technically have the force of precedent, either for courts or for the agency in disputes with taxpayers, and yet can be "persuasive." We will consider what that means later in this subsection.

(a) Courts

First, one should be aware of two important features of judicial decisions. Three partly distinct court hierarchies handle tax cases: (1) the federal court system (U.S. District Courts, Courts of Appeal, and the Supreme Court) has general jurisdiction over claims of all kinds; (2) the U.S. Claims Court, from which appeals lie to the U.S. Court of Appeals for the Federal Circuit, then to the Supreme Court; and (3) the Tax Court, with appeals to the U.S. Courts of Appeal and Supreme Court.

The last of these is the most commonly used. Appeals from Tax Court decisions are to the U.S. Court of Appeals for the federal circuit in which the taxpayer bringing the case resides, and thereafter to the U.S. Supreme Court. Tax Court judges are thought to have greater expertise in tax matters than other courts, which can be a

---

[2] See Chapter 8.B(2) for the details.
[3] See Chapter 12D(7) for the details.

reason for avoiding the Tax Court. The advantage of going there is that a taxpayer can ask this court to consider any disputed tax liability within 90 days after the IRS issues a Notice of Deficiency. The deficiency neither must nor *may* be paid in full beforehand. The Tax Court is established under Article One of the Constitution, not under Article Three, and so its judges do not have constitutionally protected life appointments; at present, the standard judicial term is 15 years. It is also useful to remember that the Tax Court considers its own past decisions to be binding precedent only for subsequent cases appealable to the same U.S. Court of Appeals.[4] Thus, when you find a decided case on all fours with the issue in a new case, you must check to see whether the earlier case arose within the same federal circuit.

Once a taxpayer has fully paid a disputed tax liability, either spontaneously or in response to a deficiency notice, he or she may petition the government for a refund. Refund cases are within the jurisdiction of the normal federal court system — district courts, courts of appeal, and the Supreme Court. The district courts have less experience with tax issues than the Tax Court, but it is not clear that this makes any difference in outcomes.

Instead of going to district court, a taxpayer can choose to file a claim for a tax refund in the claims court, whose jurisdiction is limited to refund claims, whether arising under tax or other federal law. Again, the claims court has less experience with tax issues than the tax courts. Some of its decisions have been more adventurous than experts would have expected from the Tax Court, but there is no yardstick for comparison.

The courts of appeal, including the federal circuit, do not treat each other's decisions as binding precedent. Conflicts among the circuits arise over tax issues as in other areas of law. The Supreme Court does not always deign to resolve these conflicts, though a robust history of conflict often tempts the high court to get involved.

F A Q

Q: Who wins when the Supreme Court disagrees with the IRS over a matter of federal tax law?

A: Unless Congress intervenes by addressing the issue with new legislation, the judicial holding is, well, supreme, and administrative practice has to conform to it. The IRS can read such a decision broadly or narrowly. In several notable instances, controlling Supreme Court decisions have lasted for decades, and in some instances, even Congress has brought the income tax law into conformity with the judicial view. The IRS can choose to litigate an issue, even when a judge or panel of the same court has decided a similar issue.

(b) Administrative Law

The IRS issues regulations and rulings that interpret the Code. Formally, the Department of Treasury promulgates tax regulations, which are accordingly called

---

[4]*Golsen v. Comm'r*, 54 T.C. 742 (1970), *aff'd*, 445 F.2d 985 (10th Cir. 1971).

Treasury Regulations. Most of these deal with the income tax. The IRS is bound by them in all cases that arise while they are in effect, though it can modify them prospectively, within the limits of administrative law. Some Code provisions specifically authorize the Treasury to interpret parts of the Code. The resulting regulations are sometimes called "legislative." But the Treasury or IRS interprets virtually all Code provisions in regulations that are not specially authorized; these regulations are sometimes called "interpretative." The distinction between legislative and interpretative regulations has rarely mattered to the courts, and recent cases suggest that it now matters less than ever.[5] Regulations of general application, as we have seen, bind the government in disputes with taxpayers over events that arise while the regulations are in effect. This is also true of rulings on particular fact patterns that are published as Revenue Rulings. Other rulings — most of them formally called Private Letter Rulings (PLRs) or Technical Advice Memoranda (TAMs)[6] — are issued to specific taxpayers and do not purport to apply to all taxpayers alike, largely because they are based on detailed fact patterns that would be hard to duplicate. They do not bind the IRS in other cases.

F   A   Q

Q: Given that the IRS is last in the hierarchy of authorities on tax law, do its views matter at all when a court has ruled to the contrary?

A: Most tax disputes begin and end as disputes between the taxpayer and the IRS. Within the administrative process, the views of the IRS carry great weight. Administrative interpretations inevitably influence the tax planning of risk-averse taxpayers, because the chance of winning only in a court challenge to the agency's position may be considerably less than that of persuading the agency that its own views favor the taxpayer.

The IRS also publishes an array of announcements, notices, and other statements. Some have the effect of regulations or Revenue Rulings because they are addressed to the taxpaying public; among them are, for example, updates on Code provisions that adjust dollar limits or thresholds annually to reflect inflation. Other types of IRS announcement, however, deserve notice here, namely Revenue Procedures and General Counsel Memoranda (GCMs). Revenue Procedures are technically addressed to IRS personnel, not to the public, and they state procedural standards that often signal substantive legal positions. They do so by setting forth essential factual allegations a taxpayer must make in an application for a private ruling. GCMs often speak in substantive legal terms about broad tax issues, but these are addressed to the litigation staff of the IRS and neither bind the government nor always accord perfectly with regulations and published rulings. Most introductory courses rely on few IRS materials beyond the regulations and published rulings.

---

[5] *See Mayo Foundation v. U.S.*, 131 S. Ct. 704 (Jan. 11, 2011).
[6] These labels have different meanings, and the two groups of rulings do not coincide exactly, but they do in most contexts.

(7) Constitutional Issues

The Constitution, as first ratified, did not permit Congress to impose any "direct" tax not apportioned to the population, as measured by the federal census.[7] Most taxes in the eighteenth century were indirect. Though paid by people, they were triggered and measured by features of transactions, such as the values of things being transferred or sold. Political opinion may have disfavored direct taxes, which openly target taxpayers rather than transactions or property, and are more likely to require the government to intrude on the taxpayer's privacy. Apportioned direct taxes in Britain and France directed lower-level governmental subdivisions to raise shares of a total revenue goal but let local officials decide who would pay what. The Supreme Court held an early federal income tax to be unconstitutional as an unapportioned direct tax.[8] This eventually led to the proposal and ratification of the Sixteenth Amendment, which exempts federal direct taxes on "incomes" from the apportionment requirement.

It is unlikely that any lively constitutional issue will come up, and introductory courses usually confine themselves to noting one case and perhaps a few unresolved issues that have a constitutional dimension. The D.C. Circuit recently surprised us all by holding a provision of the Code unconstitutional, but the panel then vacated its original opinion and resolved the case on nonconstitutional grounds.[9] Commentators were almost universally unsympathetic to the court's first holding. We all know, however, that nothing in constitutional jurisprudence is immutable.

At present, two constitutional issues under the Sixteenth Amendment pose difficulties for current and potential legislation. Is a federal penalty on individuals who fail to buy health insurance an unapportioned direct tax? Could a national consumption tax be levied as a direct tax, requiring annual tax returns resembling income tax returns (the "postcard" return of the "flat tax")? The Supreme Court may have occasion to decide both questions in the near future.

(8) Filling in Forms?

We have to draw the line somewhere, and this is it. Still, most tax instructors invite students to look at a few tax forms in order to orient themselves for certain substantive issues. Not a big part of the basic tax course, it may nevertheless help make the legal issues more concrete.

C. Importance of the Federal Income Tax in Revenue Terms

No one is likely to test you on this, but it is good to have some idea how much money the income tax brings in and how this compares with other federal and state taxes. Table 1.1 shows the pre-refund figures of federal and state taxes collected for 2006. (More detailed federal tax statistics are available at the IRS's website, *www.irs.gov*. State tax statistics are given in some detail at *www.census.gov*.) Social security and Medicare taxes withheld from employees' paychecks make up the employment tax.

---

[7]Const. Art. I, §9.4.
[8]*Pollock v. Farmers' Loan & Tr. Co.*, 157 U.S. 429 (1895).
[9]*Murphy v. I.R.S.*, 460 F.3d 79 (D.C. Cir. 2006), *mod.* 493 F.3d 170 (D.C. Cir. 2007), *cert. denied*, 128 S. Ct. 2050 (2008).

TABLE 1.1	Federal and State Income Tax Collected, 2006

Type of Return	Gross Collections (Millions of $)	Percentage of Total
Individual Income Tax	$1,236,259	31%
Corporate Tax	$380,925	18%
Employment Tax	$814,819	25%
Excise Taxes	$1,970	Under 1%
Gift Taxes	$57,990	Under 2%
Estate Taxes	$26,717	Under 1%
Aggregate State Taxes	$706,335	22%
Total Federal and State Taxes	$3,225,015	

F   A   Q

Q: How does the tax on corporate income differ from the individual income tax?

A: Most Code provisions concerning income and deductions and extra-statutory principles apply to both. Some deductions are not available to corporations because they are particularly tied to human functioning, such as the allowance for dependents (§§151, 152) and the medical expense deduction (§215). Others can only be taken by corporations, such as the deduction for dividends received by one corporation from another (§263). On the whole, introductory tax courses do not cover the corporate tax, but corporate tax courses assume familiarity with what is covered in an introductory course.

Conspicuously, the federal income tax is the biggest in terms of total amounts collected — almost one-third. Gift, estate, and excise taxes (on gasoline, heavy trucks, etc.) are tiny by comparison. About 35 percent of all state taxes are income taxes. State income tax law draws heavily on federal income tax law. Many concepts and rules are borrowed outright, and a significant number of state income tax calculations are based directly on numbers taken from the taxpayer's federal tax return. State property taxes, on the other hand, are a special case because, unlike virtually all of the other taxes listed here, their revenue is substantially returned to taxpayers in clearly defined benefits, like police and fire protection, roads, schools, and other municipal services. In 2006, property taxes accounted for less than 2 percent of federal and state taxes. Overall, the federal income tax is the most important tax in sheer volume as well as in legal prominence. It makes sense that it claims more attention in law school curricula than other taxes.

D. Comparing Exclusions and Deductions

Items of income are first added together and are then reduced by deductions in computing net taxable income. It is useful to focus briefly on the important difference between deducting amounts from gross income and simply not including them in the first place. In some respects, an **exclusion** is like a deduction, but whereas certain deductions are statutorily restricted, exclusions are not.

Imagine that you are adding beans to a jar through a broad-rimmed funnel — gross income is the beans. A large part of basic tax law is about telling the difference between beans and foreign objects that should not go into the jar in the first place. Items can be *included* in or *excluded* from gross income. Most tax courses begin with a survey of some principal inclusions and exclusions. There are statutory *inclusions* because, as we have seen, the sweeping definition of gross income in section 61 would otherwise leave us in doubt as to the handling of some borderline items. There are statutory and judicial *exclusions*, however, for a variety of reasons: some exclusions represent a judgment that particular items are not income, while others serve administrative purposes or implement nontax policy. We will soon be discussing some of the latter, because they are among the first topics addressed in this type of course.

A separate task follows the funneling of the beans into the jar. Sometimes beans do not just fall from the sky but grow from other beans. If some of last year's beans seed for the current crop, we must decide whether some of the resulting

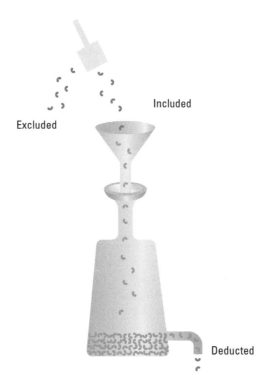

Included

Excluded

Deducted

FIGURE 1.1   THE INS AND OUTS OF INCLUSIONS AND DEDUCTIONS

beans should be eliminated to compensate for those used up in the process. This would look like the deduction of costs of earning income. It is only bottom-line income to which the income tax applies. When we deduct our costs, we adjust the proceeds to make sure we don't count what we started with, as part of something new, as profit.

Net income, not gross proceeds or gross income, is subject to income tax. Different amounts invested in different profit-making activities may produce the same net profit. We want to treat investment choices evenhandedly, both on grounds of fairness and not to bias economic agents' decisions with noneconomic incentives. It would in some instances also be unfair to put a thumb on the scale. Section F below says more about both concerns.

The metaphor of the bean jar works pretty well, but not flawlessly. One of its shortcomings may help protect us against making a mistake in understanding the income tax. Deciding what is a bean and what is not a bean is part of the first step described above. Backing out the invested beans, the seed beans, is the second step. Unfortunately, the two steps resemble each other. Both involve reducing the bean collection. Collecting the beans involves separating beans from extraneous stuff. The next step subtracts what are clearly beans from the total bean collection in order to count only new beans as new. Importantly, the stuff we keep out is, in a sense, subtracted just like the beans we take away as part of the second step. *Both steps reduce the bean collection.* Similarly, both exclusions and deductions from income reduce net income and are thus conceptually akin, though not the same thing.

Giving the bean metaphor a rest, consider the fact that most beginning tax courses deal first, and at some length, with exclusions from income, and then later deal with deductions from income. Since these two parts of the course are usually separated from each other by a considerable delay in time, you the student may have a sense of déjà vu when deductions are discussed. You may ask yourself, why are we again talking about things that should be subtracted from income? There is a reason: The policy behind the allowance of deductions is to make sure that only net income is taxed, not gross profits or proceeds. But you may still feel disoriented. So when you get to that point, remind yourself that exclusions are for stray objects, junk masquerading as income, whereas deducted amounts would indeed be income were it not for the fact that they were assets already on hand.

E. Income Tax Rate Structures, Tax Equity, and Tax Neutrality

Given that the public long ago chose income taxation for greater fairness in the distribution of tax burdens, partisan and impartial critics alike have scrutinized wave after wave of income tax law revision for fidelity to that goal. From the outset, income tax fairness has meant more than the equal treatment of similarly situated taxpayers, sometimes called **horizontal equity**. The whole point of the income tax is to go beyond horizontal equity and to tax different levels of income in a way that assures equal tax burdens overall, not only within strata of equal incomes, but between strata. How is this to be done?

Tom Paine argued that fairness required a **progressive** rate structure, one that exacts a higher *rate* of tax from someone with greater means or income than from someone with less.[10] Even an equal or flat rate makes tax burdens increase with income level. The opposite—lower rates for higher levels of income—we now refer to as **regressive**. What does fairness require? Regressive rate structures have no vocal proponents, but the debate between those who favor flat and progressive rate structures is heated. Both sides claim to stand for **vertical equity** and for avoiding regressive tax burdens, that overarching goal of the income tax.

Note that fairness and equity have nothing to do with tax neutrality. A measure is said to be tax neutral if it should not change economic agents' decisions, that is, if it will not bias the market choices people make, including the decision whether to work or not. Real-world income tax systems do not tax leisure—the decision not to work—although the rewards of profit-seeking effort are taxed. This is a clear violation of tax neutrality: It may bias people against work. Tax legislation does, however, seem to be guided by the goal of tax neutrality in many respects.

SUMMARY

■ The federal income tax accounts for the largest share of federal tax revenues—about one-third of the total.

■ The Code does not define "income," and some problems arise at the edges of otherwise uncontroversial types of income like personal service income and income from dealings in property.

■ The sources of U.S. income tax law are statutory, regulatory, and judicial. A prelegislative conception of income and of how an income tax should work influences interpretation of the legislation.

■ Both the courts and the IRS decide legal issues in particular tax cases. The Supreme Court's decisions have the highest authority. The IRS defers to them and also interprets them in the process. The IRS often defers to lower courts' decisions in disputes within their jurisdiction, but it sometimes chooses not to defer.

■ Amounts that are included in income are reduced by deductions from income in the computation of net taxable income. The exclusion of an item of potential income from the first phase—exclusion being the opposite of inclusion—also reduces net taxable income. Thus, exclusions and deductions similarly reduce net income. This important parallel between the two makes them of equal weight in the tax calculation, although exclusions and deductions are justified by very different sorts of policy in most instances.

---

[10]See Thomas Paine, 2 *Rights of Man* 639-643, in his *Collected Writings* (Library of America). Paine speaks of a "progressive property tax," but describes an income tax.

CONNECTIONS

Sources of Income Tax Law

Judicial, legislative, and administrative interpretations of the Constitution and Code have shaped the income tax law. See Chapters 3.C and E(1)(judicial and administrative roles in formulating the exclusion for employer-provided meals and lodging), 4.B and C (evolution of judicial and administrative treatment of recoveries), 5.C (judicial and statutory rules on gifts), 8.D (judicial and statutory rules on income from cancellation of debt), 8.D (judicial and statutory rules on nonrecourse debt), 9.B and C (judicial elaboration of the statutory realization requirement), and 10 (judicial and administrative rules that preserve transactional parity).

The Open Texture of Income

Unpacking the concept of income has been a challenge for the courts, the IRS, and sometimes Congress. Chapters 2 (popular and theoretical conceptions of income), 3 (principled exclusion of certain employee fringe benefits), 4.C (exclusion of certain recoveries), 5.B (exclusion of gifts), 11.A and B (exclusion of intrafamily transfers from income), and 13.B and C (theoretical grounds for excluding medical expenses and casualty losses) deal with income's disputed contours.

Exclusions Versus Deductions

The difference between excluding an item from gross income and allowing it to be deducted after inclusion relates primarily to the reasons for exclusion or deduction rather than to the computational outcome. Deductions, however, are sometimes restricted, phrased out or reduced, for taxpayers with high income or high amounts of deductions. Exclusions are rarely restricted. See Chapters 2.B, 3.E, and 13.A.

Tax Fairness

Favorable treatment of employee fringe benefits that promote environmental and health policy goals detract from the horizontal equity of the income tax. See Chapter 3.E(2). Despite the remedial justice of excluding recoveries for certain injuries and losses, the absence of equivalent benefits for those suffering uncompensated injuries and losses also falls short of horizontal equity. See Chapter 4.C(2). Personal deductions for home mortgage interest and property taxes result in unequal treatment of homeowners and renters. See Chapter 13.A, D, and E.

Tax Neutrality

The goal of tax neutrality is strongly felt in the similar treatment of recourse and nonrecourse debt under the income tax law. See Chapter 8.F. The nonrecognition of certain realized gains also serves tax neutrality. See Chapter 9.E.1. Tax neutrality helps explain the need for differences in the tax treatment of active and passive profit-oriented activities. See Chapter 12.B and Chapter 14.C.

A First Look at Income

2

The concept of income is central to any income tax system. Some systems define income by enumerating types of compensation and gain, and

O V E R V I E W

stipulating that income is any of these and nothing else. Congress has taken a different approach. It employs the undefined term "income" as a basic point of reference, leaving the courts and the IRS to apply the term according to their own lights, a daunting task even for common law jurists. Later chapters survey the details of the interpretative process. This chapter examines the problem itself. First, we see how the Code sections using the term "income" set the stage for deciding what does and what does not count as income. Then we consider how everyday assumptions about income structure our usage of the term. Finally, two important theories about income, offered by experts as advice to legislators and policy makers, round out our survey of the problem.

A. HOW THE CODE'S SKELETAL DEFINITION OF INCOME WORKS

B. GROSS INCOME, ADJUSTED GROSS INCOME, AND TAXABLE INCOME

C. THE BACKGROUND NOTION OF INCOME

    1. Income and Subjective Preference
    2. Income and Effort
    3. Receipt
    4. Receipt Plus the Right to Keep
    5. Links with Detailed Discussions in Later Chapters

D. OTHER THEORIES OF THE NATURE OF INCOME

E. TYPES OF INCOME

A. How the Code's Skeletal Definition of Income Works

As noted in Chapter 1.D, the Code does not define income, but the word *is* used in the important phrases "gross income" and "taxable income," which the Code defines in sections 61 and 63, using the term "income" in the definition. It is tempting to say these definitions are circular, but that is not so. Congress plainly intended that we read them with a background notion of income in mind. There are a number of possible sources for that notion. One source is everyday usage of the term "income." Section B explores that usage, pointing the way to discussions later in this book, but it will be useful first to consider other aspects of sections 61 and 63.

B. Gross Income, Adjusted Gross Income, and Taxable Income

Before reading Code section 61, which defines gross income, we must have a preliminary idea of the term's meaning. **Gross income** includes everything that can properly be included in the individual taxpayer's net income, ignoring deductions. From gross income, taxpayers are allowed to deduct various expenses and other outlays, and so gross income is often a higher figure than net or taxable income. Even tax experts sometimes discuss whether something is income when they mean gross income, because the context makes it clear that only the inclusion of the item is at issue.[1] Inclusion does not tell us whether the taxpayer will have positive net income, because other unrelated expenses, losses, etc., may offset that item of gross income.

F   A   Q

Q: Why do we need separate definitions of gross income and taxable income?

A: Taxable income is gross income net of all permitted deductions. It is the "income" to which tax rates are ultimately applied in computing the tax owed. Gross income, on the other hand, is whatever goes into the hopper for potential taxation (i.e., before deductions are taken). The distinction between gross income and taxable income avoids possible ambiguities in the technical language of the Code that deals with the computation of taxable income.

Example 2.1: If Mary earns $40,000 in wages and sells a short story to a magazine for $800, and nothing else of tax significance happens to her during the year, then she has *gross income* of $40,800. If Mary has these two items of gross income but also spends $300 in qualified moving expenses related to her work, she is entitled to

---

[1]See Chapter 1.E on inclusions and exclusions from gross income.

deduct the moving expenses, and her net or *taxable income* is $40,500, that is, ($40,000 + 800) − 300.

As has been mentioned, the Code defines gross income in terms of income. More specifically, section 61(a) states that "[e]xcept as otherwise provided in [the Code], gross income means all income from whatever source derived," then it offers a non-exhaustive list of items that *may* be included in gross income. The definition thus tells us that income from *any* source is gross income. This obviously presupposes that we know *income* when we see it. The list of illustrations does not override that presumption. Thus, "gains from the sale of property," an item on the list, only includes such gains if they otherwise qualify as income. Suppose that a court is asked to decide whether a taxpayer's income includes a payment from someone who totaled the taxpayer's car and buys it to settle the matter. Even though money the taxpayer receives is, in common parlance, a gain from the sale of property, we may not, without more information, conclude that the settlement is gross income. Whether it is depends on whether a recovery for loss of the car is income. As Chapter 4 explains, recoveries are always income.

To grasp the definition of a narrower category of income in section 62, we must touch lightly on the subject of deductions. It is useful to know that some so-called itemized deductions are subject to restrictions that limit their value in reducing the taxpayer's tax liability. Other deductions, such as the deduction for certain moving expenses (section 217), are not restricted. When gross income has been reduced by the unrestricted deductions, section 62 labels the subtotal **adjusted gross income** or AGI. Several of the restrictions on itemized deductions are a function of AGI. For example, section 67 provides that employee business expenses can only be deducted to the extent that, when added to certain other miscellaneous itemized deductions, they exceed 2 percent of the taxpayer's AGI. The deductions that are allowed in computing AGI are sometimes informally called **above-the-line** deductions, in reference to a line on the tax return that separates the AGI calculation from the subtraction of the restricted deductions, which are accordingly described as **below-the-line** deductions. It is useful to remember which deductions are above and which are below the line. Above-the-line treatment is generally better.

Example 2.2: An employee gets no tax benefit for the cost of tools she must buy for herself to do the work her employer assigns because of the 2 percent of AGI floor for deducting employee business expenses. But if the employer provides the tools, their value is not included in the employee's income. Because it is not included in income, it does not matter that the employee cannot deduct them. The result is the same as if they *were* included in income and a full deduction, without the 2 percent AGI restriction, were allowed. Hence, the arrangement between the employer and the employee can achieve a tax advantage for the employee.

When we subtract the restricted or itemized deductions from adjusted gross income, **taxable income** remains. This is the figure that must be multiplied by the relevant tax rate(s) or looked up in a tax table to find the net income tax due.

Two additional terms related to income deserve to make an early appearance in our discussion. **Ordinary income** is income that is not eligible for the reduced tax rates that apply to capital gain and to certain gains from the sale of business property. An **ordinary loss** is a loss from the sale or exchange of property that is not a capital asset. **Capital assets** are, broadly speaking, assets held either as investments or in some other relatively passive manner. Chapter 14 explores the precise definition of capital asset and explains the rate advantages that exist for capital gains and gains on business property dispositions and the special restriction for the deductibility of capital losses.

C. The Background Notion of Income

We noted that a background notion of income must give meaning to section 61, which defines gross income as "income from any source derived." The Sixteenth Amendment (see Chapter 1.A) authorizes Congress to tax "incomes, from whatever source derived," and also does not define income. Thus, Congress made the income tax sweep as broadly as the amended Constitution permits, using the term "income," as the amendment does, without qualification. Given that the Sixteenth Amendment left standing the Constitution's prohibition in Article 1, section 9.2, of other direct federal taxes that are not "in proportion to the census," one might expect constitutional issues to arise concerning the scope of the term "income." The opposite has been true. Since 1920, the intermediate federal courts have entertained few constitutional skirmishes over the meaning of "income." The Supreme Court has strongly signaled its unwillingness to reach out in this direction.

It is time now to explore everyday usage of the term "income" and the assumptions that usage suggests to see whether our nontechnical understanding of "income" is clear enough to give content to the constitutional and statutory uses of the term.

(1) Income and Subjective Preference

Some believe that a person has income only to the extent that he or she personally values an acquisition of something. On this view, worldly goods are not income to the unworldly because they are worthless to them. The underlying thought is that subjective value and not market value or any other objective value is the measure of income. At the outset, there is a fundamental problem with this way of thinking. Money is the standard measure of income, whether we are designing a tax system or comparing credit scores. The same amount of money cannot constitute a different amount of income to different people because their attitudes to wealth differ. If money has less value to the rich or the philosophical, its amount nevertheless determines their income. It is for this reason, before all others, that a taxpayer's personal attitudes and preferences cannot determine his or her income for tax purposes.

Subjectivity nevertheless seems to explain something basic about the design of the income tax. We return to this in Section D below, which describes three very different design approaches. These deserve separate treatment because each is a relatively sophisticated departure from everyday ideas about income, and each makes occasional appearances in expert discussions of practical tax problems.

(2) Income and Effort

In many settings, income is related to the effort or labor of the person who acquires it. Let us try out this broad definition: *Income is the acquisition of something valuable by purposive effort.* To say that someone "makes" an income by working or investing suggests that income does not include all kinds of acquisition. When a person receives an unsolicited award for good deeds or a prize for high accomplishment, these would not be counted as income. This is the basic idea. For a long time, our income tax law did not treat awards and prizes acquired without effort as income. Other countries have had similar rules. Importantly, exclusion did not presuppose the economic insignificance of awards and prizes, because many were of substantial value. If you find this approach plausible or persuasive, you are not alone. Today, however, the U.S. income tax does reach awards and prizes without regard to the effort put into acquiring them. Whatever the reason for the change, we may conclude that general opinion no longer holds effort to be a crucial attribute of a person in acquiring income. Dropping this requirement from our definition, we must now allow effortless or passive acquisition of income to be possible. So far I have used "acquisition" as a neutral term for "getting" or "having" income. We should try to specify the underlying type of event to which acquisition refers.

By the way, when European countries were inventing the income tax, several considered requiring that income must be part of a regular flow, like wages or the profits of a business, so that unusual forms of enrichment would not count as income. The underlying instinct may have been to link income with effort along the lines just discussed. In any case, no country today requires income to be part of a regular flow. (Harking back to this abandoned requirement, our Code retains the phrase "fixed or determinable, annual or periodic income" as a category in international tax rules.)

(3) Receipt

In many familiar situations, *income is money received*. Statements about income are often fungible with statements about receiving money. "My employer paid me $50,000 this year" could replace "I had income of $50,000 from my job this year," and vice versa. But the correlation between receiving money and having income is not perfect. Instead of paying in cash, my employer may give me something I will accept as a substitute for money. Whether for tax purposes or in evaluating a person's creditworthiness, barter and other in-kind transactions can result in income. In brief, cash income is not the only form income takes. (Nor is every receipt of cash income; but more on this in a moment.)

The temptation to equate income with money received exists because money is the usual measure of economic value. *Receiving something of economic value may be the underlying essence of having income*. Will that do as a definition of income? Not quite. The checkroom at a hotel receives lots of valuables that are not income to the proprietor. Checkrooms and other bailees take in lots of things, but also give them back on a regular basis. Similarly, when an agent accepts something of value on behalf of another, the agent acquires nothing and certainly has no income thereby. Income never includes valuables received without the expectation on anyone's part that the recipient shall keep them. Receipt is not *sufficient* for income.

(4) Receipt Plus the Right to Keep

We have now considered three possible leads in our effort to unpack the concept of income. Each had a glaring fault or two. We can now try to formulate a working synthesis by excluding the exceptions or counterexamples. Consider this: *Income is the receipt of something of economic value, along with the right or expectation of keeping it*. Obviously, this would-be definition puts pressure on what is meant by the right or expectation of keeping the received item. Lawyers will of course think of these as property rights. The law of property in principle decides who owns every item that can be owned. But our new hypothesis also puts pressure in a different way on the importance of receipt. To own property, you need not actually possess or control it. Someone may simply put money in your bank account. Is actual receipt of something, in other words, even *necessary* for its being income to the recipient? As lawyers, we are used to speaking of constructive possession as a substitute for actual possession, and here we could speak of constructive receipt. Note, however, that this shift would make our current attempt to define income worthless. Some notion related to but more basic than receipt would now be doing all the work, and we have not identified that more basic notion.

(5) Links with Detailed Discussions in Later Chapters

Before going further, we can look ahead to concrete developments in U.S. tax law. Whether receipt is the litmus test for income is resolved in an interesting way. As we just saw, receipt is neither necessary nor sufficient for the acquisition of income, but receipt does sometimes determine to which taxable year a taxpayer's income belongs. Chapters 4, 8, 9, and 10 fill in the details. Income can be in kind or in cash. Some employee fringe benefits exemplify this, discussed in Chapter 3, as do gifts, discussed in Chapter 5. Chapter 5 also shows that income can be acquired effortlessly, as when a taxpayer enjoys a windfall, but gifts, which may or may not require effort by the donee, are excluded from income by statutory provision.

D. Other Theories of the Nature of Income

Skepticism about the value of an informal notion of income prompted scholars to advance more explicit and technical views that influence legislative and judicial conceptions of the tax base. Two of these — the **ability to pay** doctrine and the **Schanz-Haig-Simons** (**SHS**) definition of income — stand in contrast with definitions of income by reference to its sources. Courts and commentators occasionally try to use them in solving practical tax issues. You may encounter them in the introductory tax course.

"Taxation according to ability to pay for the last hundred years or more has been a universally accepted postulate, not only amongst political and economic writers, but amongst the public at large."[2] As this suggests, ability to pay has historical roots. The worldwide movement in favor of income taxation was based on the popular belief that taxing people according to their means was the best alternative to older duplicative and corrupt patterns of taxation. Europe and eventually America and other countries seemed all to agree on this. Theorists speak interchangeably of "taxation according to means" or "taxable capacity" or "ability to pay."

John Stuart Mill gave the first technical exposition of taxation in accordance with ability to pay. He unpacked the imprecise popular conception with the proposition that fairly distributed tax burdens exact an *equal sacrifice* in well-being from every taxpayer. Most of Mill's contemporaries believed that the value of income to an individual depends on how much he or she already has, and that to distribute the *burden* of a tax equally, different amounts of money may have to be taken from

---

[2]Nicholas Kaldor, *An Expenditure Tax* 26 (1955).

different individuals. Mill explained the equivalence of burdens associated with different dollar amounts of tax by appealing implicitly to utility theory. His idea was that as income increases, each additional unit of income adds to the utility the individual enjoys, but not as much as any of the earlier units did. We now refer to this hypothesis as the **diminishing marginal utility of income**. Popular conceptions of how tax burdens should vary with income levels were not at all explicit about how that should work and certainly did not rely on utility theory.

Intriguingly, Mill claimed that equal sacrifice would impose the least aggregate sacrifice on society as a whole. But equal sacrifice has this effect only if the marginal utility of money is the same for all individuals.[3] This assumption cannot be tested empirically. It has to be accepted, if at all, on faith. For this reason, Mill's utility-based version of ability to pay has had many critics. The perils of subjectivism stirred up at least one theory that claims to be more objectively grounded.

Henry C. Simons, with a tip of the hat to work by Georg von Schanz and Robert M. Haig, recommended that income be regarded as the increase in the individual's *economic power* over a given period of time, measured by the *market value* of whatever form this increment in power takes. On the **SHS** view, income is the sum of the (newly funded) consumption and net investment over the accounting period in question, where both consumption and investment are measured in objective, market-based terms. No subjective element entered into this conception of incremental economic power gains. An individual who put a higher or lower value than the market on a given increment of newly acquired wealth would have the same income as anyone else.

Simons stressed that his definition of income focuses on "the amount by which the value of a person's store of property rights would have increased, as between the beginning and end of the period, if he had consumed (destroyed) nothing."[4] That it must be a net amount is assumed, as Simons's emphasis on the "increase" of the taxpayer's "store of property rights" implies. But he did not recognize the looming issue of which losses are properly taken into account in calculating this amount. Netting outlays and losses against gross contributions to the increase is obviously essential. Practical income taxation, however, routinely disallows the subtraction of some "personal" losses.[5] Our question concerning the inclusion of employer-provided benefits is the converse of the question whether a loss or productive expense for self-employed people who enjoy similar benefits in their profit-oriented activities should be deducted. We must reason from the first principles of SHS to complete its account of this problem.

Simons's definition falls short in at least one respect. It allows the same economic power to be counted as the income of more than one individual, as in the case of a donor and donee or charitable giver and the charity's beneficiaries.[6] Gifts, losses, and benefits ambiguously received in market transactions are among them. Speaking of gifts, Simons's fundamental defense of inclusion is that "[t]o exclude them would require introducing into the definition [of income] a distinction between one-sided transfers and payments in the nature of fair compensation."[7] This is just an assertion,

---

[3]See Richard Musgrave, *A Theory of Public Finance*, 90-102 (1959) (tracing how Mill's critics proved that his claim about least aggregate sacrifice has this logical consequence).
[4]*Id.* at 49.
[5]I.R.C. §165(c).
[6]Henry C. Simons, *Personal Income Taxation* at 134-136.
[7]*Id.* at 125.

of course, that one-sided transfers, as he calls them, are gains. Simons relies on the "simplicity and elegance" of inclusion, in effect brushing the problem aside as too slight to deserve serious discussion.

F   A   Q

Q: Do ability to pay and SHS disagree about whether specific items of possible income are indeed income?

A: The major disagreement between the two theories, which has no effect on everyday tax problems, is over the justification of progressive tax rates. Taxation in accordance with ability to pay implies that rates should be higher for higher levels of income, at least if the marginal utility of income increments at the higher levels is less than at lower levels. The SHS approach denies this justification, though it is consistent with progressive rates. Both should result in making gifts and various sorts of imputed income taxable, but advocates of both theories simply wave these awkward consequences aside on grounds of administrative convenience.

Source-based definitions of income, older than the SHS approach, are even more staunchly free of subjectivism. For example, we might say that income must be of one or another of the following types: wages, compensation for professional services, interest, dividends, gains on the sale of property, and windfalls. A list of this sort poses problems, because the description of each item on the list of included income types will also need to be interpreted. But that may be easier work for courts and administrators than the abstract problem of circumscribing income. Several European countries have source-based legislative definitions of income, and the "schedules" on which income from these sources are separately listed give the label "schedular" to income taxes of their kind.

Glenshaw Glass v. Commissioner[8] establishes that income for Code purposes is not source-based, at least at the most theoretical level. Despite that, you will find hints of a surviving source consciousness in our tax jurisprudence. We care very much about sources in deciding whether court-awarded damages should be considered income: Payment from a competitor for destroying the goodwill of the plaintiff's business is not income, but income does include payment from a customer who failed to pay for services rendered. The next section explores an overview of income from a source-based perspective. Although such a perspective has no legal significance for the U.S. income tax, it can be of use to U.S. tax lawyers, as subsequent chapters illustrate.

E. Types of Income

Much income, but not all, falls into one of three source-based categories: income from personal service (compensation), income from occasional property dealings, and income from ongoing enterprises. The distinction is not highlighted by the

---

[8]348 U.S. 426 (1955).

structure of the Code. For that reason tax instructors often leave it to the student to notice these broad categories and structure their outlines and thinking around them.

What is peculiar about each? The main thing about compensation is that it is always ordinary income; that is, it is not eligible for the lower tax rates that sometimes apply to gains from capital assets. Next most important: Compensation is normally taxed as soon as possible — there is rarely an opportunity to postpone its inclusion in the taxpayer's gross income until a later tax year than that in which the compensation is received. (We will see later that this depends partly on the fact that individuals are the main earners of income as compensation, and accounting methods concerning the timing of their income strongly favor including it in the year in which it is received by the taxpayer.) Neither of these points quite constitutes a rule. Nevertheless, both are background principles that you will find useful in organizing what you learn about compensation. By the way, compensation may be earned either by an employee or by an independent contractor who renders services.

Transactions in property are treated differently, depending roughly on whether they are more active or more passive. An investor may occasionally buy and hold property until market circumstances or those of the investor make it desirable to sell. Other property dealings are based on a plan of buying and selling property whether it has appreciated or not, and without regard to the property owner's needs and wants. The Code creates a special place for the latter activities and describes any such activity as a **trade or business**. This important phrase, like the basic term "income," is not defined in the Code. Nonetheless, we can be confident that it means the activities of an ongoing enterprise that strives to be profitable whether asset markets are up or down. Investment focused on profitable sales only in up markets are more passive than a trade or business. You will learn much more about this category of income-producing activity later in Chapter 12.

SUMMARY

- The Code defines gross income as "income, from whatever source derived," and gives a nonexclusive list of examples, but contains no definition of income.

- Congress intended to use the term "income" with as broad a meaning as the Sixteenth Amendment, which also uses the term without definition, permits. Courts, the IRS, and we must therefore interpret the Code with a background notion of income in mind.

- Our everyday concept of income is revealed in a variety of commonplaces, such as the equation of income with gains deliberately sought, the receipt of economic value in cash or in kind, and the acquisition of property rights. None of these is entirely satisfactory, but each foreshadows difficulties that the common law of the U.S. income tax has tried to resolve.

- The international trend toward income taxation drew support from the widespread conviction that tax burdens should be allocated in accordance with taxpayers' means or ability to pay.

- Gross income includes all items that may augment a taxpayer's taxable income; adjusted gross income (AGI) results when unrestricted, above-the-line deductions are subtracted from gross income; taxable income is AGI less personal, itemized, or below-the-line deductions.

■ Two main types of income are payment received for one's labor, often called personal services, and gains from selling or exchanging property.

■ Gain or loss on the sale or other disposition of property is measured by the difference between the amount realized and the taxpayer's basis in the property disposed of.

■ J.S. Mill sought to improve the imprecise popular conception of ability to pay, proposing the thesis that fairly distributed tax burdens exact an *equal sacrifice* in well-being from every taxpayer.

■ Mill's critics, including Henry C. Simons, argued that ability to pay presupposes the diminishing marginal utility of money, but that this broad thesis is unverifiable.

■ Simons offered a rival definition of income (SHS) as the market value of an individual's new wealth acquired over a given period of time, whether saved or consumed.

■ The ability-to-pay tradition and Simons's nonutility-based definition of income continue to influence theoretical and sometimes narrowly practical debates about the concept of income.

CONNECTIONS

Theoretical Definitions of Income

Although popular notions about what constitutes income lie behind the Sixteenth Amendment and most income tax legislation, experts have offered a variety of opinions on how income should be defined for tax purposes. Some theoretical definitions have impressed the courts and perhaps Congress as well. See Chapter 3.A (unwanted work-related benefits), Chapter 4.B (incompatibility of gift exclusion with both ability to pay and objective measurement of income theories), and Chapter 7.A (time-value of money rules reflect objective view of income, not ability to pay; Mill's argument against taxing savings does as well), Chapter 8.G (policy behind treating recourse and nonrecourse borrowing alike), and 13.C (treatment of losses).

Statutory Definition of Income

If we understand the statutory definition in section 61 to be qualified by exclusions that reflect grassroots rejection of the taxability of certain benefits, then Chapter 4.C (on *Clark*), Chapter 5.B (on the law person's view that gifts should not be taxed), Chapter 11.A and B (on adjustment of the individualism of the income tax to accommodate family units), and Chapter 13.B and C (itemized deductions for medical expenses and casualty losses) are all parts of that broader definition.

Sources of Income

Problems concerning broad types of income are discussed in Chapter 3 (which deals only with employees), Chapter 9 (which deals with realization and hence with dealings in property in the broadest sense), and Chapter 14 (which deals partly with business income).

Exclusions Versus Deductions

Deductions for certain expenses are always allowed in full, while others are allowed only if they exceed a certain percentage of AGI. Even when allowed, some deductions are "phased out" or reduced if AGI is greater than a certain threshold. Exclusions, which are not normally entered on the tax return (except for alternative minimum tax), are not subject to such limitations. Accordingly, if a taxpayer has a choice between excluding and deducting an item, exclusion sometimes yields greater tax benefit. See Chapter 3.E and Chapter 13.A.

Types of Income

The tax law takes strikingly different approaches to the measurement of income from trades or businesses, on the one hand, and investment activities, on the other. See Chapter 9 (delayed realization of economic gains and deferment of certain deductions of investment activities), Chapter 12 (other deductions for both types of activity), Chapter 13 (trade or business deductions), Chapter 14 (special tax rates and loss restrictions for investment activities), and Chapter 15 (cost recovery for property used in either type of activity).

Employee Pay and Perks

3

Pay for work performed is a prime example of taxable income. And so tax puzzles from the employment context provide a good starting

O V E R V I E W

point for studying the income tax. Wages and similar compensation vividly pose the question whether income and benefit are interchangeable concepts. Income can be received in cash or in kind. Putting these points together, we might well expect the employment setting to be a haven for income in camouflage. After all, employees often get to handle, use, and even keep things of value in doing their jobs. Which of these, if any, is disguised compensation? Grand theories of income try to answer the question, and we will consider them. The Code answers it by excluding several common employee benefits from gross income. The question, however, is still alive, because some benefits encountered on the job remain hard to classify. In this chapter, we come to grips with theoretical and statutory responses to employee benefits as well as lurking difficulties that so far elude the Code.

A. IN-KIND BENEFITS CONNECTED WITH EMPLOYMENT

B. SALARY PAID NET OF INCOME TAX

C. CONVENIENCE OF THE EMPLOYER

D. THE RATIONALE

A. In-Kind Benefits Connected with Employment

Money is of benefit to many who possess it. Our concern with income is based on that, but benefit is an elusive concept in its own right. Some fundamental tax problems have to do with whether apparent benefits are income. Early on, the IRS and the courts concluded that work-related benefits might look like compensation and yet serve noncompensatory purposes of the employer. When this is so, we may question whether they are income to the employee after all. Should a safe workplace or the availability of restrooms at work be taxed as a fringe benefit, though each certainly is a benefit?

Neither is a cash payment, but surely that does not settle the income question. Income can be received in cash or in kind. Any other approach would produce absurd results. A simpleminded scheme for hiding the receipt of money would be to ask someone who is prepared to pay you a sum of money to go out and instead buy something like a car or a vacation that you would have bought for yourself with that sum. Examples illustrating the functional equivalence, at least for tax purposes, of money and receipts in kind can easily be multiplied. We are of course used to thinking of things other than money as having economic value, because we live in a world of consumable items with price tags attached. By the way, retail and not wholesale values are the ones that count for tax purposes. The rule could be otherwise, but this convention is simple and avoids administrative problems that only perfectionists might want to solve.

What should we say of something received in kind that the recipient would *not* herself have bought? Unwanted gratuities, like unwanted gifts from a doting uncle, may have no value to the recipient at all. But even unwanted items are subject to the retail value rule for tax purposes, if their value is to be taken into account at all — that is, if they are to any extent gross income.

Scholars have debated whether an unwanted benefit *is* a benefit. They have also noted that unwanted benefits may be forced upon their recipients, or at least made available, as part of someone else's activity. Fine apparel, tickets to the opera, and a handsome horse to ride are employee perks for a royal servant, but having to use them can be drudgery. We know that gift-givers and employers alike may simply want to control the conduct of the people who are the objects of their ostensible benevolence. Are forced, unwanted, or simply superfluous benefits really benefits? This question lies at the root of one of the most important differences of opinion in tax theory.

Ignoring gifts and undisguised wages, work may yet spill over into employees' lives in various beneficial ways. (1) An employer may provide some of the worker's life necessities free of charge, such as food and lodging. (2) A worker may receive free or discounted samples of the boss's wares. (3) Instead of saleable wares, the boss may just give the employee a gold watch or a pen with the employer's logo. (4) Even amenities that are restricted to the workplace—a corner office, tools that never leave the workplace but "belong" to the employee—are benefits. (5) A service firm may offer to pay for a meal at a restaurant for any employee who works late. (6) The employer may give bus fare to all employees or provide free parking on the premises. (7) Some employers offer worksite childcare. Nor do these broad types exhaust the range of possibilities. (8) An airline or telecommunications firm may allow employees to consume services that form part of its unused excess capacity, which would otherwise go to waste. (9) A kindly employer (think of Dickens's Fezziwig) may give holiday parties for employees and their families. (10) In one famous case, an employer agreed to pay a key employee's federal income tax liability, presumably to protect the pretax value of the stated salary. Table 3.1 is a rough estimate (you may disagree with it) of how some of these work-related benefits serve the interests of the employer and the interests of the employee, respectively.

The tax law has faltered repeatedly in its quest for a broad principle for deciding which work-related or employer-provided benefits are income. All the more reason for this to figure conspicuously in law school tax courses. We will first consider the problems on the merits, and then examine how the Code resolves those problems.

B. Salary Paid Net of Income Tax

The tax treatment of situation (11) in the previous section was settled long ago. If an employer pays an employee's federal income tax liability, this is additional compensation for the employee and is included in gross income. In *Old Colony Trust Co. v. Commissioner*,[1] the president of a textile company whose federal income taxes were paid for him by the company contested the government's claim that this constituted additional compensation and hence income to him. The purpose of the employer's generous tax payment scheme was to ensure that "said persons and officers shall receive their salaries or other compensation in full without deduction on account of income taxes, State or Federal."[2] The Supreme Court concluded, as had the IRS and the lower courts, that "[t]he payment of the tax by the employers was in consideration of the services rendered by the employee, and was a gain derived by the employee from his labor."[3] But the troubling issue, at least for the time, was whether something happening offstage, and not involving direct receipt of value by the taxpayer, could be characterized as, well, the "receipt" of income. The case gave the Court an opportunity to state the somewhat broader principle that "[t]he form of the payment is expressly declared [by the income tax statute] to make no difference," and "[t]he discharge by a third person of an obligation to him is equivalent to receipt by the person taxed."[4] It was therefore a twofold statutory holding, though one of great importance. First, the form of a payment is irrelevant, so that in-kind receipts are just as capable of being income as receipts in cash.

---

[1] 279 U.S. 716 (1929).
[2] *Id.* at 719.
[3] *Id.* at 729.
[4] *Id.*

TABLE 3.1 Job Perks

● = yes   ○ = maybe   [blank] = no

	Condition of Employment	Used in Employer's Activity	Increases Employee's Economic Power	Increases Employee's Satisfaction (Utility)	Compensatory	Increases Productivity
Workplace restrooms						●
Corner office	●	●		●		●
Office furnishings	●	●		●		●
Extra pay to cover employee's home office		●	●			●
Company car use on the job	●	●		●		○
Company car for personal use			●	●	●	
Meals in employer's dining room	○		○	○	○	○
Meal expense account for traveling employee	○	○	○	○	○	○

Reimburse employee's other travel costs

Worksite lodging

Compulsory lodging on other employer's premises

Permissive lodging on other employer's premises

Employer-product discount, required use on job

Employer-product discount, *not* required use on job

Executive jet

Employer-paid travel frequent flyer miles

Second, discharge of an obligation by a third party on behalf of the obligor is equivalent to receipt, even if it is literally anything but that.

Example 3.1: Old Colony agrees to pay Wood an annual salary of $100,000, net of Wood's income tax obligation. A simple formula allows us to compute Wood's gross income from the arrangement. If the rate of tax is r, then Wood's income from the tax paid on his behalf, excluding the explicit salary, is

$$(\$100,000 \times (1-r)).$$

If the rate of tax is 30 percent, this formula yields additional income from the tax paid of

$$(\$100,000 \times (1-.3)) = \$70,000.$$

Wood's total salary under the arrangement at this tax rate is $170,000. You can find tutorials on the formula used here by searching the Internet for information about geometric series.

C. Convenience of the Employer

The forerunner of the IRS ruled that accommodation at or near a worksite was not income to a logger if it was provided "for the convenience of the employer."[5] Extending the idea to several other kinds of employee and to worksite meals as well, the IRS wrote the "convenience of the employer" exclusion into the tax regulations.[6]

The Tax Court applied the exclusion in *Benaglia v. Commissioner*,[7] undeterred by facts that strongly suggested the possibility of disguised compensation. The taxpayer was the manager of two luxurious Hawaiian hotels. His salary was generous, but in addition, he and his wife paid nothing to live in one of the hotels and eat in the hotels' restaurants. The government objected that the value of the meals and lodging were additional income to them. At trial, the taxpayer testified that his duties as hotel manager required him to be on site, even though he lived in just one of the hotels and was away on other business of his employer for three months of one of the years in dispute. Agreeing with the taxpayer, the Bureau of Tax Appeals, forerunner of the Tax Court, found the meals and lodging were for the employer's convenience and therefore not income.

One judge dissented, observing that the meals and lodging were a benefit to Benaglia. That was enough, he thought, to justify classifying them as income. His analysis, however, was inconsistent with tax regulations in force, which acknowledged that the benefit of employer-provided meals and lodging might not be income. (Note that section 61 regulations no longer contain a broad exclusion for "convenience of the employer" benefits.) The dissenter's point still resonates with commentators. It seems to them that even a nonportable or restricted benefit, like getting life's necessities on the employer's premises, because it is a benefit, must be income. But the law is otherwise.

---

[5]I.T. 2232.
[6]Regulations 77, Art. 52-53.
[7]36 B.T.A. 838 (1937), *acq.* 1940-1 C.B. 1.

An undisputed benefit to the employee can escape income classification. The forerunner of the IRS, the Board of Tax Appeals, and eventually Congress accepted "convenience of the employer." Code section 119 now provides that an employee's income does not include the value of lodging or meals provided for the convenience of the employer if further requirements are met. If lodging is provided, it must be on the premises of the employer, and accepting it must be a "condition of employment" to qualify for exclusion. If meals are provided, they must be "furnished on the business premises of the employer." But section 119 and the regulations do not tell us what "convenience of the employer" means. *Benaglia* remains a fundamental precedent, although it also offers no articulate explanation of the doctrine.

The issue is not whether the retail value of the meals or lodging can easily be ascertained; in most instances, their *unrestricted* retail value is no mystery. The usual treatment of receipts in kind seems inappropriate (or has so seemed to the IRS, the courts, and Congress) in part because the employee is not allowed to convert the stuff received into cash. He or she is restricted to consuming just these meals and/or this lodging.

Another factor that may be important — there is no authoritative analysis of the doctrine — is that the employee's consumption serves the employer's profit-oriented activity. We may be inclined to say, "Oh, you're so lucky to be allowed to use that *X*!" But we may also be inclined to say, "Too bad, you're being forced to use that *X*!" Which is the more appropriate response depends partly on what *X* is, but also on the employee's preferences. In either case, however, the employer's preference for having the employee engage in this bit of consumption is satisfied.

F   A   Q

Q: Can an employer bestow a benefit on an employee indirectly, as in *Old Colony Trust*, and yet require the employee to consume that benefit on the job?

A: We could think of such things as attractive surroundings, restrooms, corner offices, etc., as falling into this category. The major distinction between on-the-job perks and the employer's payment of the employee's income tax is that the former do not satisfy any obligation of the employee. Hence, the reasoning of the case does not apply to these benefits.

D. The Rationale

Many instructors invite students to think about "convenience of the employer" in terms of ability to pay or SHS. What do these views teach us about the employee perk of on-site meals and lodging? The sum an employee would pay for the freely provided meals and lodging may seem a good first approximation of the income value of these benefits. But the freedom to choose one's own meals and lodging is of course basic as well, and its market value should perhaps be subtracted from that of a one-size-fits-all choice by the employer. Ability to pay would emphasize the individual employee's subjective weighting of these two elements. Given differences in employee's tastes, there could be no single valuation of even the most similar free meals and lodging, and it is quite possible that for some employees they would have no value at all (the free lodging aboard a ship in harbor, for example, for a ship's captain who has a house nearby). So ability to pay does not solve the riddle one way or the other.

The objective approach is more promising because it looks at market values, which we can almost always ascertain, at least if we compare the employer-provided meals and lodging with exactly the same meals and lodging offered for purchase on the open market. Oops! The on-site meals and lodging, especially if they cannot be exchanged for others more congenial to the employee, may have different market values than their unrestricted look-alike counterparts, precisely because the on-site stuff *is* restricted. In fact, there may be no market at all for such items in their restricted form or status.

Meals and lodging furnished in kind on the employer's premises may therefore benefit some employees and not others from a subjective point of view like that of the ability-to-pay theory, and we cannot easily tell which employee would therefore have income on this theory. The same meals and lodging would by definition not have a market value because they are not available to be rejected, exchanged, or donated to others. Can we still speak of them as a benefit to the employee? Suppose that they benefit an employee in the narrow sense that she has more of her remaining income or savings to buy other things than meals or lodging. We cannot be sure, however, that a finicky employee will not simply choose to purchase different meals and lodging in addition to those freely given by the employer.[8] Is there even a small benefit in this case?

Code section 119 resolves the matter in favor of full exclusion of meals and lodging provided for the convenience of the employer, at least if, in the case of meals, they are furnished on the employer's premises, and if the lodging is on the employer's premises and must be accepted by the employee as a condition of employment. Convenience of the employer wins out, despite its obscure content, as a rationale for excluding from income what seems to be a clear case of benefit, though not salable and hence without market value.

E. Statutory Exclusions for Fringe Benefits

During the first decades that the income tax was in force, the tax law said nothing about employee perks as such. With section 119, however, Congress began to codify employer-provided benefit exclusions. The list now includes sections 82 (employer-reimbursed moving expenses),[9] 119 (meals and lodging), 120 (group legal services plans), 125 ("cafeteria" plans), 127 (educational assistance programs), 129 (dependent-care assistance programs), and 132 (other fringe benefits). Congress apparently intended there to be no other exclusions for fringe benefits. That has not entirely settled the matter, however, because the obscure policy behind the exclusions leaves open the possibility of nonstatutory exclusions. Code

---

[8]Although the case did not involved employer-provided meals or lodging, it is worthwhile to mention *Turner v. Comm'r*, 13, T.C.M. 462 (1954), in which a taxpayer exchanged first-class steamship tickets to Argentina, which he had won on a quiz show, for far less expensive tourist steamship tickets to Brazil, where his wife had been born. It is true that it looks as if the taxpayer got something he wanted — the cheaper tickets. But it isn't clear that he would have paid the market value of even *those* tickets if he hadn't had the more expensive tickets to dispose of.

[9]This list does not mention moving expenses that an employee pays herself, which may be deductible. Code §217. If a moving expense would be deductible under §217 and the employer reimburses it, section 82 excludes the reimbursement.

section 102(c) provides that no "amount" (presumably in cash or in kind) transferred *from employer to employee* is to be excluded from income as a gift. Job-related perks, however, were once excluded without express statutory authority, and no provision like section 102(c) has put a stop to such exclusions.

Sections 119, 120, 125, 127, 129, and 132 are for the benefit of employees only. Code section 3121(d) defines "employee" for purposes of the withholding of tax from wages. The definition classifies as an employee anyone who would be so classified under "the usual common law rules applicable in determining the employer-employee relationship," but it also expressly includes certain types of employees, some of whom would be employees under the common law rules. Although this definition technically exists only to facilitate the related definition of wages, which governs the withholding requirement, the IRS generally regards those who are subject to withholding as employees for all purposes under the Code, including the restriction of fringe benefit exclusions to be discussed below.

The common law of the income tax does not exclude the same benefits for independent contractors or the self-employed, with these exceptions. The "working condition" fringe of section 132(a)(3) allows an employee to exclude employer reimbursement for outlays the employee could have deducted under section 162 as the ordinary and necessary expenses of the employee's "business" of being employed. The work-related items that independent contractors and the self-employed can deduct under section 162 are subject to fewer restrictions (in particular, they are not subject to the threshold disallowance of 2 percent of AGI) than are employee deductions under section 162. Hence, independent contractors and the self-employed get a benefit very similar to that which is available for reimbursements of employee business expenses — without, of course, having to be reimbursed by someone else.

Example 3.2: Jones is a medical resident in a teaching hospital. The hospital provides a room with sleeping quarters for Jones to use during short free spells while working 24-hour shifts. Section 119, discussed more fully in E(1) below, excludes the value of this "lodging" from Jones's income. But when Jones finishes the residence and enters into a contract to provide consulting services for the hospital, the broad discretion the hospital allows Jones in performing his consulting work makes him an independent contractor under common law. If the hospital now gives Jones the same sleeping quarters, section 119 does not exclude their value from his gross income.

(1) Section 119

Section 119 excludes from an employee's income the value of lodging or meals provided "for the convenience of the employer" if further requirements are met. Excludible lodging must be on the premises of the employer, and accepting it must be a "condition of employment." If meals are provided, they must be "furnished on the business premises of the employer." These were the original provisions of section 119 in the 1954 Code.

In *Kowalski v. Commissioner*,[10] the Supreme Court refused to apply the 1954 version of section 119 to a perk for New Jersey state police officers that gave them an allowance for meals taken on duty at restaurants throughout the state. The Court, skirting the issue whether the highways and byways of New Jersey were "premises of the employer," held that such meals were not "furnished by the employer" as section 119 required. Soon after, Congress let state police officers elect to have their meal reimbursement excluded under section 119 retroactively, even if this would otherwise violate *res judicata*, i.e., *Kowalski*.

Then, the Ninth Circuit in *Sibla v. Commissioner*[11] held that firefighters could exclude or, alternatively, deduct meal contributions required by their employer under a racial desegregation plan that required all on-duty members of a fire station to eat together. Although the meals were taken on the employer's premises, the government argued that they were not "furnished" by the employer, as the Supreme Court had stressed excludible meals must be. The Ninth Circuit characterized the meals requirement, which indisputably came from the employer, as "a device conceived and established by the employer for its convenience,"[12] and so held the meals to be furnished by the employer. Congress responded again, finding the Ninth Circuit's reasoning entirely to its taste. In 1978, section 119 was amended to say that if an employee is required to pay a fixed charge periodically for meals that are furnished by the employer for the employer's convenience, whether the employee takes the meals or not, then that charge is excluded from the employee's income, even if the employee pays the charge out of his or her stated compensation.[13] Section 119 was further amended in 1978 to add two new interpretative rules: (1) that neither state law nor the terms of the employment contract are determinative of whether meals or lodging are intended as compensation;[14] (2) that in determining whether meals are for the convenience of the employer, no weight is given to whether a charge is made for meals or to whether the employee may accept or decline the meals.[15]

Sibla held that, even without section 119, the firefighters could have deducted what they paid for the firehouse meals as a business expense under section 162. Today, the deductibility of an expense under section 162 is characteristic of one of the statutory exclusions, namely, that of the "working condition" fringe in section 132(a)(3). The working condition fringe exclusion does more than duplicate the economic result of similar deduction. Employee business expenses, when aggregated with certain other itemized deductions, must exceed 2 percent of AGI to yield a tax benefit.[16]

Since 1996, section 119 has excluded the subsidized portion of employee housing at educational institutions and academic health centers that would otherwise *not* qualify for complete exclusion under the basic rule of subsection (a), even if the housing is furnished to an employee, spouse, or dependent as a residence. That is, the employee gets to exclude only the difference between the fair rental value of the

---

[10]434 U.S. 77 (1977).
[11]611 F.2d 1260 (9th Cir. 1980).
[12]*Id.* at 1265.
[13]I.R.C. §119(b)(3).
[14]*Id.* at §119(b)(1).
[15]*Id.* at §119(b)(2).
[16]See Chapter 12.G.

free lodging and what others—employees or students—pay for comparable on-campus housing. Section 119 also provides that meals furnished to employees by an employer on its business premises shall be deemed to be for the employer's convenience if more than half of the employees receiving the meals are for the employer's convenience.[17] The obvious pattern exhibited by the post-1954 amendments of section 119 is leniency toward peculiar cases, probably in response to lobbying. The amendments shed no light on the underlying rationale of "convenience of the employer."

Example 3.3: If firefighters, who receive free meals at the firehouse for the employer's convenience, outnumber clerical workers at the firehouse, the latter can also exclude on-site meals. Clerical workers presumably do not have to be on call like firefighters.

(2) Section 132 — Other Fringe Benefit Exclusions

In its original form, section 132 excluded four types of fringe benefits: (1) "no additional cost" benefits, (2) "qualified employee discounts," (3) "working condition" benefits, and (4) "de minimis" benefits. Each could be defended, though perhaps not convincingly, on grounds related to convenience of the employer or tax neutrality. Since 1981, when section 132 was added to the Code, exclusions have been created for (5) qualified "transportation," (6) qualified moving expense reimbursement, (7) qualified retirement planning services, and (8) qualified military base realignment and closure benefits; none of these is related to convenience of the employer. Note that (1), (2), and (4) are excludible only if made available without discrimination in favor of highly compensated employees.[18]

(a) No-Additional-Cost Fringe Benefits

No-additional-cost fringe benefits are those provided out of the employer's excess capacity to employees in the related line of business. The Code says the employer cannot incur any substantial additional cost in providing this type of benefit. Key examples are unused seats on commercial passenger flights and unused telephone bandwidth. In both cases, an employer *could* give the excess but valuable product to customers, but such largesse might undermine the employer's pricing scheme or otherwise change customer preferences. To let the excess product go to waste would deny everyone, and hence the whole economy, the no-additional-cost benefit. Arguably, employers can safely dump the benefits on employees who work in the line of business in which the product is sold to customers (this line-of-business limit is also a statutory requirement), and society will be better off. It's a nice idea, and lore has it that airline employees' and telephone company employees' unions lobbied hard for this exclusion. Skeptics object that when employers run programs that distribute alleged excess capacity among workers, there are always substantial costs; hence, the requirement of no substantial additional cost is simply not met in the real world.

Tax neutrality provides a rationale, if not a convincing one. We strive for neutrality in the application of tax measures so as not to shrink the economic "pie" of society's product by hampering the free play of markets. If the income tax thwarted

policy

---

[17]*Id.* at §119(b)(4).
[18]The rationale of the nondiscrimination requirement is taken up in Section E.2(a).

TABLE 3.2 Policy Grounds for Various Employee Perk Exclusions

● = yes   ○ = maybe   [blank] = no

	Convenience of the Employer	Other Tax Neutrality Goal	Administrative Convenience	Employee "Morale"
Meals and lodging on premises—§119	●/○		●	●
Group legal services plans—§120	○		●	●
"Cafeteria" plans—§125			●	●
Educational assistance plans—§127	○		●	●
Dependent-care assistance programs—§129	○		●	●
No-additional-cost fringe—§132(a)(1)		●	○	
Qualified employee discount—§132(a)(2)	●		●	
Working condition fringe—§132(a)(3)	●		●	
De minimis fringe—§132(a)(4)		●	●	●
Parking, mass transit, commuter vehicles—§132(a)(5)	●/○			●
Employer-reimbursed moving expenses—§132(a)(6)	●/○			●
Retirement planning—§132(a)(7)				●
Qualified pension and retirement plans—§132(m)			●	●
Military base closure benefits—§132(n)				●
Permitted home office deductions—§280A(b)	●/○			●
Stock options—§83 and §422				●
Qualified pension and retirement plans—§§401 et seq.				●

the use of excess capacity, there would also be a reduction of social welfare. Employer convenience does *not* figure in the rationale for excluding no-additional-cost benefits. If these benefits are the employer's excess capacity product, the employer would produce them anyway, so their use by employees or other donees does not promote the business.

Section 132(j)(1) prohibits discrimination in favor of highly compensated employees in the award of no-additional-cost benefits. The definition of "highly compensated employee" is borrowed from section 414(q), a provision on favorable tax treatment for certain employer-provided pensions, which indicates that Congress considered this fringe benefit capable of serving as disguised compensation for key employees, just as pension plans would be if they were permitted to discriminate.

Example 3.4: An airline offers free flights only to pilots and not to flight attendants, and the pilots are highly compensated in comparison with the flight attendants. Although the airline incurs no additional cost for the flights, their value is not excluded under section 132(a)(1) from the pilots' gross income.

Section 132 manifestly relies on various policy justifications for excluding employee fringe benefits from income. No-additional-cost fringes are supposed to avoid the deadweight loss that would result if the employer's excess capacity went unused; employer convenience is neither required nor likely here. Looking ahead, we may note that employee discounts on retail goods could be necessary to induce sales staff to use the things they sell, which can obviously assist the selling effort. Working condition benefits appear to be a small group within the larger employer-convenience category. De minimis fringes serve neither employer convenience (indeed, they defy the on-premises requirement for section 119 employee meals) nor tax neutrality in the guise of keeping excess capacity from going unused. Table 3.2 summarizes these policy grounds and makes suggestions concerning other exclusions in section 132, 401 *et seq.* Several benefits on this list serve the convenience of the employer slightly, if at all, while benefiting the employee substantially. Free parking, daycare, and educational benefits enable the employee to do his or her job better, but each is a benefit for which employees often pay for their own convenience.

(b) Qualified Employee Discounts

Convenience of the employer can explain the exclusion for discounts on clothes and similar retail goods for employees who sell or see customers in the employer's selling business. "Branding," according to current marketing wisdom, promotes sales, and so workers should flaunt the brand. The employee discount exclusion is broader, however. It extends to goods of all kinds that are sold in the line of business in which employees eligible for the discounts work. A refrigerator salesman can buy one at the employer's cost, even though customers will not know that he uses it.

Like the no-additional-cost benefit, qualified discounts are subject to the nondiscrimination rule of section 132(j). A slightly different nondiscrimination provision is found in the definition of the de minimis fringe. Hence, of the original four types of section 132 fringe, only the working condition fringe is not subject to a nondiscrimination requirement.

(c) Working Condition Fringe Benefits

An employee can exclude from income "property or services provided [by the employer] to the extent that, if the employee paid for such property or services, such payment would be allowable as a deduction under section 162 or 167."[19] Recall that in *Sibla*, the court found the firefighters could have deducted their required meals payments as business expenses under section 162 if section 119 had not allowed them to exclude an equal amount of income. The working condition fringe enlarges on that idea. Employment is considered a "trade or business" for purposes of section 162. Every employee is "in the business" not of the employer, but of being an employee.

Example 3.5: A bank teller is not in the same business as the owners of the bank, because she does not own a bank or engage in all the activities characteristic of a bank. Her job as teller, however, is considered a "trade or business" in itself.

If an employee can properly deduct an outlay for property or service as a business expense, then the employee will not have income if the employer gratuitously provides the property or service.

Example 3.6: A welder who works for a construction company buys his own protective clothing, paying for it out of his wages. The cost of the protective clothing is deductible as an employee business expense under section 162. The employer adopts a new policy and provides the protective clothing to the welder free of charge. The welder can exclude the value of the protective clothing from income. The value of the clothing does not show up at all on the welder's tax return.

Example 3.7: A doctor employed by a clinic could validly deduct the subscription price of a medical journal as a business expense. The clinic instead buys the journal for the doctor. The doctor need not report the value of the journal as gross income.

F   A   Q

Q: Can the same benefit satisfy the definition of more than one of the excludible fringes defined in section 132?

A: The working condition fringe is linked to qualified employee discounts because both have an employer convenience rationale, but case law on section 162 disallows employee business expense deductions for clothing unless it can reasonably be used only on the job—a uniform, in effect. If a firm that sells uniforms gives its sales staff qualified discounts on the uniforms so that they will wear them to work, both exclusions would apply. The overlap would not be of practical interest, however, because the working condition fringe exclusion is less restricted than the qualified discount exclusion. Only these, of the section 132 exclusions discussed so far, have a common rationale.

---

[19]§132(d) ("Working Condition Fringe Defined").

No-additional-cost fringes could also overlap with qualified discounts, but here the exclusion for the former type of fringe, which is less restricted than the latter, makes the overlap uninteresting.

The working condition fringe is not subject to the nondiscrimination rule of section 132(j)(1) because even employees who work at very similar tasks for an employer may do sufficiently different tasks to support differences in what they can deduct under section 162.

Example 3.8: A supervisor, a welder and a riveter all work for a construction company. The supervisor uses a BlackBerry to coordinate on-the-job tasks (and never uses it for personal purposes!). The welder and the riveter use very different types of tools. It would make no sense to exclude the value of the supervisor's BlackBerry only if the employer gives the welder and riveter BlackBerrys as well.

(d) De Minimis Fringe Benefits

The de minimis fringe is any property or service whose value is so small as to make accounting for it unreasonable or administratively impractical, taking into account the frequency with which similar fringes are provided by the employer to all employees. The standard example is the restaurant dinner allowance offered to law firm associates by some large firms on evenings when they work late. An early ruling allowed such meals to be excluded, and section 132 continues the exclusion. The references in the definition of this fringe to the smallness of the benefits, their occasional character, and administrative convenience all strongly suggest that employer convenience is not the rationale. Evidently, this fringe exclusion cannot advance the policy underlying the no-additional-cost fringe.

(e) Exclusions for Broad Benefits Offered to All Employees

An assortment of exclusions under section 132 are based neither on the convenience-of-the-employer doctrine nor the goal of tax neutrality. These include exclusions for the value of employer-provided (1) athletic facilities; (2) parking, mass-transit, and commuter vehicle subsidies; (3) retirement planning services; and (4) base closure and realignment benefits. Congress added this assortment of exclusions to section 132 after its initial appearance in 1984.

F. Employees' Home Offices

Code section 280A limits business deductions for home offices of the self-employed and employees alike. These limits are the subject of Chapter 12, to which the reader should refer for all the details. Here we will note only that employees are strictly barred from deducting the costs of a home office unless it is "for the convenience of the employer."[20] In *Drucker v. Commissioner*,[21] the Second Circuit reversed a Tax Court decision denying an orchestra employee's deductions for home practice

---

[20]Code §280(c)(1).
[21]715 F.2d 67 (2d Cir. 1983).

space. The appellate court reasoned that practicing at home was a "focal point" of the employee's employment-related activities, sufficient to make the home the employee's principal place of business, one of section 280A's requirements for home office deductions. The court expressly held that home practice was for the "convenience of the employer," as section 280(c)(1) requires.

F   A   Q

Q: Why does the tax law limit the exclusion of certain employee fringe benefits while actively promoting others?

A: Pensions and motivational perks, such as employee stock options, may serve defensible economic goals — persuading employees to prepare for retirement or to strive harder to increase the employer's profit — but no one can ignore the obvious connection between highly compensated employees, who benefit most from these excluded perks, and the lobbying efforts of their employers. Reining in more ingenious forms of executive compensation is the only defensible goal these exclusions advance.

G. Qualified Retirement and Profit-Sharing Plans

Most introductory tax courses deal briefly at best with the Employee Retirement Income Security Act (ERISA) of 1974, which allows employers to deduct their contributions of funds to retirement trusts for employees while also allowing employees to postpone recognition of the income they would otherwise certainly have from these contributions. The policy is to encourage employers to set up such qualified plans, within strict guidelines intended to prevent discrimination in favor of highly compensated employees. Employees must draw down their benefits by the age of 70½, at which point they must report the then value of the benefits as gross income. Survivors who receive a deceased employee's benefits must likewise report their value as gross income, without the usual protection of the step-up in basis at death for transfers from a decedent.[22]

H. Qualified Stock Options, Forfeitable Property Transfers, and Loans as Employee Benefits

Employers have found a variety of techniques for compensating favored employees on a tax-deferred or even tax-free basis. Section 422 allows "incentive stock options" of up to $100,000 per year in value to be given tax free to employees, with restrictions against discrimination in favor of highly compensated employees. This innovation dates to 1981, when $100,000 was real money. Now, section 83 is more often used to achieve the same goal without a dollar limit. It permits employers to give stock or options to favored employees without causing them to have to report their value as income until the property becomes freely transferable or all conditions of forfeiture

---

[22]I.R.C. §1014.

related to the employee's service to the employer have lapsed. The regulations under section 83 now provide safe harbors for an election under section 83(b) that can permit an employee to convert to capital gain the ordinary income potential of property transferred subject to a condition of forfeiture.[23] Until recently, employers also gave favored employees tax-deferred benefits by giving them interest-free or below-market-interest loans, but this practice is now frustrated by section 7872.

SUMMARY

- Pay for work done by the taxpayer is a paradigmatic form of income. Such compensation for personal services can be received in cash or in kind.

- Certain fringe benefits of employment, especially meals and lodging, were once excluded from income by administrative and judicial decision and are now excluded by Code section 119, at least in part because the inherently restricted use of the benefits by employees is for the "convenience of the employer."

- Code section 132 excludes many kinds of employer-provided benefits from employees' income, some for reasons related to the convenience of the employer. Most of these exclusions, however, allow compensatory fringe benefits to be received tax free.

- Employee's expenses and other outlays related to home offices are deductible only if for the convenience of the employer, but these otherwise face restrictions applicable to home offices of the self-employed.

- Employer-sponsored retirement plans as well as stock or stock option plans compensate employees with benefits that are not included in their income in the year the employer makes them available, at least if complex requirements are met. But non-discrimination between highly paid and other employees is not among the requirements.

---

[23]Treas. Reg. §1.83-2.

CONNECTIONS

Nonpreclusive Use of Items of Value

The convenience-of-the-employer doctrine excludes benefits from employees' income when the employer captures the full value-in-use of the benefit for its profit-oriented enterprise. This nonpreclusive use of the benefit by the employer is analogous to the donor's nonpreclusive use of gift property, whose value can also be enjoyed by the donee, as we see in Chapter 5.B.

Indirect "Receipt" of Income

An indirectly conferred benefit, like the employer's payment of the employee's federal income tax liability, is normally income. Although ordinary usage would not label the indirect income event the "receipt" of that income, the difference between actual and indirect receipt is irrelevant. See Chapter 10.A(1). There is some confusion in the cases, however, about whether indirectly conferred benefits should be described as constructively received. See Chapter 10.A(2).

Employee Business Expenses

The working condition fringe benefit is excluded only if a payment by the employee for the property or service conferred by the employer would have been deductible under section 162 or 167. Chapters 11 and 14 explain the requirements for such deductions, not only for employees, but also for all taxpayers engaged in profit-oriented activities. Keep in mind that an employee is always considered to be engaged in a trade or business, not that of the employer, but that of an employee in this particular job.

Employee-Oriented Statutory Exclusions

Some employee exclusion provisions are matched by similar provisions for the self-employed or for others engaged in business operations. The working condition fringe is an obvious instance, but similar results would be reached for discounts on wares given by a retailer to herself if the appropriate business connection existed. Some exclusions, however, seem special to the employment context, such as those for the no-additional-cost and de minimis fringes. See Chapters 12.D(3) and 13.G.

Employer Loans to Employees

Certain loans from employers to employees at below-market terms are subject to rules that prevent the special advantages of these loans from escaping inclusion in the employees' income. This fringe benefit is therefore not one that receives preferred treatment under the rules discussed in this chapter. See Chapter 8.H.

Getting Your Own Back: Recoveries of Damages, Damage Settlements, Insurance Benefits, and More

4

OVERVIEW

Recoveries, an odd assortment of possible income items, are not all taxed alike. Gross income includes court-awarded damages and amounts in settlement of litigation, if these replace lost wages or net profits and nothing else. A recovery for something previously taxed, however, is not income, and indeed the tax treatment of substituted value usually mimics the tax treatment of what is replaced. The like treatment of substitutes keeps events beyond the taxpayer's control from triggering an increased or decreased tax burden. Sometimes, though, it is not so easy to decide what has been replaced or even whether replacement has occurred. Moreover, not all recoveries are governed by broad principle, because the Code also excludes some recoveries from income for administrative convenience or reasons of mere politics. Recoveries are comparable in this way to the employment-related exclusions of Chapter 3, which are not all grounded on principle.

D. INSURANCE RECOVERIES

E. HOW NON-DEATH BENEFITS OF LIFE INSURANCE ARE TAXED

F. DAMAGES AND SETTLEMENTS

    1. *Commissioner v. Glenshaw Glass Corporation*
    2. *Raytheon Production Corporation v. Commissioner*
    3. Contingent Fees

G. TAX TREATMENT OF TENANTS' IMPROVEMENTS TO LEASEHOLDS

H. OTHER PROPERTY IMPROVED WITHOUT REALIZATION

I. "RECOVERY" OF BASIS

A. What "Recovery" Means in This Context

A **recovery**, as the word suggests, is the return of something to its rightful owner. One may recover the thing itself, and if its loss was never deducted, there is nothing for the tax law to be concerned about. The item is already on the owner's balance sheet. No gain or loss is realized. But if what is recovered is a replacement for the original, the tax law must take note. The recovery may be wholly or partly income.

Treating like things alike plays a large part in the taxation of recoveries. In many situations, this is the only rule of thumb needed to find the right solution. Sometimes, however, it offers only fuzzy guidance — for example, when likeness itself is open to question. Are frequent flyer miles a replacement for part of the already-taxed funds a taxpayer used in buying tickets from the airline, or are they compensation for the taxpayer's fidelity to the airline? They are the latter, certainly, when the taxpayer's employer buys the tickets but the taxpayer has freedom to choose one airline over another. Is payment to the "donor" of rare blood gross income or payment for a commodity that must be presumed to have a basis equal to the price paid and therefore not income? The Tax Court has concluded that such payment is gross income.[1] But it was IRS practice to attribute a cost basis to the marital rights a spouse exchanges for a divorce property settlement.[2]

F	A	Q

Q: If a recovery for a loss is excluded from gross income, can the taxpayer who is not able to recover for a similar loss claim a deduction instead?

A: No, loss and bad debt deductions are narrowly circumscribed. Some realized losses are not deductible, and whether a recovery could have been excluded does not govern deductibility. We study the details of loss and bad debt deductions in Chapter 12 on personal deductions and Chapter 13 on business deductions.

---

[1]*Green v. Comm'r*, 74 T.C. 1229 (1980).
[2]*U.S. v. Davis*, 370 U.S. 65, at 73 n.7 (1962).

B. The Development of Recovery Exclusion

Early on, courts and tax officials decided without statutory guidance that recoveries for physical injuries and certain other losses should not be taxed. These early decisions left the contours of the exclusion vague. Conspicuously, they did not say whether or to what extent the *reason* for the recovery mattered. A recovery for some untaxed and nonexempt item of benefit to the individual need not be excluded to avoid double taxation, because the item is facing tax for the first time. Yet it is sometimes hard to determine whether the thing replaced has been taxed already or is tax-exempt. Consider how often lawsuits and private settlements of litigable claims are based on combinations of legal doctrines that have little to do with each other. Measures of damages for tort and contract wrongs, to mention those with which first-year law courses deal, are not exclusively concerned with the plaintiff's previously taxed property. Hence, not all judgments and settlements deserve exclusion. Those based on multiple claims are hard to classify for that reason alone.

Courts and administrative officials reasoned tacitly in this way when they first invented the exclusion for recoveries. They did not delineate the range of recoveries that could be excluded. We can ignore items that were formerly excludible but no longer are. (One such example is a corporation's recovery for injury to its goodwill, which would now be treated as a taxable gain.[3]) What matters is that the courts concluded after analyzing more types of recovery that not all are alike.

It would make things easier if we could say that only recoveries for previously taxed items of value are excludible. The exclusion of damages for life-and-limb torts shows that this is not so. It is almost accurate to say that excludible recoveries are limited to those for previously taxed items *or* for items that should never be taxed (life and limb). The key is that in both cases we want to avoid taxing a proxy for something that itself could be owned without (further) taxation.

Sidebar

RECOVERIES AS FEES FOR THE "USE" OF THE INJURED PERSON

Even uncomplicated recoveries for personal physical injury pose a theoretical problem. Regarded as fees for "use" of the injured individual, they look like taxable compensation. The reason for this exclusion is almost as easy to grasp as that for the exclusion of an economic replacement for something whose value had already been taxed. For, had that individual not been injured, his or her healthy condition would not have been taxed as income. We come equipped, so to speak, with lots of assets — limbs, functioning neurological systems, our personal dignity — that we are not required to include in gross income. Exclusion of the substitute for wholeness, therefore, seems proper.

(1) A Broad Exclusion for Fault-Based Recoveries: *Clark v. Commissioner*

One venerable case, however, complicates our lives and clouds the sky of the government. In *Clark v. Commissioner*,[4] the taxpayer's attorney made a wrong choice in

---

[3] *Farmers & Merchants Bank v. Comm'r*, 59 F. 2d 912 (6th Cir. 1932) (recovery for injury to goodwill excludible without proof of goodwill's basis); *contra Raytheon Prod. Corp. v. Comm'r*, 144 F.2d 110 (1st Cir. 1944) (recovery for lost goodwill is excludible only to the extent taxpayer proves it had a basis in the goodwill).
[4] 40 B.T.A. 333 (1939), acq. 1957-1 C.B. 4.

preparing his tax return, and Clark owed more tax than he otherwise would have. The attorney magnanimously paid the difference. Clark claimed this payment on his behalf was a recovery for a loss caused by a third party. The government disagreed, invoking *Old Colony Trust*, for the proposition that when someone else pays your taxes you have gross income. See Chapter 3.C. The court, however, accepted Clark's reasoning, analogizing the recovery to those for breach of promise to marry and for personal injury, among others. In the court's view, the tax advisor simply made the taxpayer whole for a loss the tax advisor had caused, and it didn't matter that this involved paying a tax for which Clark was liable after the mistake had been made. Still, the rationale of the case is not clear. Several of the types of recovery cited by the court replace human capital—good health or marital rights—"assets" that are acquired tax free. Clark's avoidable tax burden was not an injury to life and limb or the like. All we can say without qualification is that the combination of the attorney's mistake and the recovery left him no better or worse off.[5] Moreover, the holding did not turn on whether what was lost was already taxed or tax exempt, as in most of the other recovery exclusions the court mentions. The IRS says that *Clark* stands only for the exclusion of recoveries of taxes the taxpayer would otherwise not have owed, basically confining the case to its facts.

Example 4.1: Jim, a construction worker, accepts a job working on a major building project. To take the job, he quits his current job, sells his home, and moves to the new work location. Assume that the move was economically reasonable. The employer then announces that the project will not go forward. Jim sues and recovers both for his loss on selling the house and for the wages he would have earned at his old job. The loss on the house would not have been deductible and the wages would have been taxable if they had been earned. Yet Jim looks like Clark in having been made to suffer these losses by the fickle employer. If Jim invokes *Clark*, he may at least persuade the IRS to compromise with him because the analogy is hard to dispute.

Example 4.2: Jill knows that under section 1031 you can sometimes exchange business property for replacement property without having to pay any tax on the transaction. Her lawyer says, "Sure, we can do that," and doesn't ask whether the property is encumbered by debt. It is, though. As a result, Jill ends up owing tax on the exchange, which has otherwise been handled by the lawyer. She threatens to sue for malpractice, and the lawyer pays her a substantial sum to avoid the malpractice claim. Does Jill have income? Almost certainly, she does, but like Clark, she wouldn't have had this tax liability if it weren't for the lawyer's mistake.

---

[5] If this were the key to the exclusion, *Farmers & Merchants Bank*, *supra* note 1, which the *Clark* court did in fact cite, would still be good law.

F   A   Q

Q: Would the reasoning in *Clark* apply to a taxpayer's recovery for a return preparer's mistake that resulted in a penalty and interest but did not change the amount of tax due?

A: Let us assume that a return preparer misunderstands the tax law and on that basis shows less income than the taxpayer objectively owes. The IRS discovers the error and assesses a penalty and interest for the late payment of the deficiency in tax. The return preparer pays the penalty and interest for the taxpayer. Is this recovery excludible from income? Yes, even though this fact pattern does not include one peculiar element of *Clark*: The underlying tax liability actually changed in that case and is not affected by the return preparer's mistake here.

C. Statutory Treatment of Certain Recoveries

We have seen that section 104 codifies several recovery exclusions that were originally judicial and administrative. (Code sections 101-140 are exclusion sections.) The codification of these exclusions leaves open the question whether they would otherwise have to be excluded anyway on general principle or even on constitutional grounds. We will return to that question shortly.

Four frequently encountered types and one somewhat unusual type of recovery are not counted as income:

- Workers' compensation awards,
- Damages for personal physical injury,
- Benefits of accident or health insurance, and
- Certain health or sickness benefits for military and other government workers abroad.

The common element is obvious. Each type of benefit or award makes the taxpayer whole for a loss related to bodily health or well-being.

(1) Damages for Personal Physical Injury Excluded Under §104(a)(2)

Section 104(a)(2) excludes "any damages (other than punitive damages) received . . . on account of personal physical injuries or physical sickness." Note the restriction to *physical* injury or *physical* sickness. It is meant to deny the exclusion for other sorts of tort recovery, especially reputational and psychological distress damages. Congress imposed it only in 1996, after a zigzag sequence of court rulings and earlier legislative tinkering. The government had litigated claims for the exclusion of a wide variety of tort and statutory damages on the theory that when the damages were for emotional, dignitarian, reputational, or other nonphysical losses, the exclusion might be denied unless the damages would not constitute income under section 61. Courts disagreed in a variety of respects. Congress finally resolved the fracas by cutting the exclusion back even more than the IRS had proposed. At the same time, Congress added that "emotional distress" is not a physical injury or sickness for purposes of section 104(a)(2), except that damages for medical care attributable to emotional distress did still qualify for exclusion.

(2) Tax Equity of These Exclusions

Early cases like *Clark* assimilated the recoveries now dealt with in section 104 to a wider class that seems to include all personal tort recoveries and perhaps any compensation for losses from standard human endowment: basic physical and dignitarian equipment that most people are lucky enough to have, the almost universally shared starting point for life's demands. Of course, excluding recoveries does nothing for those who are born without these basic things or who suffer losses of them without being able to recover for those losses. Perhaps that inequity is lessened to some extent by the fact that section 104 now delineates a narrower class of exclusions. The tax law's treatment of misfortune is not thereby made less unjust, but the hint is that the remaining exclusions are intended to serve a different purpose.

Section 104 and the two next sections of the Code are related in an important way. Section 104(a) excludes accident and health insurance recoveries. Section 105(b) excludes from employees' gross income the benefits of employer-paid accident and health insurance, and section 106 excludes the value of employer-paid accident and health insurance coverage. Although Congress confined its largesse to a subset of all deserving taxpayers—those whose employers offer this perk—these exclusions do help the government to provide health benefits, as court-awarded damages for injuries also do. The subsidy is indirect; it results from not taxing the recipient on the value of the benefit, but this nevertheless makes it cheaper for the employer to make a given level of benefit available to the employee.

Sidebar

COMPARISON OF TORT AND CONTRACT RECOVERIES

Recall that tort recoveries for personal physical injuries resemble recoveries for breach of contract, in that both make the victims of wrongs whole and both reduce the wrong suffered by the plaintiff to a sum of money. From this lofty perspective, section 104(a) and section 186 are related. The latter excludes recoveries for contract breaches. Importantly, section 186 excludes recoveries only to the extent that the losses covered would have been deductible.

D. Insurance Recoveries

Two kinds of insurance payout—most death benefits of life insurance and property loss benefits—are excluded from income. The death benefit exclusion in section 101 is express. The exclusion for property insurance recoveries is implicit—tax experts trace it to the language in section 165(a): "Except as otherwise covered by insurance. . . ." This does not actually say that property insurance benefits are excluded, but Congress knows the IRS interprets it that way—an excellent example of implicit congressional approval of an administrative interpretation. Section 123 expressly excludes certain living expenses received by an individual under an insurance policy when the individual's principal residence is not available because of a casualty or the threat of casualty.

Both exclusions make sense for a different reason than the exclusion of recoveries that restore human capital, despite a superficial kinship. Life insurance benefits replace something like capital: The loss of a financial provider and the loss of financial reserves are similarly debilitating. Moreover, both kinds of benefit replace insured losses. These similarities, however, do not take us very far. The death of a family's provider is not like the loss of a limb or one's hearing. In the latter cases, what is lost belongs to the basic store of human capacities that the tax law never reaches. In the former, the loss replaces a flow of untaxed gifts, but the financial resources lost when a loved one dies would in most instances have been taxed at least when the decedent earned them. In contrast, most life insurance benefits are not taxed at all.

Although only some types of insurance benefits are excluded, there is reason for excluding all of them. All basic insurance involves the pooling of risks. A number of people contribute after-tax dollars to a common reserve to cover losses that only some will suffer. When the pooled money goes to those with losses, the group is not collectively better off. Wealth has simply been redistributed. The security of being insured may have macroeconomic significance, but aggregate taxable income is not increased.[6] We noted in Chapter 2 that some tax theorists believe aggregate taxable income should never exceed net national income. This view supports the exclusion of insurance benefits, which only move existing wealth around among the insured.

Not all insurance benefits, however, are excludible. We noted at the outset that when benefits replace anticipated but as yet untaxed income, the recipient normally has income, so that the insured fares no better than similarly situated persons who have not suffered losses. Hence, payments under the insurance some businesses carry against lost profits or business interruption is income.

> ### Sidebar
>
> **THE FLOW OF INSURANCE BENEFITS AND RECOVERY THEORY**
>
> Life insurance and health or accident insurance are different in one important respect: The beneficiary of ordinary life insurance is not the person whose life is insured, but the person covered by health or accident insurance is at least one of the beneficiaries. Life insurance benefits are therefore not a recovery for the person whose death triggers them, but health insurance benefits are a recovery for the insured person and his or her family. In practical terms, however, life insurance is usually bought to cover the loss of income from the death of the insured. In this respect, it too can be regarded as providing a recovery.

The living expense exclusion of section 123 violates this general principle. Living expenses are not deductible, and when another party pays them for you, the benefit should be income on the principle of *Old Colony Trust*. Congress nonetheless decided to exclude the difference between normal expenses for the taxpayer and household and extraordinary living expenses occasioned by a casualty or when the government denies a taxpayer access to his or her principal residence. The Code contains no similar exclusion for the value of a rental vehicle paid for by car insurance after an accident or breakdown. It is unlikely that the IRS audits for these stray items of income, but it could justifiably do so.

---

[6]Insurance companies invest the premiums they receive in exchange for coverage, and the investment income is subject to income tax, but the burden of that tax is removed because the insurer gets to deduct losses paid. The details are beyond the introductory tax course, but the curious student may want to have a look at I.R.C. §§803-805, which permits life insurance companies to deduct benefits, and §832(b)(5), which permits a non-life insurance company to deduct losses paid on insurance contracts. Section 834 excludes certain investment income from a non-life insurance company's income, anticipating the deductibility of losses this will be used to pay. The insured as a group usually benefit as well from investment gains of the insurer, which faces no net tax burden if they are distributed in benefits; this is a tax subsidy by the government for both the insurer and the insured. The point about wealth redistribution only applies to reserves consisting of premiums alone.

In summary, the current tax treatment of payments received under insurance contracts appears to be inconsistent, no matter which reason for exclusion we consider. The statutory treatment of insurance recoveries does not resolve the puzzles raised by nonstatutory recovery exclusions.

E. How Non-Death Benefits of Life Insurance Are Taxed

Two broad types of life insurance are sold in this country. **Term life** insurance gives beneficiaries a specific dollar benefit upon the death of the insured if that occurs within the stated term of the policy. **Endowment life** insurance, which goes under such names as "whole life," "universal life," and "flexible life," combines features of term life with an investment account. The policyholder, who need not be the person whose life is insured, is entitled to a given amount of money if the insured survives to a specified date and the policy premiums have been kept current. Under many such policies, this amount is a gradually increasing figure that begins modestly—only after the policy is in force for only a few years—and rises finally until it equals the maximum death benefit payable on the policy at the death of the insured.

F   A   Q

Q: Is the forced savings feature of endowment life insurance the most important benefit of such insurance for many who purchase it?

A: For tax purposes, we do not consider this kind of benefit as something over and above the savings a policy owner accumulates. The peace of mind that the purchaser of ordinary life insurance enjoys in contemplating the security of her family and loved ones is also not considered for tax purposes as something apart from death benefits actually received by them.

Because an endowment policy combines life insurance with a savings feature, the tax exclusion of the death benefits could in principle be limited to that part of any payment at death in which the policyholder had a vested right without regard to the death of the insured. The basis of the taxable payout would be the sum of all premiums paid minus the portion of those premiums that would have purchased the term life policy standing alone; that is, the net gain would equal the amount not realized as a death-conditioned benefit minus the policyholder's basis in that benefit.

Example 4.3: Arnold, at the age of 25, purchases an endowment life insurance policy with a death benefit of $100,000. The policy will pay Arnold's beneficiaries this amount if he dies before reaching the age of 65. It will also pay Arnold, during his life, a sum less than $100,000, if he requests it, after the policy premiums have been paid for two years. The sum is $1,000 in year three, $1,500 in year four, $2,000 in year five, and gradually increases to $100,000 over the remaining 35 years before his 65th birthday. The annual premium is $2,000, and the annual premium of a simple term life policy with the same death benefit is only $300. If Arnold dies on his 45th birthday, having paid all of the premiums until then, the tax analysis could be as follows: Of the $100,000 that goes to the beneficiaries of Arnold's policy, $1,700 of each of the 20 premiums paid, or $34,000, is Arnold's investment (basis) in the endowment or savings aspect of the insurance contract. Some part of the total is a return on that investment, which can be determined by reference to the amount Arnold could have withdrawn under the terms of the contract at age 45. Let's say this is $10,000. Then, only the remainder, or $56,000, is truly a death benefit.

The foregoing analysis *could* serve as grounds for allowing Arnold's beneficiaries to exclude only $56,000 from income under section 101(a). But that is *not* how the government interprets section 101.

For simplicity, and perhaps out of sympathy for the survivors of the insured, the entire amount paid as death benefit is excluded. Note, however, that if Arnold withdrew the available $34,000 just before he died, the policy (following the pattern of many such policies on the market) might still be in force, allowing his beneficiaries to receive $100,000 despite his withdrawal. Therefore, the contract is not so straightforward a combination of the term and savings components, and perhaps it makes sense on a deeper level for the whole death benefit to be excluded, as it is under current administrative practice.

TABLE 4.1	Tax Inclusion, Exclusion, or Partial Taxation of Recoveries
Damages	**Inclusion/Exclusion**
Lost wages, independent contractual service compensation, or business profits	All ordinary income
Lost tax-exempt income	All excluded
Lost value of capital asset	Exclusion of amount equal to basis, the remainder taxed as capital gain
Lost business property	Exclusion of amount equal to basis, the remainder taxed as quasi-capital gain under §1231
Lost goodwill	Exclusion of amount equal to basis, the remainder taxed as quasi-capital gain under common law treatment of goodwill as capital asset (see *Raytheon*, below)
Nondeductible economic loss (*Clark*)	All excluded
Personal physical injury	Excluded under §104(a)(2)
Loss of life	Life insurance benefit excluded under §101; court-awarded damages excluded under §104(a)(2)
Insurance recovery for property loss	Excluded under §165 to the extent of taxpayer's basis in lost property

One final point: If the initial policy owner sells a life insurance policy to another person, the exclusion of death benefits received by the new owner is denied for all but his or her basis in the policy. The object is clearly to prevent arbitrage in death benefits, which would be unseemly and might even provide a motive for murder. What is not curtailed is the exclusion for the original owner of a life insurance policy, no matter how slender an interest this person may have in the life of the insured. Corporations now regularly insure large numbers of their employees to win fairly predictable death benefits. Such "corporate-owned life insurance" has come in for much criticism, and Congress has recently outlawed it, by limiting COLI death coverage to specified individuals.

F. Damages and Settlements

Some litigators think of themselves as generalists who do not need to have specialized knowledge of any area of the law, least of all tax. Nothing could be further from the truth. The amount of tax knowledge needed, however, is modest. How does tax matter in the conduct of a lawsuit? When the relief sought is damages, the desired outcome is of course a recovery, and recoveries are sometimes income, sometimes not. We have seen that section 104 excludes certain kinds of damages and settlements from income. Whether a jury award or a settlement falls within that exclusion depends on the nature of the claims the judgment or settlement covers.

As we have seen, the tax treatment of a recovery often mimics that of what is replaced, but not always. If what was lost has already been taxed or is exempt from tax, the recovery is not taxed. In litigation, the complaint, as modified by subsequent proceedings that modify the complaint, indicates the grounds on which the plaintiff believes a recovery is proper. The plaintiff in effect tells the world that this is the nature of the claim. That is strong evidence in a subsequent dispute between the settlement's recipient and the IRS over the extent to which the recovery must be included in income. Findings of the court may of course alter this putative characterization of the recovery. Similarly, the terms of a settlement may state bluntly that the money is being paid to replace wages (taxable) or as compensation for a physical injury (excludible under section 104(a)(2)). But vague characterizations, such as "for opportunity costs," can make matters worse.

(1) *Commissioner v. Glenshaw Glass Corporation*

Perhaps the most famous case on the tax characterization of damages is *Commissioner v. Glenshaw Glass Corporation*.[7] The taxpayer had won exemplary damages for the defendant's fraud and the federal antitrust laws had trebled these damages. The Supreme Court dismissed the suggestion that the exemplary and punitive damages were not income because they were not a "gain derived from capital, from labor, or from both combined," as the Court itself had characterized income in *Eisner v. Macomber*,[8] although no windfall had been in question there. Instead, the *Glenshaw Glass* Court held that income could be derived "from any source whatever" and that Congress had intended to exercise the "full measure" of its taxing power under the

---

[7]348 U.S. 426 (1955).
[8]252 U.S. 189 (1920).

Sixteenth Amendment, which allows Congress to levy direct taxes on income "from any source derived."

(2) *Raytheon Production Corporation v. Commissioner*

As a practical matter, *Glenshaw Glass* tacitly expresses a presumption that damages are income. The taxpayer must always show how and why a portion of a money judgment or settlement should *not* be treated as such. This comes through vividly in the earlier *Raytheon Production Corporation v. Commissioner*,[9] which held that damages for the destruction of part of a taxpayer's business were gross income to the extent that the taxpayer could not prove it had a positive basis in what had been destroyed. ("Basis" is one's investment in an asset, adjusted to ensure non-taxation when the asset is used or disposed of; see Chapter 6.A.) The court acknowledged that damages for lost goodwill, as the business injury was characterized, could be characterized as a "return of capital," but refused to give the taxpayer the benefit of the doubt by so characterizing any of the recovery. The court commented significantly that it ruled out the possibility of treating the recovery as one of lost profits, which would have been ordinary income instead of capital gain, because the taxpayer's pleadings in the antitrust proceeding had not indicated that lost profits were at issue. Again, pleadings have tax implications.

Example 4.4: Agnes and Cecilia, software designers, formed a corporation in which they held 51 percent and 49 percent of the stock, respectively. Both devoted their full efforts to making the corporation successful and received small salaries. When the stock of the corporation had appreciated, Agnes fired Cecilia for alleged wrongdoing and invoked their buy-sell agreement to repurchase Cecilia's shares at a low price. Cecilia sued for wrongful discharge and to recover the full value of her stock. The court awarded her damages without indicating the portion awarded on each of her claims. Since the pleadings covered both claims, the government took the position that Cecilia's victory was all ordinary income, arguing that there was no finding of the stock's value. Absent contrary evidence, the government's position would normally succeed in litigation over the extent of Cecilia's income.

(3) Contingent Fees

A separate issue concerning litigation and taxes is of vital importance to contingent fee plaintiffs. The successful plaintiff is often surprised to learn that she must pay tax on a part of the court award she never sees. Although the plaintiff's attorney withholds a percentage of the damages under the contingent fee arrangement, the whole award is treated as received by the plaintiff and in part then disbursed back to the attorney.

In most instances, a successful plaintiff who pays a contingent attorney's fees can deduct this as a cost of obtaining the recovery. More precisely, the plaintiff may be able to deduct attorney's fees as a business expense or an expense incurred for the production of income—that is, under section 162 or section 212, respectively. The deduction for expenses related to employment, however, is limited. Such expenses must be aggregated with other "miscellaneous itemized expenses," and only the

---

[9]144 F.2d 110 (1st Cir.), *cert. denied*, 323 U.S. 779 (1944).

excess of these over 2 percent of adjusted gross income are allowed, and even then the taxpayer's total itemized deductions may be limited by the standard deduction or by the gradual phase-out of itemized deductions for high-income taxpayers; Chapter 13.G explains this limitation in detail. In brief, the deductibility of attorney's fees is precarious for employees.

When the Supreme Court recently confirmed that a litigant is not entitled to treat a contingent fee as earned directly by her lawyer—the litigant must first pass "Go" and pay the tax on the fee[10]—Congress showed Title VII plaintiffs some mercy, permitting discrimination plaintiffs to deduct their attorney's fees and court costs "above the line," thus avoiding the restrictions to which employee business expenses are otherwise subject.

G. Tax Treatment of Tenants' Improvements to Leaseholds

When a landlord retakes possession after the tenant abandons the leasehold or defaults on the lease, the landlord is entitled to whatever improvements the lessee made, unless the lease specifically gives the tenant the right to remove some or all of them. In the eyes of the common law, the landlord is just getting back what he gave up for a period of time, because improvements are deemed part of the land itself. Recall that the description of the real estate in a deed to a house and land only identifies the parcel on which the house stands and traditionally does not mention the house. Is the landlord's recovery of the leasehold, when improvements that increase the property's value have been added by the tenant, a recovery only of what the landlord already owned or the acquisition of something new and, hence, income?

Because the improvements flowed from the agreement between the landlord and tenant, it may be tempting to regard the entire transaction as one in which the land simply grew more valuable, rather than as one in which the landlord not only got back what he or she already owned, but also received a new and separate asset, whose value should be treated as a windfall for tax purposes.

After the Supreme Court in *Helvering v. Bruun*[11] decided that any value-increasing improvement could be regarded as newly acquired, so that the logic of recovery does not apply to it, Congress enacted section 109, which declares that "[g]ross income does not include income (other than rent) derived by a lessor of real property on the termination of a lease, representing the value of such property attributable to buildings erected or other improvements made by the lessee." Note that Congress did not dispute the Court's reckoning that there may be income in such circumstances; the provision only says that such income need not be reported as such. In any event, we need not worry about whether the category of "recovery" should be stretched to justify the now statutory exclusion.

---

[10]*Comm'r v. Banks*, 543 U.S. 426 (2005); I.R.C. §62(a)(20).
[11]309 U.S. 461 (1940). See Chapter 9.D(2).

H. Other Property Improved Without Realization

Suppose that intangible property is modified by legislation or private contract; for example, a warranty is added to an executory contract for the sale of equipment. Should we regard a taxpayer's use of the modification to her advantage as the recovery of something in which she has no basis and which she must therefore include in gross income? This puzzle and others like it are perhaps best dealt with not as recovery issues, but as realization issues. In any event, no case law or administrative response affords guidance in terms of recovery, though *Cottage Savings Association v. Commissioner*[12] and regulations on security swaps indicate that a change in the bundle of rights a security represents is almost always a realization event, because the modified or replaced security is distinct from that owned before.[13]

I. "Recovery" of Basis

To avoid confusion, it must be emphasized that recoveries of the sort discussed so far in this chapter do not include what are often called "recoveries of basis," which can never be income to the taxpayer. When a taxpayer disposes of property, the difference between the proceeds of the disposition (the "amount realized," to use the term section 1001 coins for this) and the property's basis is a gain, if positive, or a loss, if negative. The taxpayer can be said to recover the property's basis in either case. If there is a gain on the transaction as a whole, the taxpayer is not taxed on a portion of the proceeds equal to the basis of the property disposed of. In the case of a loss, the taxpayer can deduct the excess of his or her basis over the amount realized, so that this part of the property's basis serves to offset the taxpayer's income from other sources.

We also speak of recovering basis in connection with depreciation and annuities. Depreciation, discussed at length in Chapter 15, allows a taxpayer annually to deduct a part of the basis of property used in a trade or business. This scheme of deductions allows the taxpayer to get the benefit of the property's basis over a number of years. Similarly, in computing taxable income, an annuitant subtracts an aliquot part of the price of the annuity from each payment he or she receives. We describe this too as recovery of basis.

Example 4.5: Alfred buys a printing press for $500,000 to use in a newspaper business. The business fails, and the poor market for used presses results in Alfred getting only $200,000 for his press when he liquidates the business. At that point, he had taken tax depreciation deductions that reduced the basis of the press to $450,000. He has no gain, of course, on the sale, and gets to keep the $200,000 he actually receives without having to pay tax on it. His deductible loss on selling the press is $250,000, and this allows him to avoid tax on income from other sources, because the deduction reduces his taxable income and thereby shelters $250,000 of other gross income. We say he "recovers his basis" by selling the press on these terms, with the benefit of deducting the loss.

---

[12]499 U.S. 554 (1991).

[13]*Comm'r v. Olmsted Inc. Life Agency*, 304 F.2d 16 (8th Cir. 1962), held that an insurance company's cancellation of a retired agent's "renewal royalties" for the past sale of life insurance and the substitution of annuities for the royalty rights was a "novation," i.e., the substitution of a new contract for the old contract, but nonetheless was not a realization event. The court did not use the word "recovery," though it might have said the agent merely recovered what he already owned.

In Chapters 6 and 9, dealing with basis and realization of income or loss on property dealings, you will be reminded not to confuse recovery of basis with financial recovery of money or property.

SUMMARY

- In general, recovered money or property is treated as a substitute for what it replaces and is taxed or not, according to whether what is being replaced would be taxable.

- Gross income includes damages and settlements that replace only lost wages or net appreciation of destroyed property.

- A recovery that replaces a physical endowment is excluded from income if it falls within any of the categories excluded by section 104.

- Recoveries for nondeductible losses may be excludible, as *Clark* illustrates, but the scope of the exclusion is not clear.

- Death benefits of life insurance are fully excluded under section 101, unless the beneficiary bought the policy, and then only to the extent of the beneficiary's basis.

- Property insurance benefits are excluded from income by expansive interpretation of section 165.

- Withdrawal of value from an endowment life insurance policy is excludible only to the extent of basis.

- Recovery for injury to business goodwill or going-concern value is deductible only to the extent of the taxpayer's basis in them.

- Punitive damages and statutory damages not limited to excludible personal physical injury or to the basis of business goodwill are included in gross income.

- Pleadings and settlement documents are usually crucial evidence of what a recovery replaces and hence of whether and to what extent it is includible in gross income.

CONNECTIONS

Loss Deduction

When a recovery makes good a taxpayer's loss of some kind, the prior deductibility of the loss naturally has a bearing on whether the recovery is excluded from income. The discussion of transactional parity in Chapter 10 sheds further light on this.

Basis Adjustments

If recovery makes up for a partial loss in the value of property, the original basis of the entire property may be adjusted. The amount recovered is treated as an amount realized on the disposition of a partial interest in the property. Because part of the entire property's basis must be allocated to the partial interest, some (or, in rare cases, all) of the recovery may be excluded. This kind of recovery is tantamount to a deduction of the allocated partial basis from the amount realized. See Chapter 7.B.

"Recovery" of Basis

To clarify the foregoing connection, we should note the following. The word "recovery" is unfortunately in general use both for items that make up for injuries or financial losses and for the quite different matter of taking the basis of property into account in depreciating or determining the tax consequences of a disposition. Chapter 7 extensively discusses recovery of basis.

Origin-of-Claim Doctrine

What a recovery replaces usually dictates whether it counts as income or not. Similarly, the "origin" of a litigable claim is the key issue in determining whether the litigation expenses are deductible. Since recoveries and litigation expenses belong to different categories—potential income items and potential deductions—the latter are discussed separately in Chapter 13.

Realization Doctrine and Landlord Windfalls

Helvering v. Bruun, discussed in Section G, apparently enlarged congressional and administrative discretion to decide when a taxpayer realizes a gain or loss in property dealings. Chapter 9.B(2) discusses this aspect of the case.

Attorney's Fees

On below-the-line deduction of attorney's fees, see Chapter 13.G on itemized deductions.

Gifts, Windfalls, and Other Haphazard Gains

Theory can account for most standard exclusions from income. Others make sense to all *except* the theorist. Gifts are the classic case. The idea that they might be taxed strikes most ordinary people as outrageous. But pundits have failed to see what is so special about them. Giving satisfies the donor and the donee is made better off, so why shouldn't both be taxed — the donor on acquiring the means of making the gift and the donee on receiving it? Similar questions are raised about other more or less fortuitous items like government benefits, insurance recoveries, scholarships, the Nobel Prize, lottery winnings — the list is long. This chapter is about exclusions that experts are not comfortable with or actively oppose. We can please most of the people most of the time, and the income tax chooses to try to do that here. What the expert minority thinks matters, though, and sometimes changes the outcome at least slightly. Congress makes the final call.

O V E R V I E W

A. FORTUITOUS ACCESSIONS TO WEALTH IN GENERAL

B. GRASSROOTS RATIONALE OF THE GIFT EXCLUSION

1. Theories of Income and the Case for Inclusion
2. Taxing Gifts Would Destroy the Equation of Total Private Income with Social Product
3. A Macroeconomic Reason for Excluding Gifts
4. Distinguishing Gifts from Other Fortuitous Gains
5. Intrafamily Gifts

C. CASES ON THE MEANING OF "GIFT"

D. BASIS ISSUES RELATED TO GIFTS

E. THE BASIS OF INCOME AND RESIDUAL INTERESTS IN GIFT PROPERTY

F. GIFTS THAT FORM PART OF OTHER TRANSACTIONS

G. NET GIFTS

H. PRIZES AND AWARDS, SCHOLARSHIPS AND FELLOWSHIPS

A. Fortuitous Accessions to Wealth in General

Lucky finds and other unmerited gains are taxed no differently in the United States than the fruits of labor and capital. Other countries see it differently and do not tax some or all of them. If serendipitous gains are ever not income, the source of a gain plays a part in determining whether it is income. Alas, for finders and keepers here, our courts have repeatedly held that sources are irrelevant.

Sidebar

EXCLUSIONS FOR TRANSFER PAYMENTS

The value of food stamps is not included in a recipient's income, but unemployment benefits are, even if distributed pursuant to a special governmental stimulus program designed to alleviate the hardship of joblessness. A large fraction of Social Security retirement benefits is included in the income of taxpayers with gross income from other sources above certain thresholds, but recipients with less income are allowed to exclude them.

We begin, not with a gift, but with a lucky find. In *United States v. Cesarini*,[1] a couple bought a piano for their daughter for $15 and seven years later discovered $4,467 in old currency inside while cleaning it. They first reported the find as income, and then amended the tax return to deny that it was. Before the court, they argued that section 61 does expressly include treasure trove (the common law category to which their find arguably belonged) in gross income, and that no pattern of treating other lucky finds differently could be discerned elsewhere in the Code. The Seventh Circuit rejected their arguments, quoting section 61: "Gross income means all income *from whatever source derived*, unless excluded by law." This would seem to establish inclusion as the default treatment for all haphazard gains. But sources sometimes do matter.

Although the *Cesarini* holding is good law, ordinary people may harbor doubts about the underlying point. To see how the law has developed, we first consider all haphazard gains from a general perspective, and then focus more closely on gifts, the near cousin of windfalls. Section B.4, below, briefly compares the disparate treatment of gifts and true windfalls and the underlying rationale.

B. Grassroots Rationale of the Gift Exclusion

(1) Theories of Income and the Case for Inclusion

Most people do not consider gifts income. A number of theoretical approaches support a different view. If "benefit" is your favorite test for whether something is

---

[1] 296 F. Supp. 3 (D.C. Ohio 1969).

income, then gifts benefit both the donor and the donee. If "consumption" strikes your fancy as a part of the definition of income, both the donor and the donee "consume" the gift. "Accession to wealth"? Again, yes as to both donor, on first acquiring the gift property, and donee, when the property is passed on. Someone may object that these approaches allow "double counting" of the income item, because they may attribute the same *thing* as income to more than one person. But without a more elaborate theory of income, that is no objection.[2]

Example 5.1: Susan gives Jane $200 for Jane's campaign for a place on the town council. Jane uses the money to pay personal expenses unrelated to the campaign. Susan cannot deduct the contribution, and Jane must report it as income. The money a private individual gives a political candidate is not deductible, and that same money may be included in the recipient's income if he or she uses it for personal purposes.

Example 5.2: Technogame, Inc., pays its principal software designer $5,000,000 for one hour's work. The IRS challenges Technogame's deduction of this payment as lavish and extravagant wages. The IRS may win because an employer is not allowed to deduct a lavish or extravagant salary paid to an employee, although the employee must include it in income.[3]

(2) Taxing Gifts Would Destroy the Equation of Total Private Income with Social Product

The sum of society's wealth is not increased when one member of society transfers something to another. In this respect, gambling, gift giving, and insurance contract payments are alike. The similarity, however, has not persuaded the public or the legislature that all should be treated alike for tax purposes. Most people think it reasonable to count gambling winnings as income, but regard gifts differently. Whether a transfer increases the national wealth is, therefore, not the key to understanding the different tax treatment of gifts, windfalls, and insurance payments for losses.

(3) A Macroeconomic Reason for Excluding Gifts

In *Eisner v. Macomber*, which held bona fide stock dividends *not* to be income, the Supreme Court said in dictum that income is gain derived from labor or capital or the two combined. Theorists of the pre-income tax era had identified labor, capital, and lands as the main "factors of production."[4] The first advocates of income taxation believed individual income was simply the division of national product among individuals and could also be reduced to the gains attributable to such factors of production. *Macomber* appeared to interpret the Sixteenth Amendment in the light of this received wisdom. In *Commissioner v. Glenshaw Glass, Inc.*, however, the Court

---

[2]This chapter does not address the special character of gifts to charity and others to which taxpayers' contributions are deductible, despite the fact that they are also gifts; we leave them for separate consideration because they advance public policy concerns and are in fact treated differently from "private" gifts.
[3]Code §162(a).
[4]252 U.S. 189, 207 (1920). Economists eventually came to consider land just another kind of capital.

repudiated the dictum,[5] noting instead that the Amendment speaks of "income, from any source derived." No list of sources, even as broadly described as "labor" and "capital," limits the scope of "income" as the term is used in the Constitution or in Code section 61.

Case law accordingly shows no sympathy for the popular conviction that income does not include gifts, lucky finds, lottery winnings, and other serendipitous gains.[6] Your grasp of the law and of tax theory are not faulty, however, if you remain uneasy about these matters. On the contrary, you *should* be aware that for most purposes, income is *usually* the product of labor or capital or both. Yet the venerable thesis that income must come from certain types of productive activity, which would favor excluding gifts from income, would not explain the *in*clusion of windfalls.

(4) Distinguishing Gifts from Other Fortuitous Gains

To explore the matter further, compare the general characteristics of gifts and wind-falls. Both are fully at the acquirer's disposal; no part of their value has been used up in the process of being transferred from a previous owner to the present owner. But a donor is not allowed to deduct the value or the basis of the gift, so the gift's value has probably been taxed at least once. Lost money or other property may be deductible by the person who lost it and the tax refundable. The government stands to lose no revenue on a gift transfer, but may lose revenue on a windfall unless its value is taxed to the recipient.

On the other hand, a finder, like the recipient of a gift, is better off to the extent of the acquired property's value, no matter where it came from. This common element may be the deciding factor in classifying both as income for two main theoretical frameworks, the ability-to-pay and the SHS objective definitions of income. As we saw in Chapter 2.C.2, some have been drawn to the idea that the passivity of donors and donees, or of lucky finders, differentiates these serendipitous additions to wealth from those acquired with effort. Our own Code once seemed to defer to that idea, at least for prizes based entirely on merit, such as the Nobel Prize. It is impossible to say whether the need for revenue or the difficulty of articulating the principle behind this would-be distinction persuaded Congress to include all prizes in income.

(5) Intrafamily Gifts

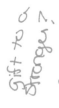

Given the failure of theoretical arguments to chasten the grassroots view of gifts, it is not surprising that income tax laws always ignore theory in this respect. Take it as a fundamental fact about income taxation: Gifts, unless they have close ties with business or employment, are not income to recipients. Code section 102(a) so provides.

---

[5]348 U.S. 426, 430-431 (1955). An interesting point: If *Glenshaw Glass* had affirmatively held that source cannot constitutionally be used in identifying gross income (in deciding whether gross income includes any would-be accession to wealth), then the Constitution would require that both gifts and windfalls, or neither, be considered gross income. The Code expressly excludes gifts and not windfalls, suggesting that gifts would otherwise be included in gross income. This may not be necessary as a matter of constitutional law.

[6]Life insurance benefits are excluded for most recipients. I.R.C. §102(a). Property insurance recoveries are universally considered to be excluded, but the only hint in the Code to this effect is contained in §165(a), which allows many losses not covered by insurance to be deducted. Gambling winnings are included in income — there is no statutory exclusion for this — but gambling losses can be deducted up to the amount of gambling winnings for the year. I.R.C. §165(d).

Income tax systems have little choice but to disregard many transfers between parents and children, especially when parents and children are functioning as a single unit. The sheer number and frequency of benefits shared or shifted within a family blurs their boundaries, making it difficult to determine the net result for any family member. Consider an allowance given to a child on the leniently enforced condition that chores be done against the backdrop of the parent's obligation to support the child. It is not worthwhile to keep track of such things or worry about their classification. In any case, the intrusion by government into the fabric of the family[7] would be unacceptable. It is not surprising that income tax systems ignore most transfers among family members.

F   A   Q

Q: Would it count as a gift to "throw" a game, allowing the prize to go to your opponent?

A: While the outcome of a game hangs in the balance, refusal to compete may be illegal but is probably not a gift to the other side within the meaning of section 102.

It might work, however, to limit the gift exclusion to gifts between family members who share a household, such as during child-rearing years and when parents are elderly. Other intrafamily gifts might be taxed without intrusion on the family at its most intimate. Policing the boundary, however, would not be easy. Tax-sensitive parents could make transfers to children during the privileged period for gift giving that the parties might later decide to label as gifts or as loans, depending on the balance of tax consequences.[8] Instead, we (and most, if not all, other countries) exclude not only all intimate family gifts, but all gifts, despite the variety of their purposes and economic effects (see Table 5.1 on the following page). The slippery slope from the former to the latter pushes tax systems to treat all gifts alike, exempting donees from income tax on the value received, despite their great differences in purpose and economic effect.

Not surprisingly, tax common law has struggled to distinguish gifts from other effortless gains. We next consider a few important cases. Though each deals with what a gift is, none openly treats this inquiry as having a policy dimension of any kind. This antiseptic approach allows the courts to remain open to the possibility that a transfer can be a gift to a business associate or to an employee.

---

[7]*Moore v. City of East Cleveland*, 431 U.S. 494, 498 (1977) (describing intrusive definition of "family" for zoning purposes as "slicing deeply into the family itself").

[8]Parents often do lend money to children, taking back promissory notes, which they later "decide" and perhaps always intended to "forgive," thereby permitting the debtor/donee children to claim deductions for interest paid on the notes and to have a basis in the alleged gift property measured by the face value of the notes. The IRS can, of course, dispute the reality of the loans and contend that the gifts were actually complete when the "loans" were set up, but current law treats recharacterization of loans as gifts as depending on the facts of the particular case.

TABLE 5.1 Purposes and Effects of Various Gifts

● = yes   ○ = maybe   [blank] = no

	Necessary for Child Rearing	Optional for Child Rearing	Intergenerational Transfer	Life Partner Transfer	Donor Narcissism	Commercial Interest Served
Children's clothing, food, lodging	●					
Childcare outside the home	○	○		○		○
Some toys for children	○	○				
More toys for children		●				
Children's higher education			○		○	
Gift to grown child			●		○	
Gifts to spouse/partner			●	●	○	
Gift to business associate					○	○
Gift to former employee						●
Gift to needy stranger					○	●

C. Cases on the Meaning of "Gift"

The main decision on gifts is *Duberstein v. Commissioner*,[9] which consolidated two cases. In the first, Berman gave Duberstein a Cadillac. The two were business associates, and Duberstein had referred customers to Berman over the years. Duberstein mildly resisted but then accepted the car and acknowledged at trial that it was related to the customer referrals. There was no contract between the two requiring future business cooperation. Held, no gift. In the second case, the trustees of a wealthy church made a gratuitous lump sum retirement payment to Stanton, the church's resigning investment and property manager. The relationship between the board and Stanton may have been troubled toward the end of his tenure, but the board resolution authorizing the payment said it was a token of gratitude. The case was remanded for further findings of fact.

The Court extracted the meaning of "gift" in section 102(a) from earlier cases.[10] Putting their teachings together:

1. A gift you *have* to make is no gift.
2. Even a voluntary transfer is not a gift if made with a profit-oriented or compensatory purpose.
3. The right kind of intention is one that "proceeds from a 'detached and disinterested generosity,' . . . 'out of affection, respect, admiration, charity or like impulses.'"

Quasi-rule (3) may collapse into (2) because the catchall phrase "or like impulses" may cover any reason other than profit or compensation of the payee for past services, but that is not made explicit. The *Duberstein* Court did not reason by analogy with paradigmatic gifts made by parents to children in the nest. Some courts and the IRS, therefore, think the substantive motives cited in (3) provide a core test.[11] Others, like the Ninth Circuit in *Olk v. Commissioner*,[12] interpret "like impulses" more broadly; a croupier in *Olk* was not allowed to treat as gifts the gratuities he received from superstitious gamblers, even though he was in no position to do them any favors—the court shrewdly reasoned that superstition is neither generous nor benevolent.

The broad *Duberstein* standard is problematic. *United States v. Harris*[13] was the tax fraud prosecution of two sisters who claimed that regular payments and other gratuities they received from an older man were gifts and not pay for companionship. The government could not establish *mens rea*—which is, of course, a requirement for any criminal conviction, even when the crime is tax fraud. No one, the court thought, could form a sufficiently specific wrongful intent when the legal definition of gift for tax purposes is as vague as *Duberstein* left it. This of course does not mean that the government cannot nail a would-be donee for *civil* fraud. The burden of proof is on the taxpayer in that context. The defendants in *Harris* might easily have lost in a civil fraud contest, precisely because proof of a gift is difficult.

---

[9]363 U.S. 278 (1960).
[10]*Id.* at 285-286.
[11]*See, e.g.*, Rev. Rul. 99-44.
[12]536 F.2d 876 (9th Cir. 1976).
[13]942 F.2d 1125 (7th Cir. 1991).

Duberstein is the leading case on the meaning of "gift" in Code section 102, but it also deals with a recurrent and central, if narrower, problem. An employer will often want to compensate an employee and one business associate will often want to reward another with an excludible "gift" rather than taxable payment for services, because the payor thereby gets more bang for the buck. When *Duberstein* was decided, there was no automatic disqualification of this strategy for rewarding effort in a tax-exempt fashion. Shortly thereafter, Congress stepped in to give the IRS the per se rule it wanted for employees, adding section 102(c) to the Code in 1986, which provides that an "amount transferred by or for an employer to, or for the benefit of, an employee" is never an excludible gift.

Thus, the gratuitous transfer to Stanton would not be eligible for exclusion today, even if the church's intent were disinterested, benevolent, etc. Note that Congress did not directly alter the *Duberstein* standard for transfers outside the employment context. Section 274(b), however, placed a low ceiling on section 162(a) deductions for business gifts, without affirming or denying that gifts between business contacts are possible. A donor cannot deduct more than $25 per donee for any taxable year. The total amount to be deducted is not limited, only the total value of "gifts" to any person. Note that the exclusion of the gift is not affected: The recipient may still exclude the gift if it is indeed one within the meaning of section 102(a). Effective denial of the deduction for large nonfamily gifts makes sense. If a business "donor" could deduct the value of substantial gifts, their value would escape tax as donor or donee income, whereas family gifts are normally taxed in full as income of the donor or as income partly of the donor and partly of the donee (see Section E below).

Is a business gift possible? We saw that one of the taxpayers in *Duberstein* sought to exclude as a gift the large retirement gratuity his employer gave him, and the Court remanded for further findings and decision (the lower court agreed and found the gift eligible for exclusion). The exclusion should be in doubt, however, whether the payor was entitled to a deduction or not. Though *Duberstein*'s demarcation of the class of gifts is fuzzy, recall point (2) in the above summary of its ruling: Even a voluntary transfer is not a gift, if made with a profit-oriented or compensatory purpose. Yet the Court did not rule out the possibility of a business gift. Congress used the word "gift" in section 274(b) without hinting that business gifts are not also excluded by section 102(a), and nothing in either section supports the case for exclusion. The regulations under section 102 are silent on this point.

Example 5.3: Richard, a very rich man, invites his best friends, of whom many are business associates, to his wedding. Everyone who attends the wedding receives a lavish present. On his tax return for the year, Richard claims deductions for the value of the gifts to business associates. Given the similarity of the gifts to the wedding guests who were not business associates, it is plausible to conclude that Richard did not intend the gifts he deducted to further specific commercial or economic ends. A court could (as in the *Stanton* case) find that Richard's primary motive was benevolent and not profit seeking.

D. Basis Issues Related to Gifts

Problems about whether a transfer is a gift occur along the dividing line between purely benevolent transfers and those tied to the donor's economic well-being. Many gifts are well within the bounds of benevolence. Those not made in cash, however, raise another kind of question. A gift in kind must have a basis in the hands of the donee. If that basis equals the value of the property, the gift poses no special problems, because neither the donor nor the donee can have a gain or loss by reason of the transfer when value equals basis; the difference between these two amounts is always zero.

When value and basis differ, gain or loss should be attributed to one of the parties. The donor has the economic gain or loss; why not the gain or loss for tax purposes? Isn't the making of a gift a disposition, and isn't disposition a paradigmatic realization for purposes of section 1001? See Chapter 9.A. But the broad rule is that donors do not realize gain or loss on making either charitable or private gifts. Because no gain or loss is realized, none is recognized, and the donor has no *income* tax consequences in either case. (He or she may have an obligation to report and pay gift tax on the value of the gift, under a statutory scheme that imposes a unified tax on lifetime and testamentary gifts.)

Example 5.4: Croesus purchased a modern painting for only $200 when the painter was unknown. The painting is now worth $2,000,000. He gives it to the Museum of Modern Art. He realizes no gain or loss on making this charitable contribution. This is so even though Croesus would have realized a gain of $1,999,800 if he had instead sold the painting for the $2,000,000 it would have brought on the market. (Croesus is entitled to deduct the painting's entire present value of $2,000,000 as a charitable contribution under section 170, but we discuss charitable contributions more fully in Chapter 12.F.)

Example 5.5: Same facts except that Croesus gives the Andy Warhol painting to his niece Cleopatra. As in the previous example, Croesus realizes no gain or loss on making the gift.

Just as inter vivos donors face no income tax consequences, the estate that distributes money or property to beneficiaries has no income tax consequences on the transfers themselves, although an estate that stays open for a period of time may be liable for tax on its income. What are the consequences for *recipients* of gifts in kind?

Recipients of gift property do not share the immunity of donors and their estates. Whether acquired by purchase or by gift, the later transfer of the gift property is normally a realization event. Donees face all the usual consequences of property dispositions. To know the tax consequences of a realization event, section 1001 tells us that we must know the basis of the property disposed of. What then is the basis of gift property?

The Code deals differently with lifetime and testamentary gifts. At one time the entire value of the estate of a decedent, out of which testamentary gifts were to be made, was subject to an estate tax at what were once substantial rates, although inter vivos gifts in kind are rarely subject to the ostensibly parallel gift tax because of a high annual exemption.[14] In short, the two kinds of gift, lifetime and testamentary, impose different costs on the donor, and it has been thought that this difference justifies a difference in the donee's basis.

Testamentary gifts come to their recipients with a **stepped-up basis** equal to the fair market value of the property on the date of the decedent's death or on a date six

---

[14]For years, few estates have paid the estate tax, whose rigor the statutory threshold and various dodges greatly diminished. The estate tax was repealed for 2010 but the repealing statute reinstates the tax at moderately high rates from 2011 on.

months later, if the executor elects to use this alternative valuation date.[15] This is roughly the same basis the new owner of the property would have had on buying it — the new basis is equal to the "cost basis" that section 1012 would prescribe for the same property purchased at fair market value on whichever of those dates the executor chooses.

Inter vivos gift property has a **split basis**.[16] There is one basis for measuring gain after the gift is made, and another basis for measuring loss. It works like this. The recipient of a gift in kind takes the property with his or her benefactor's basis as far as gain on the sale or other disposition of the property is concerned. Any gain the donor would have had on a sale of the property at the time of the gift or later, the donee will also have. Admittedly, the tax to be paid by the donor and the donee, respectively, on selling the property at that time may differ because of other differences in their tax situations — they could face different marginal rates, or enjoy different reductions in taxable income because of unrelated losses, or have different credits against overall tax liability. But the gross income added by virtue of the disposition of the property will be the same in either case.

For measuring a loss, however, the basis of inter vivos gift property is restricted to the lower of (1) the donor's basis, or (2) the fair market value of the property at the time of gift. Thus, if a taxpayer makes a gift of loss property — property whose basis is greater than its fair market value — the recipient cannot benefit from that loss. The disallowed loss is the difference between the basis and the fair market value *at the time of gift*. Actually, the donor's full basis can still come to aid of the property's new owner if the property rises above its fair market value at the time of the gift. The reason is important for applying the split-basis rule correctly. The difference between the basis of the property in the original owner's hands and the fair market value of the property when the gift is made is not *subtracted* then and there from the property's basis, so as to be lost for all purposes. The new owner gets to use the old owner's basis if the value of the gift later rises so as to exceed that basis, which means that the inherent loss may produce a benefit.

It may seem that understanding the split-basis rule is hard enough without having to be concerned about its rationale. But we really should do that as well, because it turns out that the rationale is subtle at best, and perhaps just wrong. The only conceivable purpose for the split-basis rule is to prevent a donor from transferring the tax benefit of the loss to a donee. A low-tax-bracket donor might be tempted to do this if the object of his or her benevolence were in a higher bracket, because between the two of them the net taxes saved will be greater. Let's pause to note the reason for this general proposition.

Example 5.6: Dad gives Daughter stock with a basis of $1,000 and a current fair market value of $800. The built-in loss is $200. Dad, who is retired, is in the 10 percent marginal tax bracket. Daughter has a higher annual income and is in the 28 percent marginal bracket. The tax benefit of a loss is the amount of the loss multiplied by the taxpayer's marginal tax bracket; for example, a loss of $200 is worth $56 to a taxpayer whose marginal rate is 28 percent, because 28 percent of $200 is $56, and this is the amount by which the taxpayer's tax liability is reduced on claiming the deduction, but it's worth only $20 to a taxpayer in the 10 percent bracket because 15 percent of $200 is $30.

---

[15]Code §1014(a)(1) & (2).
[16]*Id.* §1015(a).

Hence, low- to high-tax-bracket gifts of loss property result in a net tax savings for the donor-donee unit and a net loss for the government.

So far, so good. Unfortunately, the split-basis rule does not prevent gift-giving arbitrage through gifts of gain property. A high-tax-bracket donor may be tempted to give property with a basis that is higher than its fair market value to a low-tax-bracket donee, again because between the two of them the net taxes saved will be greater. The math is parallel to that for gifts of loss property.

Example 5.7: Dad has not retired and faces a marginal tax rate of 28 percent. Daughter is a student and pays 10 percent on all of her net income from part-time work. Dad gives Daughter stock with a basis of $1,000 and a current fair market value of $1,200. The built-in gain is $200. The tax burden of incurring the gain, should Daughter sell the property right away, is only $20 for her — her tax rate of 10 percent multiplied by the gain of $200. If Dad had realized the gain instead, his tax on the gain would have been $56 — his tax rate of 28 percent times $200. So if Dad and Daughter are a kind of unit for economic purposes, which they may be because Dad helps to support Daughter while she is in school, together they suffer the lower tax burden, and the government stands to lose the higher tax Dad would have paid on disposing of the property.

Gifts of gains from high- to low-bracket taxpayers and gifts of losses from low- to high-bracket taxpayers thus pose parallel threats to the fisc and allow a form of tax arbitrage at taxpayers' election.

We should remember that the gift exclusion is most clearly justified for gifts within families. Intrafamily giving seems most commonly to run from older to younger taxpayers, and older taxpayers are more likely to be in higher tax brackets than younger taxpayers. If so, then gifts of gain property from parents to children, grandparents to grandchildren, etc., are prominent among those favored by the split-basis rule, for it is from higher- to lower-bracket taxpayers that gifts of gain property yield tax benefits under the rule. Gifts from lower- to higher-bracket taxpayers are barred from producing similar benefits. Although, as the foregoing examples illustrate, older taxpayers may be in lower brackets than their younger relatives, this is unlikely be true of the much older taxpayers who are most likely to make large gifts to their descendants; these are generally wealthy taxpayers who have high taxable incomes even in retirement.

The split-basis rule is non-neutral unless we assume the foregoing demographic information about who makes gifts to whom and about the parties' respective tax brackets. Few tax experts think highly of the rule's efforts to block loss shifting, even though the purpose of frustrating tax savings through loss shifting has the support of most experts in some other tax contexts.

E. The Basis of Income and Residual Interests in Gift Property

A gift in kind must have a basis so that the taxpayer and the government alike can reckon the taxpayer's gain or loss on its later disposition. The split-basis rule handles that problem for inter vivos gifts, one donee at a time. Often, however, a donor chooses to divide the income stream from the residuary interest in gift property.

For example, a testator may leave the family farm to a spouse for life and to their children at the spouse's death. How is the basis of the property each receives to be determined? One way would be to allocate the available basis, whether the stepped-up basis of section 1014 or the split basis of section 1015, in proportion to the fair market values of the divided portions of the gift as of the date of the gift or basis determination. But that was and is not the Court's way.

F   A   Q

Q: What about divided gifts of property that all vest on the effective date of the same testamentary gift?

A: The stepped-up basis of the entire estate is normally divided among them in proportion to their values on the effective date. Code section 1022 provides a special rule for certain estates with effective dates after 2009.

The entire basis goes to the corpus or residuary interest. In *Irwin v. Gavit*,[17] the Supreme Court held that interests assigned to beneficiaries out of the income of testamentary trust property were entirely taxable as income. The interests were not entitled to a stepped-up basis (under the predecessor of section 1014) equal to the face value, which would have exempted some or all of their value from income. The Court in dictum allocated the full stepped-up basis of the entire property to the corpus, so that only the residuary legatee's income was reduced.[18] Nothing in the case turned on when the basis of the corpus should be determined, but section 1014, the contemporary version of the stepped-up basis rule, points us to the date of the decedent's death or an alternative valuation date within six months thereof.[19] Thus, stated in full, the basis of a divided testamentary gift is the full value of the property on the valuation date fixed by the decedent's death and executor's election, if any, and that basis is assigned to the non-income interest of the residuary beneficiary. Presumably, though this has never been litigated, the split basis of an inter vivos gift whose income and residuary aspects were divided between different donees would go entirely to the residuary interest, with no tax relief for the income beneficiary.[20]

Example 5.8: Aunt Jane leaves a ten-year Treasury note to her niece and nephew, with the income to go entirely to her niece and the amount to be received when the bond matures to go to her nephew. Just before making the gift, she purchased the bond for $9,100. It pays interest at 3 percent per annum of the bond's face value, which is

---

[17]268 U.S. 161 (1940) (Holmes, J.).
[18]"[W]e think that the provision of the act that exempts bequests [by excluding them from income] assumes the gift of a corpus and contrasts it with the income arising from it, but was not intended to exempt income property so-called simply because of a severance between it and the principal fund."
[19]I.R.C. §2032(a) allows the executor to elect a valuation date that is normally six months after the decedent's death unless the property to be valued is sooner distributed or disposed of.
[20]In fact, inter vivos gifts of income and residuary interests are typically made through trusts, which are themselves income tax-paying entities. The very structure of the income tax provisions dealing with trusts presuppose the rule stated above—that income beneficiaries have no basis in their interests and that residuary beneficiaries get the entire benefit of the section 1015 basis—but these provisions implement that presupposition in a complex statutory manner that is beyond the scope of this book.

$10,000. The amount to be paid at maturity is $10,000. The niece receives $300 in interest annually for ten years, and the nephew receives nothing during those years. After the tenth year has run, the nephew receives $10,000. The full amount of the interest income is gross income for the niece; if she has no deductions or losses from other sources, she pays tax on the $300 at her marginal rate of 28 percent, and so the net value of the gift to her each year is only $216. The nephew has a gain of $900 on receiving the redemption distribution — the difference between his basis of $9,100 and the amount of the distribution $10,000 — and the rest of the distribution is not included in his income.

Let us examine the alternative to the foregoing orthodox method of basic allocation. Partial sales of property pose the problem of allocating the original basis of the entire property between the parts sold and retained. The allocation is made in proportion to the values of the parts when the property is first acquired.

Example 5.9: Developer buys a tract of land for $3,000,000. Her basis in the entire tract is therefore $3,000,000. Developer sells part of the tract for $1,000,000 after the whole tract has risen in value to $4,000,000. If the part sold was worth $500,000 when Developer acquired the tract, $500,000 is the basis attributable to it for purposes of measuring the gain on this sale. Hence, Developer has a gain of $500,000 on the sale of the part of the tract.

Following this pattern, we would determine the value of the income and residuary portions of a divided gift and apportion between them the total available basis — stepped-up or split — according to their values. By analogy with the rule for partial sales of cost-basis property, we would use the values of the income and residuary portions at the time when the gift is made. The residuary portion would then be valued not at its expected value when the residue is to be distributed, but at the *present value* of that anticipated future acquisition. Present values, as we learn in Chapter 7, can differ dramatically from future values to be received. Similarly, each anticipated installment of the income to be paid to the income beneficiary would be valued with a discount for the lapse of time before its anticipated receipt.

Example 5.10: On the facts of the previous example, Niece's anticipated receipts of $300 in annual interest would be worth not $3,000 ($300 times ten years), but, if the right discount rate is 4 percent and the interest payments are received at the end of each year, only $2,443. (If you use Excel, the financial function "PV" gives this answer.) Nephew's anticipated receipt of $10,000 after ten years, again using 4 percent as the discount rate, is worth only $6,756. Aunt Jane's cost basis of $9,100 would be allocated between these two portions according to their respective values. The income interest would have a basis of $2,417, and the residuary interest would have a basis of $6,782, so that the niece's installments in the aggregate would yield gross income of $583 and the nephew's residuary distribution a gain of $3,218.

Thus might the tax benefit of the basis be spread between income and residuary beneficiaries of divided gifts. Does fairness require this approach? No. Divided gifts can be designed to take after-tax consequences into account, and so the beneficiaries have only the donor's choice to blame for any lopsided tax treatment of their respective portions. In summary, there seems to be little here to justify change in the law, apart from the worry that donors may not get it right.

F. Gifts That Form Part of Other Transactions

A transfer of property can be partly a gift and partly a sale or exchange. One common variation on this theme is the "bargain sale," in which the seller sells an item at a lower price than market value to gift part of that value to the buyer. We must use the phrase "bargain sale" carefully. Tax experts use it with conscious irony to describe transactions that have both sale and gift aspects. But sometimes a bargain is just a bargain. Some sellers offer the public the opportunity to buy things at below-market prices for purely commercial reasons, not out of benevolence or generosity. To tell the difference between a gift disguised as a sale and a sale at a favorable price, we must know what is going on between the seller and the buyer. As *Duberstein* indicates, it is the seller's intent that controls whether a transfer is a gift, yet intent must manifest itself objectively.

Example 5.11: Virago, an online retailer, offers brand-name point-and-shoot cameras at prices guaranteed to be 10 percent below that of any competitor. Jill, a casual customer with no ties to Virago management or employees, buys a camera and gets the discount. Virago is not making a gift of 10 percent of the value of the camera to Jill.

Example 5.12: The owner of a local camera shop sells Jill a point-and-shoot camera at a 10 percent discount because he knows Jill is graduating from law school and he is feeling generously inclined because of the occasion. He continues to sell the same camera to others without giving a discount. Jill has received a gift.

Who benefits from the combination of gift and non-gift elements? If the seller would have paid a higher tax on selling the property at fair market value, a disguised gift yields a tax benefit for the seller. Some of the tax that would otherwise be due is avoided by the low-price sale, at least if the gift is not treated as a gift. There is no taxable benefit for the donor if he or she would have had no gain on selling the property at the bargain price. But not all sales yield gain. The sale of property for less than its fair market value is a foolish strategy for avoiding tax, unless the gain apparently forgone by the seller actually still benefits him or her in some roundabout fashion, such as when the sale is to a family member or other favored person.

G. Net Gifts

Closely related to bargain sales are gifts on which the donee agrees to pay the *gift* tax for which the donor is liable. These are called **net gifts**, because the gift is only the portion of the value of the property net of the tax the donee pays as quid pro quo. (Section 2504 gives a different meaning to the term "net gift" for certain gift-tax calculations.) Under the once-and-future federal gift and estate tax, some gifts are completely exempt because the base of the gift tax excludes for every donor up to $13,000 a year in gifts to each of any number of donees (section 2503(b)). Gifts above this **annual exclusion** (as it is familiarly called) are added, as it were, to a running tab of lifetime gifts. These nonexcluded gifts may become taxable if a decedent's combined testamentary gifts (bequests through his or her estate) and lifetime gifts in excess of the annual exclusion exceed a specified dollar threshold called the "unified exemption equivalent amount." We are not concerned with the details of the unified gift and estate tax. But net gift agreements are predicated on the fact that a donor may incur a gift tax after having made gifts exceeding a rather high total value.

Example 5.13: Grandma has been generous with gifts to her grandchildren over the years and has given gifts whose total value, after applying the annual exclusion, have used up her unified exemption equivalent amount. She wants to make another big gift this year to her grandson. He agrees to reimburse her for the gift tax she must pay with the gift tax return she files on making the gift. This is a net gift arrangement. Grandson receives a gift whose net value is the difference between the value of the gift and the gift tax that he pays for Grandma.

A net gift combines gift and non-gift elements, and like the combined gifts discussed previously, net gifts may give the donor a taxable quid pro quo. The whole point of the arrangement is to reimburse the maker of the gift for a tax legitimately owed. This is squarely within the *Old Colony Trust* holding that a taxpayer has gross income to the extent that another pays his or her tax liability. The *Clark* holding is that a recovery for taxes legitimately owed is *not* gross income to the recipient when it was the payor's fault that the tax liability arose in the first place. In net gift situations, the recipient of the gift does not control whether the gift should be made and so cannot be responsible for the tax liability of the taxpayer.

One would think that nothing remains to be said about the amount of the reimbursement income. In *Old Colony Trust* situations,[21] the amount of the gross income resulting from the third party's payment of the taxpayer is always the amount of the tax paid. An odd alternative possibility exists, however, in the net gift context, and the Supreme Court oddly made that alternative the rule.

Remember that the taxpayer who makes a gift of appreciated property does not realize the property's inherent gain. One who sells or exchanges property, however, *does* realize and normally recognize any gain or loss — this is the standard treatment of such dispositions under section 1001. So a transaction that is part gift and part recognition event must be parsed. In *Diedrich v. Commissioner*,[22] the Court decided that the taxpayer who makes a net gift has gross income only to the extent that the tax paid by the donee exceeds the taxpayer's entire basis in the gift property. In this instance, the gift consisted of stock worth $300,000, held with a pre-gift basis of roughly $50,000, and the gift tax paid by the children of the taxpayer on receiving the stock was $60,000. The Court allowed the full basis to offset the benefit of the tax

---

[21]279 U.S. 716 (1929); see Chapter 3.A.
[22]454 U.S. 813 (1981).

payment, so that the taxpayer was held to have only $10,000 in gross income from the transaction.

More traditional treatment would have divided the gift into two parts, one of them for which consideration ($60,000) equal to its fair market value was received, and the other for which there was no consideration. This follows the pattern of analysis for partial sales or exchanges. First, we identify the value of the part of a larger piece of property on which gain or loss will be recognized, and then we ascertain the basis of that part of the whole property, which is inevitably less than the property's entire basis. On the facts of the case, this would have been easy to do because the stock was of homogeneous value. Hence, if it had been acquired by purchase for $50,000 in the first place and had grown in value to $300,000 over the intervening period, a $60,000 portion would have a basis equal to one-fifth ($60,000/$300,000) of $50,000, or just $10,000. The donor's gain on the portion of the stock sold to the donee would be $50,000, the difference between the proceeds of the "sale" ($60,000) and the basis of the part of the stock sold ($10,000). But no, the Supreme Court chose the less cumbersome, taxpayer-friendly route, allowing the basis of the entire property to offset the gain on a mere part.

This resembles the favorable but rare treatment accorded to the taxpayer in *Inaja Land Co. v. Commissioner*,[23] to be discussed in Chapter 6.B. There, local government exercised its eminent domain power to take an ill-defined easement over land owned by the taxpayer, and the Tax Court decided that because it was impossible under the circumstances to determine what percentage of the total value of the land the condemned interest represented, the taxpayer must be allowed to recover the property's entire basis before having to recognize any gain on the compensation given for the easement. The difficulty of ascertaining the relative values of the part and the whole was the premise, however, of the holding. In *Diedrich*, the Supreme Court announced what appears to be a broad rule for all net gifts, perhaps for all conditional gifts such as those in which the donee directly compensates the donor for part of the value of the gift. The extension of the holding should not be taken for granted, given the strain between the exception and the approach otherwise generally applicable to partial sales.

H. Prizes and Awards, Scholarships and Fellowships

To describe prizes and awards, even the least easily anticipated, as fortuitous would stretch the meaning of the word. The whole point of a prize or award is to recognize the merit, need, or some other attribute of the recipient, and many recipients have made some effort to get them. Game-show contestants and academic grant applicants, of course, strive for what they get. Nevertheless, some prizes and awards surprise or at least come as strokes of luck to some taxpayers.

The family resemblance of prizes and awards to gifts may be the source of a grassroots belief that they too should not be taxed as income. Before 1954, the Code itself was agnostic as to their treatment. With the 1954 Code came section 74, in its original form, which declared prizes and awards generally to be includible in gross income, but made exceptions for those primarily made to recognize achievement in certain fields of endeavor if the recipient had done nothing to get them. Section 74

---

[23]9 T.C. 727 (1947), *acq.*, 1948-1 C.B. 2.

has since restricted the exclusion to two situations: (1) The winner transfers the prize or award to a charity without using or enjoying it, or (2) it is an "employee achievement award" for length of service or for safety. Now, even Nobel Prize winners must give up a sizeable portion of their admittedly sizeable prize to the government.

Under Section 117, scholarships and fellowships (not necessarily different types of academic awards) are excluded from gross income if used for qualified tuition and related expenses, but any portion that is payment for teaching, research, or other services by the student required as a condition of receiving the otherwise excludible amount must be included in gross income. Some grant programs for students that do not qualify for the exclusion, because the grant money is not earmarked for qualified tuition and related expenses, are nevertheless not considered wages for purposes of tax and Social Security contributions by either the grantor or the student and may be excluded on other grounds as applicable, such as working-condition fringes.[24] The IRS has also graciously allowed exclusion for athletic scholarships if the educational institution does not require the student to participate in a sport, or any other particular activity, and cannot terminate the student for nonparticipation. These restrictions smack of the gratuitous—like gifts!

SUMMARY

- Gross income includes fortuitous accessions to wealth without limitation as to their source, unless they are expressly excluded.

- Gifts of money are entirely excluded; gifts of property are excluded from income but come with a split basis that may result in the donee being taxed on pre-gift appreciation.

- Testamentary gifts normally have a fair market value basis to the heirs, devisees, and legatees—the fair market value being fixed at the date of the decedent's death or, if the executor makes an election, at a date six months later.

- The stepped-up basis of testamentary gifts goes entirely to gifts of corpus, in the case of split gifts—income to one donee, corpus to another—so that income gifts are entirely included in the donee's gross income.

---

[24]Treas. Reg. §1.3141(b)(10).

CONNECTIONS

The Return of a Windfall

Property law often gives a finder the right to undisturbed possession of the found item, but someone with a higher claim based on prior possession or title can reclaim the item. If the item is found in one year and returned in a later year, the claim-of-right doctrine requires its value to be included in the finder's income in the earlier year and allows the finder to deduct its value when found in a later year, with correction for the difference in tax rates if the value is greater than $3,000. See Chapter 10.A(3).

"Gifts" from Employers

Section 102(c)(1) denies the gift exclusion to gifts from the taxpayer's employer. Fringe benefits for which Code sections 82 (employer reimbursed moving expenses), 119 (meals and lodging), 120 (group legal services plans), 125 (cafeteria plans), 127 (educational assistance programs), 129 (dependent care assistance programs), and 132 (other fringe benefits) provide exclusions are not considered gifts for purposes of the denial of exclusion in section 102(c)(1); the more specific exclusions in the listed sections are controlling. See Chapter 3.

Realization

The gain or loss inherent in property is not realized when the owner makes a gift of that property to a tax-exempt donee under section 170(c) or to a private donee, such as a family member. See Chapter 9.A.

Basis of Gift Property

A taxpayer, therefore, does not get to use the basis of property he or she owns as a sort of tax shelter against gain when making a gift, because the classification of giving as a nonrealization event precludes the donor from recovering the gift property's basis in her hands before the gift is made. See Chapter 6.B.

Basis

6

We measure gain or loss on a property sale by comparing the seller's investment with the sale proceeds. If the proceeds are greater than the

investment, there is a gain. If less, the seller loses part or all of the investment and suffers a loss. These ideas guide us in thinking about property transactions for financial and tax purposes alike. Normally, the cost of an item is also the owner's tax investment or "basis" in the asset. Basis and cost may continue to be the same, and the owner's gain or loss on disposing of it may be the same from both financial and tax viewpoints, but not necessarily so. Accordingly, taxable gain or loss is the difference between the proceeds of a sale ("amount realized") and the *adjusted* basis of the property sold. As this implies, basis is not to be taxed. We can turn this around to expose a broader rule. An asset's basis is either its historic cost or that part of the asset's value that should be treated *as if* it had already been taxed. It is excluded from income when the asset is sold. If the asset is used in business, a fraction of the basis can be deducted for each year of that use. This chapter first explains how basis ordinarily figures in the computation of gain and loss. Next, we consider some unusual applications of the concept. Finally, we survey the parallel between property dealings, to which basis is the key, and other profit-oriented activities, in which it plays a smaller part. Not all introductory courses present this material in a single unit, and so the connections noted at the end of the chapter amplify this first close look at the concept of basis.

A. Fundamentals

The origin of the concept of basis lies in our everyday understanding of profit and loss in property dealings. When a person buys property, the purchase price is significant for later transactions. Importantly, this amount is subtracted from the proceeds in measuring the gain or loss on any sale or exchange of the property. The cost of improving or carrying the property before the sale or exchange would have been part of the owner's investment, and so would also be subtracted from proceeds in measuring gain or loss.

Example 6.1: Mary buys a car for $25,000 and pays an after-market merchant another $1,000 to install a GPS in the car's dashboard. When Mary sells the car for $24,000, her loss is not $1,000, the difference between the sale proceeds and her original cost, but $2,000, the difference between the sale proceeds and her original cost *plus* the cost of installing the GPS. If she had sold the car for $27,000, her gain would have been $1,000.

Similar reasoning applies when we measure the income derived from the sale of property. Normally, the money that goes into buying or improving an asset has already been taxed. If the invested money had been received tax free, say, as municipal bond interest that is not subject to federal tax under Code section 103, we should still treat the money going in as if it had already been taxed. In either case, the amounts paid to buy and improve the property should escape tax when they come back out of this investment.

Example 6.2: Mary buys a car for $25,000 and has a GPS installed in it for an additional $1,000. When Mary sells the car for $24,000, her $2,000 loss may be deductible. It is deductible in full if she bought and held the car, not for her own use, but as a mint specimen of its make and model to be sold to a collector of such cars at a later time. If she bought the car for personal use or as an investment and sold it for $28,000, she would have had a taxable gain of $2,000. (Losses on personal-use vehicles are not deductible; see Chapter 13.C.)

Note that the cost of property in an economic sense is always someone's cost, and that when someone else acquires the property, the property often has a different cost — that is, the cost to that person. Similarly, property has a basis *for* a particular taxpayer, and different taxpayers who may own the same property at different times will in all likelihood have different and unrelated bases for that property.

Example 6.3: Mary's cost and additional investment in her car added up to $26,000. This was also her basis in the car. If she sells the car to Bill for $24,000, Bill's economic investment in the car is $24,000, and so is his basis. (Economic investment and basis do not always match, but they do in this circumstance.)

F   A   Q

Q: How is the basis of an asset related to the asset's fair market value?

A: Basis often corresponds to the amount for which an asset was originally purchased plus any subsequent investment. This amount is a matter of the asset's history and is not tied to its fair market value. Therefore, the fair market value of the asset can be greater or less than the asset's basis, varying with fluctuations in the market for this particular asset or for assets of the same kind. The basis and fair market value of an asset are the same when the asset is purchased in an arm's-length transaction.

The Code refers to basis in many contexts. Code section 1001, a provision with the broadest application to transactions in property, tells us that the difference between the **amount realized** on a sale or exchange of property and the basis of the property is a realized gain, if a positive amount, or a realized loss, if a negative amount. It also tells us that **realized** gains and losses are **recognized**, that is, taken into account for income tax purposes for the year in which they occur, unless the Code provides otherwise for the specific type of property or transaction. Section 1001(b) defines **amount realized** as "the sum of any money received plus the fair market value of the property (other than money) received" in a sale or other disposition. Hence, the term has a meaning very much like that of the familiar term "proceeds." But amount realized takes on additional meaning by virtue of its use in section 1001(a), which tells us that gain or loss is measured by comparing basis with amount realized. It has roughly the same meaning as proceeds, but may be measured differently to give effect to other specialized Code provisions.

F   A   Q

Q: How does the amount realized on a property disposition differ from the gain realized on the transaction?

A: A seller may recoup her investment in an asset on selling it and also make a profit. In such cases, the consideration received from the buyer includes recovered investment and profit. If the sale is at a loss, the proceeds fall short of the seller's investment in value. The amount realized on a disposition of property is the amount against which we measure gain or loss for tax purposes; it is usually equal to or closely related to the proceeds of the deal.

Section 1001 thus emphasizes the fundamental difference between realization and recognition. Elsewhere the Code provides that gain or loss shall not be recognized in certain transactions in order to prevent tax consequences from affecting a taxpayer's choice whether to engage in the transaction or, in other words, to preserve the neutrality[1] of the tax system with respect to economic choices. Where the sale or exchange of property is concerned, the prospect of paying tax on anticipated gain may weigh against nontax reasons for going forward with the transaction.

Nonrecognition, however, is the exception. Section 1001 states the general rule that gain or loss shall be recognized, or taken into account for tax purposes, on a property disposition, unless the Code provides otherwise.

Now that gains and losses have come up, it is important to know that section 1001 does not make even realized *and* recognized losses deductible. That is the work of section 165, the basic Code provision on losses. While allowing most business and investment losses to be deducted, section 165 stringently limits the deductibility of other losses of individual taxpayers.[2] These are deductible only if they "arise from fire, storm, shipwreck, or other casualty, or from theft."[3]

> ## Sidebar
>
> ### HOW IS BASIS DETERMINED?
>
> Code section 1012 provides that the basis of an asset acquired by purchase is its cost. Cost basis corresponds closely with what we would simply refer to as the cost of an asset in a nontax context. Other Code provisions require that we adjust an asset's basis, raising or lowering it to reflect events that bear on the tax consequences of holding the asset.
>
> Section 1016 states some of the rules that require the adjustment of basis. These rules usually assume knowledge of more elaborate rules elsewhere in the Code, most of which are beyond the scope of an introductory tax course. Some, however, are discussed in Section G below.

Example 6.4: Grasshopper does not bother to insure his personal residence or keep it in good repair. Eventually, the dilapidated house becomes worthless. Grasshopper realizes and recognizes a loss equal to her basis in the home, but this is a "personal" loss, that is, not one incurred in a trade or business or in a profit-seeking activity, and so the loss is not deductible. If the house had been destroyed by fire, Grasshopper could have deducted a loss equal to her basis.

B. Early Recovery of Basis

As we have seen, basis usually comes into play when a taxpayer disposes of property (though not in making a gift, see Chapter 5.D and E). A taxpayer then has a sort of tax shelter against gain to the extent of the property's basis. The previous section provides illustrations of this. Gain realized is the positive difference between amount realized and basis. Basis can also come into play in other settings.

A taxpayer may sometimes recover basis before disposing of property. If the property is divisible, the sale or loss of a part triggers the recovery of only that part's basis. The basis of the whole is normally apportioned among the parts according to their separate values at the time of acquisition. A block of stock purchased for a single price poses no problem, because shares are fungible and are traded at a common market price. If a taxpayer buys a block of shares, each has a basis equal

---

[1]See Chapter 1.F.
[2]See Chapter 2.D, footnote 5.
[3]See Chapter 13.C on personal casualty losses.

to its pro rata portion of the purchase price. But assigning a basis to the parts of other types of property may be more difficult.

We can assign a separate basis to part of a tract of land, even though the part was not separately priced, but this requires that we know the value of the part when it was acquired. Appraisal techniques and standards that would be used for nontax purposes are used here as well. When real estate basis apportionment is an issue in litigation between the IRS and a taxpayer, it is normal to seek the services of an all-purpose real estate appraiser.

Example 6.5: Mary buys a large farm to hold for future development or sale. Some of the land is wooded, some is not. A portion of the farm is wetlands. Not all of it has easy access to public roads, being cut off by the wetlands. Mary finds a buyer for a portion with access to roads. A licensed real estate appraiser will compare this part of the whole farm with similar properties in the neighborhood that have recently been sold. Comparing their features and adjusting for known differences in market conditions, the appraiser will give an expert opinion as to the value of the parcel Mary wants to sell. This valuation might be used in negotiating the sale of the parcel to a developer. If Mary has held the property for a long time, however, a different valuation is needed for apportioning the basis — a valuation as of the date of Mary's acquisition of the whole parcel. The value of the part at that time is its cost basis. The valuation techniques used are the same for both purposes.

Note that the appraised values of the parts must add up to the price paid for the property. Since real estate appraisals rarely come out this way — even the appraised value of the entire property is not required by any rule of appraisal to equal what the owner is willing or able to sell the property for — the insistence of U.S. tax law on finding that the value of the parts should equal the price paid for the whole means that appraisals must be disregarded in some circumstances. Nevertheless, appraisals are the only source we have for basic information about the values of property. More will be said on this topic in Chapter 8, which discusses realization more extensively.

In rare circumstances, it is not possible to value the parts of some property, and an exception to the general rule must be devised. In *Inaja Land Co. v. Commissioner*,[4] the taxpayer was the owner of land used as a commercial recreational site, and a governmental subdivision took easements over the site by eminent domain. Normally, the owner's gain or loss on the forced sale would have been calculated by subtracting the basis of the easements alone from the amount received for it. (Remember: This would have been the value of the easements when the entire tract of land was bought, not its value at the time of the taking.) Here, the taxpayers persuaded the Tax Court that the easements were open-ended; the government could divert more or less water over the land, which left the burden of the easement and even the dimensions of the affected portion of the land indefinite. This also made the easements impossible to appraise. The land as a whole had cost the owner $60,000, and the amount received for the easement was $49,000. Given this difficulty, the court allowed the owner to exclude the entire amount received as compensation. In effect, the court gave the owner the benefit of the doubt, because it was possible that the basis of the easement would have been very large in relation to the cost of the whole property.

---

[4]9 T.C.727 (1947), *acq.* 1948-1 C.B.2.

The court did not elaborate on the treatment the taxpayer would receive on later selling what remained of the original property interest. Experts agree that the original basis of $60,000 would be reduced by the recovery of a basis of $49,000 for the easement, so that the remaining property would have a basis of only $11,000. Thus, if the taxpayer later sold the remaining property for $100,000, the gain would be $89,000.

The lesson of *Inaja Land* is very limited: Confronted with a basis apportionment problem, it is not unreasonable to allow the entire basis to be recovered before reckoning there to be any gain. Other courts may choose to deal with this problem differently if facts even remotely like those of *Inaja Land* come up again. But early recovery of basis makes sense as a way of preventing the taxation of an uncertain gain.

Burnet v. Logan,[5] an earlier case, seemed to approve tax treatment like that in *Inaja Land* for a wide category of situations. The taxpayer had sold a working oil interest under a contract that entitled her to annual installment payments that depended on the market price of the oil produced. The anticipated payments were therefore of uncertain amount. The Supreme Court held that her gross income did not include any portion of the payments actually received until their total exceeded her basis in the interest she had sold. This **open transaction** treatment, the Court appeared to say, was appropriate whenever the price for which property was sold remained uncertain over a multiyear period, even if part of the price was fixed and certain. For years, manufacturers of military equipment and certain others used the open-transaction method in reporting income from long-term contracts.

Congress responded by creating a special "installment sale" method in sections 453, 453A and 453C, for the timing of income from purchase payments spread over more than one year. If a purchase agreement requires the buyer to make any payment after the end of the taxable year of the sale, the income from the sale as a whole is recognized in parts proportional to the installments to be received. In the language of the Code, "the income recognized [from a disposition to which the rules apply] is that proportion of the payments received in that year which the gross profit (realized or to be realized when payment is completed) bears to the total contract price."[6] If the full price is partly contingent, the value of the uncertain portion is estimated, taking the probability and time value of money into account.

Example 6.6: Ann sells unimproved land held with a basis of $40,000 to Brenda for $100,000, with a down payment of $20,000 and annual installments in each of the following eight years of $10,000 each. The fraction of each installment that Ann must recognize as income is 60 percent, the ratio of the $60,000 gross profit to the total $100,000 contract price. Of the down payment, Ann recognizes income of $12,000 (60 percent of $20,000). Of each subsequent installment, Ann recognizes $6,000 (60 percent of $10,000).

If the holder of the installment obligation disposes of it before all of the installments are received, the portion of the seller's original basis that has not yet been recovered is subtracted from the amount received for the obligation in determining the gain at that point.[7] The payments to be received on an installment sale contract

---

[5]283 U.S. 404 (1931).
[6]I.R.C. §453(c).
[7]*Id.* §453B.

are deemed equal to the amount of all payments that are not contingent as to amount, plus the fair market value of any contingent payments.[8] In other words, a value is placed on the uncertain portion of the anticipated payments, using ordinary financial valuation methods for determining the value of contingent future payments. Usually, this means that the uncertain portion of the contract price is set equal to the discounted present value of the uncertain part of future payments, multiplied by the probabilities that each will be received.

The purpose of the installment sale provisions is to offer the taxpayer somewhat less generous treatment than the open-transaction approach. Gain is not postponed until basis is fully recovered, but neither is the gain recognized as soon as the disposition is final under applicable state law. The latter is the treatment applicable to ordinary dispositions. A compromise element in the rule allows gain to be recognized only at the very end of the installment process if that gain exceeds the sum of fixed and definite amounts to be paid plus the fair market value of contingent amounts to be paid. The installment sale rules do not apply to dealer dispositions of personal or real property, because recurrent sales are likely to provide a rough matching of income and basis recovery year by year.[10]

Example 6.7: McGregor agrees to sell a garden to Potter for payments of $10,000 a year for nine years, plus 10 percent of Potter's profit on selling the garden if she does so in the tenth year. The probability that she will sell the garden in the tenth year is 50 percent, and the present value of 10 percent of her profit is $10,000. The contract price is therefore $100,000. If McGregor's basis in the garden is $20,000, 80 percent of each installment received is income. If Potter fails to sell the garden in year ten, McGregor's remaining basis of $2,000 can be deducted as a loss for that year.

Obviously, the installment method is less generous to taxpayers than open-transaction treatment. But open-transaction treatment has never been the norm. The installment method is decidedly more favorable than the default rule, for all of the gain on a disposition is normally recognized as income

Sidebar

COMPARING THE STANDARD OPEN-TRANSACTION AND INSTALLMENT-METHOD TREATMENTS OF DISPOSITIONS

Section 1001 prescribes immediate recognition of all realized gains and losses, unless the Code elsewhere provides relief. Immediate recognition allows basis to be recovered immediately but also requires income to be recognized no later than when the taxpayer has a right to it, even if it is to be paid later.[9] Other Code sections allow a taxpayer to recover the basis of property before or after gain or loss is otherwise realized. Special cost recovery methods allow basis to be taken into account before realization, thus accelerating the benefit of loss recognition or deferring the pain of gain recognition. Open-transaction treatment, in the rare cases in which such treatment is permitted, allows gain to be disproportionately deferred to a later tax year. Installment-method treatment under section 453 allows the owner of an asset sold or exchanged for one or more installments to be received in a later tax year to treat the installments as consisting proportionately of gain (or loss) and recovered basis.

---

[9]Technically, this depends on the taxpayer's accounting method, but on both the cash receipts and disbursements method and the accrual method, the exchange of property for an installment obligation triggers income inclusion. Treas. Reg. §15A.453-1(d)(2) makes it clear that receipt of an installment obligation is a receipt of property, and its value is the fair market value of the obligation. Thus, if the taxpayer elects not to use the installment method under I.R.C. §453(d), even a cash-method taxpayer has received the fair market value of the installment obligation as soon as it is exchanged for the property being sold.

---

[8]*Id.* §453(f)(8).
[10]*Id.* §453(b)(2)(A).

in the year the deal is final for state law purposes, even if some or all of the payment is to be received later.

Example 6.8: A sells B her personal residence in year one, accepting B's promissory note and mortgage for $200,000, delivering a general warranty deed to B. A hands over the deed at the closing to B; there is no escrow of payment or title documents. Under every state's law, the sale is final at the time of closing, even if the note and mortgage permit B to pay A over a conventional 30-year mortgage period.

Rather than duel with the IRS about whether the proceeds of a sale will be uncertain enough to justify use of the open transaction doctrine, a taxpayer automatically qualifies for better-than-the-worst treatment. The installment method is a compromise. It serves only as a new default rule; the taxpayer may elect not to use it, but if the election is not timely made, the taxpayer is bound by it for the entire transaction and payment period.

Where gifts and charitable contributions are concerned, prior recovery of basis may determine the amount of the taxpayer's deduction for the transfer, not just temporarily but for good. *Diedrich v. Commissioner*[11] permits the maker of an inter vivos gift to exclude from income payment by the donee of the gift tax, up to the donor's full basis in the gift property. A less generous alternative would have been to analyze the transaction as part gift and part sale. On this approach, the donor would recover only part of the basis of the property transferred to the donee, in keeping with the normal apportionment of basis. Generally, if property acquired for a single price is divisible, the cost basis of the whole is apportioned among the parts according to their separate values when acquired. *Diedrich* accords the donor treatment that is even more favorable than the *Inaja Land* exception to the general rule, because once the gift is made, the donor no longer holds any interest in the transferred property, and the reduced basis cannot make a later sale or exchange *by the donor* yield a disproportionately large gain.

F   A   Q

Q: Is *Diedrich* consistent with the rule of section 1011(b)?

A: No. Section 1011(b) follows the general rule that *Diedrich* disregarded. It prescribes that the basis for determining the gain or loss on the sale aspect of a bargain sale shall be the basis of the whole property multiplied by the ratio of the value of the part sold to the value of the whole. A "bargain sale" to a charitable organization is a sale for less than full consideration. Accordingly, the donor does not get to shelter the proceeds of the bargain sale with the entire basis of the property transferred, but only with that portion of the basis apportioned to the portion sold.

---

[11]457 U.S. 191 (1982).

C. Tax Burdens on Property and Business Activities

Is business activity treated more favorably under basis recovery rules than profit-oriented dealings in property? Earlier we observed that basis is closely connected with the realization requirement. Only property can have a basis, and gain or loss is realized only in property dealings. The links between property, basis, and realization run deeper still. They form a triad of concepts that have only rough counterparts in the tax analysis of other profit-oriented activities. We speak of recovering rather than "deducting" basis to compute realized gain or loss, but basis recovery is directly comparable to the deduction of the expenses of earning income, and a single rationale stands behind both types of adjustment. Nevertheless, expense deduction and basis recovery do not follow the same timing principles.

The usual tax treatment of property dealings postpones the recovery of basis until gain or loss is realized. In contrast, the costs of income-producing activities are usually deductible when they are incurred and not only if and when the activity yields income. This boldly different treatment of property dealings and profit-oriented activities only seems unfair to the former and lenient to the latter. The truth is less objectionable.

The two patterns of tax treatment are basically equivalent: (1) early deduction of costs with full taxation of the eventual yield, and (2) capitalizing costs with a deduction for them from the eventual yield. The effect of allowing a deduction for a sum of money in one year and including that same sum in income in a later tax year is the same as allowing no deduction at the outset but then not taxing the income of the tax-reduced amount for that same period.

Example 6.9: Suppose a taxpayer has $1,000 in hand and can choose between two tax treatments of the income this money can produce. The first treatment would allow the taxpayer to invest the whole $1,000 at 8 percent for one year. At the end of a year, the taxpayer will receive $1,080, all of which is taxable at the taxpayer's normal rate of, say, 25 percent. The net amount in the taxpayer's hand after the year will therefore be $810. The other treatment would tax the $1,000 right away, before it is invested, and then not tax any part of the proceeds of the investment. In other words, only $750 of the $1,000 is available to be invested, because a tax of $250 is first imposed. After a year, $750 earns $60 = $750 × .08. The taxpayer is allowed to keep the full $810 = $750 + 60. The outcome of the two alternative treatments is therefore the same.

This relationship does not depend on the length of time or the tax rates involved, so long as the same tax rate applies to both the invested amount and the yield.

Example 6.10: If A invests $100 in a traditional IRA, A is allowed to deduct that amount, so the investment goes in tax free. If the return after some time is 10 percent, the gross yield is $110, but this is fully taxable. A tax rate of 20 percent leaves A with only $88. Had A invested instead in a Roth IRA, A would have had to pay tax first on the $100 available for investment, so that only $80 would have gone in. If the return after the same period of time is still 10 percent, the gross yield is $88, but the rules for the Roth IRA exempt this yield from tax. Note that the after-tax yield is the same in each case. Note also that the amount of tax paid is less in the second case than in the first, but since it is paid at an earlier time, its present value at the time paid was the same as the then value of the larger tax in the first case, which is paid later. The time value of money exactly offsets the nominal tax difference on these facts.[12]

If the two patterns of taxation are equivalent, you may wonder why anyone would ever prefer one to the other, and why Congress would offer them both as it does in the case of the two kinds of IRA. Several factors can destroy the equivalence. If the taxpayer's marginal rate of tax changes from the time of investment to the time of disinvestment, the advantage will go to the method that reduces the amount of tax overall, usually the method that allows the deduction or recovery of the cost when the taxpayer's marginal tax rate is highest. Change in the value of the currency can also destroy the equivalence.

TABLE 6.1	Matching of Income and Costs in Profit-Seeking Activities			
● = yes [blank] = no				
	Deductible	Capitalized	Gross Yield Taxed	Net Yield Taxed
Most business outlays	●		●	
Most investment outlays		●		●
Long-term business capital outlays		●		●

D. How Basis Affects Annual Accounting

Although the goal may be to tax lifetime income, the tax law rigorously divides life into taxable years.[13] Costs are deductible in the year incurred or paid, and not in another year, except by largesse of the net operating loss rules.[14] Rigorous emphasis on annual accounting periods, however, is tempered for property dispositions by section 1001, which defers recognition of income until it is realized, and then permits basis to be subtracted from the proceeds in computing gain or loss. Instead of allowing the cost of property to offset only income the property produces in the year when that cost is incurred or paid, the cost of property becomes the property's basis — we say it is capitalized rather than deducted — and this generally serves to postpone recovery of the cost until the property is sold or exchanged.[15]

---

[12]I.R.C. §§408, 408A. The time value of the tax to be paid would not be the same if the return on the investments were not taxed at the same intervals. This would be the case, for example, if one of the investments were allowed to grow tax free until disinvestment, although the return on the other was subject to tax annually.

[13]*Burnet v. Sanford & Brooks Co.*, 282 U.S. 359 (1931).

[14]I.R.C. §172 (allowing NOLs to reduce earlier and subsequent years' taxable income); see also §108(b) (reducing NOLs when an insolvent taxpayer's income due to cancellation of indebtedness is reduced).

[15]See Chapters 13.A and 14.A and B.

The design of the income tax thus makes really good sense for property held long-term, producing no income along the way, and eventually surrendered all at once for money or other property. Even though its value may fluctuate during the holding period, whether it will is normally a matter of conjecture, and interim fluctuations may be offsetting.

The patient approach of taking only realized gains and realized losses into account is akin to the open-transaction approach. If the gain or loss were only computed after a venture is complete, all of its gross income and deductions would be netted at a single time, rather than as many times as the number of taxable years through which the venture extended. This is exactly how the "venture" of holding property long-term is analyzed: The costs of acquiring and preserving the property are all added to its basis, which means that these costs are subtracted only when potential gain or loss on the whole property is realized.

Strictly speaking, this special treatment of property investment is not an alternative to annual accounting. In fact, if property does yield income other than when disposed of, that income is compared with certain expenses of holding the property that are *not* capitalized or added to basis, and the taxpayer's accounting method governs when and how this is done. But for the simple case of property passively held for eventual sale or exchange, without a timetable, it is as if the investment activity were treated as single transaction.

E. Adjusted Basis

Anyone who studies the Code will often come across the term **adjusted basis**. Basis is adjusted upward when more post-tax or tax-exempt value is invested in an asset and downward when the asset's owner recovers or uses some of the basis in a transaction or by reason of an event other than complete disposition of the asset. Section 1016 lists a number of situations that call for such adjustment, but the list is incomplete; other basis-adjusting rules are found elsewhere in the statute. The idea of a fluctuating basis deserves our general attention at this point, although the details belong to the subject matter of other chapters.

Why adjust basis? A simple example will answer the question. Although basis and cost are the same in some situations and remain so, events that take place between the purchase of property and its disposition can change the calculation of gain or loss at disposition. Suppose, for example, that a taxpayer's building is partly destroyed by fire, for which there is no insurance coverage, and the taxpayer correctly deducts the loss as a casualty. (Casualty losses are deductible whether they afflict business or personal property, though with restriction in the latter case. See Chapter 13.C.) If the taxpayer has income for the casualty deduction to offset, there is a tax benefit. The fire loss also deprives the taxpayer of part of the building, so that any subsequent profit on the investment is likely to be reduced. The initial basis of the property, measured by its cost, is adjusted downward when the casualty loss is deducted, and only the remaining or adjusted basis is available to be subtracted from the amount realized when the building is later sold, in calculating gain or loss. Similarly, if the taxpayer, instead of losing part of the building to a fire, had added a new wing to it — at additional cost, of course — that additional cost should be added to the basis of the building, and then subtracted from the amount realized when the building is sold. The chief types of event that call for adjustments to basis can be characterized as further investment in the property, such as the cost of defending title to land, or recovery of previous investment in the property.

F. Property Used in a Trade or Business

Basis plays a large part in the tax treatment of property used actively in a service, retail, or other ongoing activity for profit, not just held for some vaguely planned disposition in the future. The Code frequently speaks of the former type of activity as "trade or business" and of the latter as "property held for the production of income."[16] These are the only two categories of profit-oriented property use. A profit can also be made on the disposition of property, such as a home, not held primarily for profit. Property virtually always has a basis, and it is important to remember that that applies to all three kinds.[17]

A major difference between the two categories is that related expenses may be deductible or not, depending on which category the property belongs to. Accordingly, not everything we spend on property we already own must either be deductible or added to basis. Improvements by either a homeowner or an office-building owner are nondeductible and *are* added to basis. But repairs are not added to basis, even though home repairs are not deductible (repairs to an office building are deductible and also do not augment basis). Repairs keep a thing what it already is, whereas improvements add to it. This is the key to whether the outlays in question result in basis adjustments. When we spend either to acquire or to improve property we already own, the amount spent is added to basis. Other amounts spent may be deductible or not, depending on whether the property is held for the production of income (deductible if so, nondeductible otherwise). Deductibility is not the determining factor for basis adjustment. Some deductible events, like casualties, reduce basis. There is no outlay in these situations, only an event that reduces the value of the property.

Depreciation and amortization are permitted methods of recovering (deducting) the basis of property used in a trade or business.[18] To depreciate property for tax purposes is to deduct a part of its basis for each taxable year that it is expected to produce income. Similar tax treatment of intangible property used to produce income is called "amortization." The gradual recovery of basis is not meant to give business activity a tax edge over passive investment. It should only aid the taxpayer and the government in matching business income with the costs of producing that income. Income tax is fundamentally *not* a tax on gross proceeds or receipts, but should instead only burden gains. Since the stream of a business's revenue is spread over many taxable years, it is important for both the taxpayer and the government to match income and costs; opportunism on the part of either would violate tax neutrality. As property is depreciated or amortized, its basis is recovered and accordingly reduced, following the pattern of downward adjustment for basis recovery that we saw at the beginning of this chapter in connection with *Inaja Land.*

---

[16]See I.R.C. §212.
[17]There are a few very unusual situations in which the Code leaves us in doubt as to the basis of anything that could be considered property, none of them relevant to the introductory tax course.
[18]See Chapter 15 *passim.*

SUMMARY

■ Basis is the tax counterpart of cost or investment in property, and like investment is adjusted upward or downward as events that occur after acquisition of the property require.

■ The realization requirement normally makes property owners wait until they dispose of property to recover the basis. Recovering basis is the same as deducting it from the amount realized.

■ Investment in property and the use of property in a trade or business are treated similarly in this respect: Outlays directly associated with property in either setting are capitalized, that is, added to the property's basis.

■ An activity that is characterized as a trade or business for tax purposes, however, can deduct most other outlays — that is, those not capitalized — as long as they have a reasonable connection with the enterprise, whereas outlays arguably associated with a pure investment activity but not directly linked with specific property are not deductible.

■ Because basis is normally subtracted from property-related profits only when the property is disposed of, basis provides a device for matching gains and costs that would otherwise have to be manipulated through accounting rules. Basis rules, however, are not accounting rules, which means that the IRS has less discretion to control the matching process for property dealings.

CONNECTIONS

Basis, Realization, and Gain or Loss

The tax consequences of owning and disposing of property, regardless of the nature of the activity in which the property is used, turn on the relationship between the property's basis, the realization of some or all of the property's value, and the measurement of gain or loss on realization. Section 1001 establishes this basic relationship as the default rule of the Code. See Chapter 9.

Disadvantage of Having to Capitalize

Chapter 7 explains why delayed recovery of basis, which correspondingly delays reduction of the taxpayer's tax liability, tends to increase the tax burden on the taxpayer.

Early Recovery of Basis

As *Inaja Land* illustrates, a taxpayer may be allowed to recover a disproportionate part of his or her basis in property upon disposing of only a part or partial interest in it. Tax shelters have sometimes taken advantage of this idea, relying on formal steps to establish a basis in property that lacks economic substance.

Chapter 9.C(3) gives examples of this strategy and describes the unfavorable judicial response.

How Basis Shelters the Taxpayer from Gain in Some Situations

Holding property with a basis, however, is certainly better than holding the same property with no basis, because when realization occurs, basis shelters the owner from gain or entitles the owner to deduct a loss, unless the property is used without a profit orientation. Chapter 9 goes into this broadly, and Chapter 15 explains how depreciation provides a special application of the shelter principle for business uses of property.

Special Basis of Nonrecourse Financed Property

Chapter 8 explores the peculiar rule that allows a borrower to include the amount of a nonrecourse obligation in the basis of property acquired or improved with the proceeds of the obligation. Since the borrower's personal credit is not subject to the claims of the lender or other obligee, this is one instance in which being allowed to "capitalize" an outlay is a kind of tax break.

Why Tax Timing Matters: The Value of Money over Time

7

Many tax rules are about when, not whether, the taxpayer has income. Why? A bird in the hand is worth two in the bush. Invested money grows

O V E R V I E W

and borrowing costs something. More generally, money or its equivalent is worth more the sooner it becomes available. By way of corollary, the earlier a loss occurs, the higher the cost of restoring it. The income tax must of course be sensitive to the effect of time on value. A tax postponed is a tax reduced, because the taxpayer can pocket some of what that tax can earn before it is finally paid. The value to the government of a postponed tax is also less because the government must borrow and pay interest or delay other spending to put the expected revenue to immediate use. A tax paid early is a heavier tax because the government then has earlier access, without cost, to what would have been paid later. Income tax rules therefore must respond to the time-value of money. Tax-planning strategies are often based on avoiding or gaming those rules. Tax casebooks do not always group these strategies and correlative features of the tax law together, but this chapter does, in the hope of easing the learning curve.

A. HOW DELAYED TAX LIABILITY LOWERS THE TAX RATE

B. "OPEN TRANSACTION" TREATMENT

C. COST RECOVERY IN DIFFERENT KINDS OF INCOME-EARNING ACTIVITY

A. How Delayed Tax Liability Lowers the Tax Rate

Merely postponing the payment of a tax reduces the burden of paying it, because the taxpayer can invest a smaller amount now and "grow" the amount needed later. Invested money often grows with a high degree of predictability.

Example 7.1: Ozzie would have owed $15,000 in income tax for last year, but then he discovered a Code provision that allowed him to deduct $10,000 saved for retirement on condition that the $10,000 should be included in his income ten years later. Ozzie validly contributed $10,000 for last year to a retirement plan. Deducting this, he saved $3,000 in taxes for that year and invested it in a savings account that pays an after-tax rate of 7.2 percent per year simple interest. After ten years, the savings account balance is $6,000. He withdraws everything from the retirement account and the savings account. He must report additional gross income of $10,000 for the year of the withdrawals, but he has earned $3,000 post-tax on the savings account, and this conveniently pays tax on the $10,000 with something to spare. Was the $3,000 in tax that he initially postponed ever paid? Yes and no. The postponement strategy allowed him to earn the amount needed to pay the tax without disturbing his other resources. So he paid the tax but the net effect was the same as nonpayment.

In an introductory tax course, you will probably not have to compute the return on investments. You must become aware, however, that even a modest periodic rate of return can yield surprising gains if the yield is added to principal (**compounded**) at regular intervals. (A periodic rate of return is one stated as a percentage of the principal for a specified period, such as per annum, per month, semiannually, etc.) Below we look at some numerical examples. Take note of two common terms: **Principal** is the original amount invested (or deposited in a savings account in our example); **simple interest** is interest that is added to principal at the end of a period and not as it accrues during a period: in other words, an annual rate of simple interest is compounded annually. Interest can be compounded more frequently—daily or monthly, for example.

Example 7.2: Gates deposits $100 in a savings account that pays 5 percent simple interest annually. If he leaves the money in the account for two years, he earns $5 in interest for the first year. This is added to the $100 principal at the beginning of the second year. At the beginning of the third year, interest of $5.25 is added to his principal of $105, and the balance is now $110.25. If the savings account had paid 5 percent compounded daily, the balance would have been $110.52.

Money invested at 7.2 percent simple interest doubles its value in ten years. If the government let you have a ten-year grace period for paying the $100 in taxes you owe, an investment at an after-tax rate of 7.2 percent of just $50 at the start of the grace period will enable you to pay the full amount of the tax by the end of it. Admittedly, this is a high interest rate, but lower rates also give gratifying results. Small differences in the annual simple interest rate make the doubling period change drastically: 18 years at 4 percent, 14 years at 5 percent, 12 years at 6 percent. Money invested at 8 percent doubles in nine years. Unfortunately, at 3 percent it takes money about 25 years to double. For those who like this sort of thing, a convenient formula is provided at the end of the chapter.

F   A   Q

Q: Does interest only compensate a lender for inflation?

A: When inflation is extremely low, money usually earns interest that includes a market value for riskless lending, with an upward adjustment for the risk posed by the specific borrower. When inflation is substantial, a further upward adjustment compensates the lender for the nominal loss in value of the loan due to inflation.

Money whose availability is postponed until a future date shrinks in value. The farther off your payday, the less the money is worth now. You could grow that distant amount over the time in question by investing a smaller amount at the prevailing market rate of interest. We just observed that money invested for nine years at 8 percent, with annual compounding, doubles in value. Turn that around: Money that will only become available nine years from the present is worth half the amount now if the prevailing rate of return on money invested reasonably is 8 percent per annum. Money that will become available ten years hence is worth half the amount if the prevailing rate is 7.2 percent, and so on. Any spreadsheet software package and many websites allow you to calculate the time value of money backwards and forwards, given the present or future value of the money, the interval of time, and the rate or return on a present investment. See Section G for a more mathematical treatment.

Now consider one of the most conspicuous tax applications of these principles. We include property appreciation in the owner's income for tax purposes only when the appreciated value is realized, and that is often later than when that value can be measured with some confidence. This gives the taxpayer the privilege of delaying the payment of the tax on that income. The time value of money makes the delayed payment

Sidebar

INTEREST AND DEFERRED CONSUMPTION

Early-nineteenth-century economists speculated that interest reflected the *personal* value of a loan to the borrower and was therefore determined by the strength of the borrower's preference for early access to money that he or she would later have to acquire anyway to repay the loan. Today, we know that the market for loans is sensitive to a variety of circumstances, including the insecurity of lenders, the demand for loans, the riskiness of lending to specific borrowers, and possibly sunspots.

worth less to the government and less burdensome to the taxpayer, because the *present value* of the future tax payment is always less — by how much, we can easily compute if we know the prevailing rate of return on invested money and how long it will be before the payment is due.

Other rules and sometimes special circumstances enable taxpayers to postpone an inevitable tax liability, even though realization is not relevant. This chapter deals with such scenarios and with how the time value of money figures in them, creating problems for the income tax.

B. "Open Transaction" Treatment

Income is taxed year by year. This makes time value an issue everywhere in income tax analysis. As we have seen, the tax on an item of gross income is a heavier burden if the income belongs to an earlier year rather than a later one and the taxpayer would pay the same dollar amount of tax in either year. The difference may be great or small in real terms. It is certain, however, that the effective tax *rate* is increased by earlier taxation, just as it would be reduced by later taxation. "Late and soon, getting and spending" fare differently under the income tax. Attributing income-paid deductions to the most appropriate year is a vital part of tax administration. Which year is most appropriate depends on economic reality — income and deductions belong to the year in which they are earned or suffered. Administrative convenience and nontax goals, however, may also influence tax timing rules.

Consider how these goals compete with each other in the treatment of transactions that straddle more than one tax year. The courts and the IRS once reluctantly granted "open transaction" treatment case by case, essentially waiting to measure the income from the transaction until valuation and other issues were resolved, and allowing the income to be reported after the dust had settled. In *Burnet v. Logan*, discussed in Chapter 6.B, the taxpayer sold a working interest in oil reserves to an oil production company in return for a percentage of the wholesale value of the oil that would eventually be produced. The Supreme Court allowed her to recover her entire basis in the working interest before having to include any part of the payments she received in her gross income. Treating the earlier years' payments as all basis recovery, which is, after all, a kind of a cost deduction, and attributing her gain to later years only resulted in a lower tax on the entire transaction — a tax postponed is a tax reduced. The Court, however, felt compelled to allow this tax break because the total amount the taxpayer was to receive in payments for her working interest depended on facts that could not be predicted with any probability, or so the parties had stipulated.

F   A   Q

Q: Why does the tax law insist on measuring income annually instead of on the open-transaction method?

A: The reason is a combination of administrative convenience and the time value of money. Year-by-year taxation allows the government to draw a line under past years' economic activity — with exceptions for difficult cases. But the time value of money strongly reinforces the pressure for measuring income at frequent intervals. Economic values are time dependent. The choice of dates for measuring net income is therefore inevitable, and annual intervals satisfy that need.

The government would have done extremely well if the taxpayer had been allowed credit for her basis only when the series of payments was complete, restating her gross income from the working interest for that year and as many previous years as would be necessary. This would not do for all "open transaction" situations, because the statute of limitations on returns from previous years might prevent the taxpayer from making the needed downward adjustment to earlier years' gross income; that problem, however, could be solved by revision of the statute of limitations. Why would this alternative, with an appropriate mechanism in place, be unsatisfactory?

Tax neutrality comes to mind again. If the open-ended sale of a working interest had the effect of subjecting the seller to heavier taxes in the earlier years and providing relief later, taxpayers would be crazy not to structure these sales differently, so that basis could at least be recovered proportionately over the payments' multiyear span. The contract for the purchase of Mrs. Logan's working interest might make her a coproducer of the oil, with different rights and obligations. Or the deal might not be made at all, frustrating both Mrs. Logan's and the oil company's wishes.

Property sales in which the seller has a positive basis, for a price contingent on future events, are problematical in two ways: (1) The total amount to be received is unknown until the nominal amount of all payments is ascertainable. Some part of the total will always be return of basis and therefore not income. If the entire price is contingent, the seller may suffer a loss on the entire transaction. Thus, a practical problem of measuring the gain arises because of the contingent amount of the payments to be received. (2) But measurement of the gain is problematic even after the amounts of all the payments are known because of the time value of money. A payment of $50 in the first year has the same time value as a payment of $100 in the ninth year if the prevailing market rate of interest is 8 percent.

Generally, then, the time value of the payments is not the same as their nominal values, and the difference should be taken into account. But time valuation is always determined with respect to a point in time. Which should be used? Two obvious competitors are the dates of the first and last payments. To equate the total contract price with the present value of all the payments as of the first payment date would be to treat the seller as having the entire benefit of the sale before it is either economically available or ascertainable. To equate the contract price with the value of all the payments as of the date on which the last is received would be to understate the seller's income in those cases in which at least part of the gain is economically available and ascertainable before the year of the last payment. The IRS, without specific statutory authority, takes the position that the effective date of the sale, determined under state law, should be used as the reference point for attributing gain to the seller, if not necessarily for measuring its time value. Although arbitrary, this approach has the advantage of administrative simplicity.

C. Cost Recovery in Different Kinds of Income-Earning Activity

Now that we have confronted the problematical aspects of basis recovery for open transactions, it is time to compare these with other types of property transactions that have more definite boundaries. Three major types of activity that yield income are labor, dealings in property, and business activity that combines labor and property. (This should remind you of *Glenshaw Glass v. Comm'r*,[1] which warned that not all income falls into one of these three categories.) The timing of deductions related to each should be noted.

The timing rules for pure labor income and for income from a business activity that combines labor and property are broadly similar. A taxpayer's income from personal services alone and associated deductions are attributed to the taxable year when received, if the cash method is used, or when earned, if the accrual method is used. Expenses are deducted when paid, on the cash method, or when the obligation to pay them is incurred, on the accrual method. These accounting rules allow income to be attributed to separate years. For many service activities, deductions are few and easily matched with the tax years in which they support income production. Compare all this with dealings in property alone, without associated services.

When a taxpayer buys and sells property as the core activity of a business, the cost basis property is deducted as it is sold. The cost of inventory is deducted when it is sold, but special rules allow taxpayers to deduct the basis of the last inventory acquired as that of the inventory first to be sold. The normal rule is called "first-in-first-out" or FIFO, and the alternative rule is called "last-in-first-out" or LIFO. (On the distinction between inventory and other property, see Chapter 13.B.) Here, the important point is that no deduction is allowed for the costs of property involved in profit-oriented dealings in property until the property is actually disposed of.

A taxpayer engaged in a service business may also buy and sell property that is not inventory, stock in trade, or property that is otherwise the focus of the business.

Example 7.3: When a law firm owns the office building in which it carries the practice of law, its primary business is that of rendering professional services. Yet, it has business income if it sells the office building at a profit. This kind of property transaction is treated in a manner that is a compromise between the normal treatment of dealings in property and the treatment of expenses incurred to carry on a business. Property used in the business is usually depreciable or amortizable, which means that its cost is gradually recoverable over the period of its service to the business. When such property is sold, the depreciation or amortization of its basis may not yet be complete — there may be basis or historical cost that has not yet been meted out in deductible increments under depreciation or amortization rules — and in such a case, the remaining portion of the property's basis is deducted from the amount realized in computing the gain or loss on the transaction.

---

[1]See Chapter 2.F.

D. Realization and Time Value

Property transactions can, of course, yield income just as manual labor does. But there are differences, and one stands out above all the rest. The compensation an individual or independent contractor receives is virtually always income for the year in which payment is received. The law does not require this coincidence. Those who render services just will not work in most instances for substantially deferred compensation. This comes close to ensuring, where compensation is concerned, that taxable income and economic income are assigned to the same tax accounting period.

By contrast, dealings in property can yield economic income that is not taxed right away. A property owner whose property appreciates can just sit back and wait, controlling the tax timing of income recognition by her power to decide when to dispose of the property. An unrealized gain is not income for tax purposes.

Example 7.4: Stock you own goes up in value by $667 after a while, and then just stays at this value until you finally sell it ten years later. If you had sold the stock right when it first went up in value, you would have had a gain of $667, on which the tax at 15 percent would have been $100. If instead you keep the stock, the unrealized gain is not taxed until you sell it—ten years later, in this example. If you had a savings account that paid after-tax interest at a rate of 7.2 percent, $50 set aside there when the stock's economic gain occurred would enable you to pay the full $100 tax when it fell due ten years later. The realization requirement can effectively reduce the tax rate by postponing the payment of the tax.

When property is sold or exchanged or otherwise disposed of, gain or loss *is* realized. For now, we are only concerned with the broad idea that the reporting of unrealized gain is not compulsory—unrealized gain is not recognized—with rare exceptions.[2] What is the reason for this broad policy decision? Unrealized gains and losses can disappear as property values fluctuate, and appraisals of some types of property would be costly and uncertain. Income taxation of property income in most countries is restricted to realized gains and losses.

At first glance, the time value of money together with the realization requirement appear to create a major discrepancy between how property dealings and other

> **Sidebar**
>
> **THE POSSIBILITY OF TAXING UNREALIZED GAINS AS THEY ACCRUE**
>
> The divergent treatment of income from personal services and income from property dealings rests on the realization requirement, which in turn rests in part on the practical problem of valuing property without the benefit of market finality. Could it be otherwise? Today, national and international markets for a variety of goods and commodities provide reliable information about property of types that are comparatively fungible — agricultural commodities, publicly traded stock and trust interests, many commercially manufactured goods, and some intellectual property. Real estate markets witness the sale or exchange of fewer properties; comparable sales offer weaker indications of market value. Income tax systems may soon take advantage of reliable market information and abandon the realization requirement for taxing some of the items mentioned above, but probably not for taxing dealings in real property.

---

[2]Money or property received under a claim of right in exchange for other property, but without final establishment of that right, would not usually be considered realized. We discuss the claim of right doctrine in Chapter 7.

income-producing activities are taxed. If that were so, both fairness and tax neutrality would be severely undermined. But there is more to the story.

E. Inflation's Effect on the Value of Money over Time

When the value of the currency in which money is invested decreases over time, values stated in unadjusted units of the currency increase. If inflation alone accounts for the currency's drop in value, the apparent uptick in value of the investments valued in that currency is not real. For example, if there is 4 percent inflation in the value of the dollar over one year, $1.04 after the year has run will on average buy what $1 would have bought at the beginning. A payment due after one year, adjusted for inflation, would therefore represent only a nominal gain of 4 percent and no real gain at all.

F   A   Q

Q: What is a "fixed" rate of interest?

A: Interest rates are usually not adjusted for changing rates of inflation. They are instead stated in *fixed* terms — that is, fixed without adjustment for inflation. The obligation to pay 5 percent in one year would yield a 5 percent gain in the absence of inflation, but the same obligation will yield a gain of only .95 percent if inflation is running at 4 percent. That is because one cent is only .95 percent of 1.05, slightly less than 1 percent.

No one knows with certainty what rate of inflation, if any, will apply to future periods of time. Fixed rates of return are therefore risky, but they are often all we have. For that reason, tax planning based on fixed rates of return is also risky. By the same token, tax timing rules that are designed to frustrate such tax planning may overcompensate for the time value of money, turning inflationary bubbles into taxable income.

Example 7.5: Joe bought a house to live in for $100,000 in January 1980. He sells the house in January 2008 for $250,000. Using the Commerce Department's online inflation calculator, $171,310 is the inflation-adjusted value of Joe's initial investment at the time of the sale. Hence, only $78,690 of the gain realized is real and the rest is apparent. Nevertheless, the gain for tax purposes is $150,000, roughly twice the real gain. Section 121 allows Joe to exclude the entire gain from gross income if he has lived for an aggregate of at least two years in the house. If not, and if he has not held the house as a capital asset, the apparent gain is fully taxable as ordinary income. Today, that result is highly unlikely, because it is so easy for this gain to qualify as a capital gain, and the applicable rate of tax for such gains is low — just 15 percent — which would almost perfectly adjust his tax burden for inflation. It would be as if he were subject to a tax rate of 30 percent only on the real gain of $78,690.

As the example shows, capital gain taxation may compensate for inflation. A single lower rate for all capital gains is too generous for relatively short holding periods. Yet one year is the holding period for the 15 percent capital gain rate of tax under current law. (Capital gain taxation is discussed in detail in Chapter 14.) For simplicity, we will follow the Code's lead and ignore inflation in the remainder of this discussion. That does not mean, however, that it would not be more accurate to adjust for it.

F. Installment Sale Treatment Revisited

As we saw in Chapter 6.A, section 453 allows a taxpayer who sells property to report the gain on most installment sales in increments as the installment payments are received. The installment sale regime thwarts the urge of sophisticated taxpayers to indulge in schemes for the early recovery of basis and later recognition of income. Generally, the ratio of the profit on the contract to the full contract price determines the fraction of each installment that must be treated as gain. Obviously, this installment method implicitly permits the taxpayer to recover basis with each installment as well. The regulations under section 453 tell us what to do when the contract price is partly contingent or undetermined at the time of the sale. Roughly, only the certain part of the contract price is considered in determining how much of each installment is treated as income.

G. Correlation of Deductions with Income

It is a fundamental feature of income taxation that costs are subtracted from revenues in calculating income. Recall that the cost of investment property is usually deducted only when the property is sold. As we saw in Section C, the same is true for inventory: Its cost is also deducted when it is sold, although inventory cost is computed using special rules. The recognition of income is delayed until it is realized by the disposition of property, but the deduction of what is invested in property is delayed until then as well. By contrast, many of the costs of earning other sorts of income can be deducted as soon as the costs are incurred and not only when the income itself becomes available. Early versus late deduction of costs to some extent balances the effect of the realization requirement. To see how significant this balancing is, we must delve into the arcane equivalence of expensing and yield exclusion.

H. The Interactive Tax Treatment of Costs and Yields

As Section B explained, allowing a deduction for the amount invested in a profitable activity and taxing all the revenue of the activity is equivalent to *not* allowing a deduction for the investment but allowing the entire yield of the investment to be excluded from income. Thus, if one kind of profit-making activity gets to take deductions for its costs as they are paid or incurred but must include all the profits in income, and another kind of profit-making activity must capitalize its costs and deduct them when the profits arrive, then the two are taxed equivalently, absent inflation. This means that dealings in property, with the advantage they enjoy under the realization requirement, are no better off than service businesses that are allowed to deduct salaries but are taxed on the full amount of their revenue. This conclusion is discussed with respect to basis recovery in Chapter 6.C.

Example 7.6: Jane has $1,000 to invest, but she must first pay tax on that amount at her tax rate, which is 30 percent. After paying the tax, she is left with $700, and she invests this amount in property that appreciates at a rate of 4 percent per annum. After one year she has $728—that is, her original $700 plus 4 percent of $700 or $28. Let's suppose that the proceeds of the investment are entirely tax exempt. When the dust settles, Jane is left with $728. (Jane's pattern of taxation is no deduction upfront with full yield exemption.)

Example 7.7: Jim also has $1,000 to invest, and he is allowed to deduct this from income at the outset of his investment (suppose that it's a different kind than Jane's investment, and subject to different tax rules). He invests the entire $1,000 at 4 percent per annum and has $1,040 after one year before paying his taxes. The entire $1,040 is taxable at 30 percent, so that after tax, Jim is left with $728, just as Jane was. (Jim's pattern of taxation is full deduction upfront with full taxation of the yield.)

Immediate deduction of an amount invested in an activity (deduction up front) is sometimes called "expensing." Conclusion: Expensing is equivalent to yield exemption. This proposition is true as long as tax rates do not change over the course of the activity, and when there is no inflation.

What light does this shed on the difference between investments benefiting from the realization requirement and others? One consequence of the equivalence of expensing and yield exemption is very important: *Deduction of the cost of an enterprise before the accounting period in which it yields income reduces the tax rate on the enterprise as a whole.* To see this, take the comparison of Jane and Jim a step further. If Jim had not been required to pay tax on the entire yield of his investment, which he was allowed to deduct at the outset, he would have done better than Jane, who, having been denied the deduction of her investment at the outset, can only do as well as Jim if the entire yield of her enterprise is tax exempt. If Jim were allowed to deduct his investment at the outset but did not have to include the whole yield of the enterprise in income at its conclusion, his tax rate would be lower than Jane's, which is 30 percent.

The tax regime Jane faces in Example 7-6 is like that of the investor in capital assets under the Code, except that Jane gets to receive the proceeds of her investment completely tax free, whereas the investor in capital assets does pay tax on the gain, although at a rate lower than the ordinary gain rate but not quite zero. In the other example above, Jim is allowed to deduct his input costs up front, as trade or business owners may under the Code for inputs purchased early in the business cycle. But not all expenses of a trade or business can be deducted at the outset, and tax accounting methods are designed to spread trade or business deductions over the duration of the activity.

I. Further Illustrations of the Time Value of Money

(1) Growth of Money over Time

Here are a few more illustrations of the time value of money. Obviously, $100 invested at 3 percent simple interest per annum yields $103 after one year. If you were to reinvest the entire $103 at 3 percent for a second year, and continue to do this for a total of five years, the yield would be $115.92, slightly more than the $100 plus five times $3. This slightly growing yield can become surprisingly large after years of reinvestment of principal and previously earned interest. Invest $100 for ten years at 4 percent and you get $148, almost as much as $100 invested at 5 percent for ten years if the interest is added to the principal each year to bolster growth only for the 4 percent investment. Allowing the return from each period of investment to remain "in" and also earn interest is the key. We say the interest is compounded each year if the interest is added to the principal at each year's end and allowed to earn interest along with it. More frequent compounding increases the rate of growth.

How much will $100 be worth after n years if it is invested at 5 percent interest compounded annually? Each year the principal grows by 5 percent. This is .05 times the principal. Add this to the principal and the total is 1.05 times the principal. If the return is added to the principal each year, the amount on hand after two years is 1.05×1.05 times the original amount, or $(1.05)^2$ times that amount. It is simpler to write this as $(1.05)^2 \times$ the original amount. Generalizing, the original principal, which is growing all the time, will have grown to $(1.05)^n \times$ the original amount after n years.

(2) Reversing the Process: Discounting to Present Value

Just as amounts invested grow surprisingly quickly when interim returns are added to the principal, so is the present value of money to be paid in the future often unexpectedly small in comparison with the future payment. It stands to reason that if the compounding of returns on an investment makes it grow much faster than we might expect, so too is the true cost of paying someone that future amount correspondingly small. Again, you are not likely to have to do the math in your introductory tax course, but it is important to have a good intuitive feeling for the idea of "discounting" a future sum to present value. The following examples are just intended to give you a sense of how it works.

You must come up with $10,000 to pay an obligation that is due five years from today. How much must you invest today to have the money at the required time? If a savings account pays after-tax interest of 5 percent annually, and you intend to leave the initial deposit and the interest in the account until needed, then you can obviously achieve your goal by depositing less than $10,000 now. Whatever amount this is, it will grow by 5 percent each year, and that accumulating growth is added to the principal to earn 5 percent itself during the next period. It's pretty easy to calculate that after one year, the (new) accumulation is 5 percent or .05 of the original amount, and it is still there, so that the total on hand now is $1 + .05$ or 1.05 times the original amount.

Divide $10,000 by 1.05 and you get the amount that must be invested at 5 percent to earn $10,000 after one year: $9,523.80 = \$10,000 \div 1.05$. Divide $10,000 by 1.05 twice and you get the amount to be invested to earn $10,000 in two years: $9,070.29 = \$10,000 \div 1.05^2$. (Dividing one number by another twice is the same as dividing the first number by the other squared: $(\$10,000 \div 1.05) \div 1.05 = \$10,000 \div 1.05^2$.) By now the idea should be obvious. To get back to the number of dollars that after n years of being invested at 5 percent will have grown to $10,000, we divide $10,000 by 1.05^n.

How much must you put into the savings account? Call it k. Then after a year,

$$k + (5\% \text{ of } k)$$

will be in the account. it is simpler to write this as

$$k + (k \times .05)$$
$$= k \times (1 + .05)$$
$$= k \times (1.05).$$

Left in the investment vehicle, this amount grows by 5 percent during the second year. This works out to the above amount plus 5 percent of itself, or

$$k \times (1.05)(1.05) \text{ or } k \times (1.05)^2.$$

We can reverse the process if we know what the outcome will be after two years. Suppose that principal plus interest after two years is $100. Then k can be computed as follows:

$$\$100 = k \times (1.05)^2.$$

Divide through by $(1.05)^2$:

$$\$100/(1.05)^2 = k \times (1.05)^2/(1.05)^2 = k$$
$$= \$90.70.$$

If the government allows you to put off paying a tax of $100 for two years, and if you are able to earn an after-tax rate of 5 percent per annum on some investment, you are forgiven $9.30 of the tax, because by investing just $90.70 now, you can earn the necessary $100 to pay the tax with.

J. Tax Shelters Based on the Time Value of Money

Tax shelters that have at least one foot in reality often rely on the idea that a taxpayer who buys into a specially contrived activity may be able to use deductions from it to reduce his or her tax liability from other more ordinary activities, such as providing services for pay, at least temporarily; even if the delayed tax must be paid later, the taxpayer captures the post-tax time value of the postponement of the tax that would otherwise have been paid. By depreciating the basis of an apartment house, say, the owner suffers no out-of-pocket loss and yet lowers taxable income right away. True, the later sale of the real estate is likely to bring the taxpayer gain, precisely because the depreciation deductions have lowered the basis of the property, and this gain will be taxable. But that is in part the tax that was postponed by the depreciation of the building. So the effect is that the time for paying the tax has been postponed. By investing the postponed tax amount in the interim, the taxpayer can make money. Tax has to be paid on the yield, but the taxpayer will inevitably show a profit.

In 1986, after a long period of aggressive tax shelter activity, Congress revised section 465 and enacted section 469, both of which operate to deprive individual taxpayers of the chance to profit by exploiting the time value of money. Section 465 does this by making the taxpayer match deductions from most nonrecourse-financed activities with the termination of the activities or with reduction of the nonrecourse debt. Section 469 does so by disallowing the use of most *passive losses* — losses arising from activities in which the taxpayer is not an active participant — against income of the taxpayer from other activities, like employment. These two Code sections are not usually discussed at length in an introductory income tax course. They are mentioned here to reassure you that the barn door is no longer wide open.

SUMMARY

■ An amount reinvested with its yield grows more rapidly than an amount on which the yield accumulates without being added to the principal. For example, a 3 percent yield compounded annually doubles your investment in 25 years, a 4 percent yield in 18 years, a 5 percent yield in 14 years, a 6 percent yield in 12 years, a 7.2 percent yield in ten years, an 8 percent yield in nine years, and so on.

■ Because an investment grows over time, the amount that must be invested to yield a stated sum over a known time interval can be computed by reversing the compounding calculation. If r is the rate of return per period (e.g., months or years) expressed in decimal terms, and n is the number of periods, the present value of the amount k to be paid or received n periods from the present is

$$\frac{k}{(1+r)^n}$$

■ Many tax rules are designed to ensure that taxpayers are not able to postpone taxation, unless the government chooses to allow this for policy reasons, because postponement reduces the cost of the tax to the taxpayer and reduces the value of the tax to the government.

■ If gross income from a multiyear transaction comes in early and expenses are incurred later, postponement of the measurement of income until the transaction is complete would result in the government losing some of the time value of tax of the income. Even if income and deductions arrive in mixed amounts over the duration of the transaction, there could still be some loss to the government of this sort. For these reasons, the accounting rules prescribed by the IRS strongly disfavor open-transaction accounting.

■ For the same reason, Code section 453 strikes a compromise between open-transaction accounting and immediate reporting of the entire gain on a sale that contemplates installments of the full contract price to be paid later than the year in which the deal is final for state law purposes. Commercial annuities are treated similarly.

CONNECTIONS

Compensation for Services

The tax consequences of earning money or property by personal labor are rarely delayed for income tax purposes. Retirement schemes, some of which have the explicit approval of the Code or the IRS, do sometimes permit the tax consequences of compensation to be deferred, as discussed in Chapter 3.H.

The Realization Requirement and the Time Value of Money

Property gains and losses that can sometimes be measured with great certainty, as in the case of fluctuations in the value of securities traded on public exchanges, are yet not taken into account until realized, usually by sale or exchange of the property. The delay permits and requires taxpayers who own property to delay taking these gains and losses into account for tax purposes. See Chapter 10.B, E, and F.

Depreciation of Nonrecourse-Financed Property

In Chapter 8.F, we learn that nonrecourse debt is normally included in the basis of the property it encumbers. This permits the borrower to take deductions for depreciation and other purposes before actually investing already-taxed dollars in the activity in which the property is used. See Chapter 15. These "early" deductions allow the borrower to postpone tax on other income the deductions shelter, allowing the borrower to enjoy the time value of the postponed tax at the government's expense. Recall, however, that sections 465 and 469 deprive individual taxpayers of most opportunities to profit by taking otherwise legitimate early deductions.

Early Recovery of Basis

Though rare, opportunities to recover all of an asset's or activity's cost before the asset is disposed of or the activity completed also allow the taxpayer the benefit of the time value of tax postponed on income from other sources. See Chapter 6.B.

Original Issue Discount and Other Disguised Interest Schemes

Until 1984, debt instruments often gave creditors economic equivalents of interest without explicit payment of the interest. The result was to postpone taxation of the interest at an obvious gain to the creditor/taxpayer under time value principles. See Chapter 8.H.

Borrowing and Debt

8

Borrowing does not add to one's income for tax purposes, as long as the debt is outstanding. The lender still owns the money or property and

experiences none of the tax consequences associated with a disposition. Repayment of the loan principal is also a nonevent for tax purposes. A debtor cannot deduct principal payments, whether in installments or a lump sum, and the creditor has no income on getting back what is rightfully hers. From these first principles, pervasive consequences flow. We must consider how the income tax regards the use of borrowed funds to acquire other property: Does the acquisition have a basis, and if so, what? We must also separate out the payment by the debtor of interest and its receipt or accrual by the creditor, because these certainly do have immediate tax consequences. Finally, we must consider whether transactions described by taxpayers as not involving loans, debt, or interest can safely be treated as such for tax purposes.

A. RATIONALE OF LOAN TREATMENT

B. INTEREST ON DEBT

C. RELIEF FROM LIABILITY

D. CANCELLATION OF DEBT

E. RECOURSE AND NONRECOURSE DEBT

F. THE BASIS OF NONRECOURSE-FINANCED PROPERTY

G. ORIGINAL ISSUE DISCOUNT AND OTHER ELUSIVE FORMS OF INTEREST

A. Rationale of Loan Treatment

The standard explanation of how borrowing and debt affect income is as follows. The obligation to repay a loan burdens the borrower's net worth. In fact, the downward pressure exactly equals the lift provided by the amount borrowed. The liability offsets the value of the cash or other assets added to the borrower's balance sheet. As the borrower pays off the loan, he or she uses funds obtained in some other way, and the relief of the debtor's obligation is paid for with after-tax dollars or tax-exempt income.

Because the loan is not income, putting it to use also has no effect on the borrower's income. The Code makes sure that money is always treated as having a basis equal to its face value, and this is true of borrowed money as well. Borrowed property has a basis, when sold or exchanged, equal to its fair market value when borrowed. This becomes the initial basis of new property acquired in exchange for the borrowed property.

Example 8.1: Nathan borrows $20,000 to finance the start-up of a landscaping business. No line exists on the tax return for reporting the borrowed funds as gross income, because they are not gross income. Nathan simply returns the $20,000 without having spent any of it. There are no tax consequences.

Example 8.2: Same facts, except that Nathan uses the $20,000 to start the business. The business earns a net $40,000 in the first year, and he repays the loan right away. His loan repayment can be thought of as coming either from the borrowed $20,000 or from the new post-tax $40,000 on hand. Either way, he is left with $40,000, he has paid tax on an amount that left him with a post-tax $40,000, and he no longer has the $20,000 loan proceeds. All the money he now has is post-tax.

F	A	Q

Q: What dictates this approach to borrowing under the income tax?

A: It is a policy choice, not an eternal verity, although all income tax systems take this approach. To treat borrowed funds as income, with an offsetting loss on repayment of the loan, would make consumption paid for with loans or credit taxable as a component of income. Many think this would be inconsistent with a basic premise of income taxation: Unfunded consumption is not part of the tax base. In addition, the complexity of adopting a different approach to the basis of property acquired with borrowed money or property would be daunting.

The exclusion of borrowed funds from the income tax base is arguably necessary for maintaining the distinction between taxing income and taxing consumption. The consumption taxes that dominated European and American federal taxation before the nineteenth century certainly did not spare consumption financed with borrowed money. People felt that these duplicative taxes on a wide variety of consumption items cynically targeted the necessities of life. The income tax shifted some of the tax burden from consumption to savings and investment. The sensitivity of the public to this point has apparently disappeared. Recent proposals that would replace the income tax with a consumption tax all include borrowed money in the consumption base.[1]

Example 8.3: James, a law student, borrows $35,000 a year to finance his tuition and living expenses. He has no income. Under a consumption tax, whether imposed like a sales tax or paid annually with a tax return, James will pay tax on this borrowed money if he spends it on consumption. A sales tax, which can function as a consumption tax, applies to borrowed funds because it does not exempt sales when the buyer uses borrowed money, such as when the buyer uses a credit card.

B. Interest on Debt

The **principal** of a loan is the amount borrowed. **Interest** is the fee the borrower pays for the use of the principal. We also speak of principal and interest with respect to debts that do not arise from borrowing, such as the principal amount of a fine and the interest to be paid on that fine when it is overdue. In this chapter, we are primarily concerned with the principal of loans and debts and their tax consequences.

The payment of interest has straightforward tax consequences. Section 163 generally makes interest paid deductible if it relates to a trade or business other than that of being an employee. Most interest paid to finance investments or for other profit-oriented activity is deductible unless it exceeds the investment income of the taxpayer for the year. Interest that is not business or investment related, with several exceptions, is labeled "personal," and is not deductible.

A huge exception exists for home mortgage interest, either from debt incurred to buy, build, or improve a principal residence or as a home equity loan—there are dollar caps for the amounts of each type of home-related debt on which interest is deductible. For most middle-class people, home mortgage interest is most of the interest they will pay in their lives. Given that home owners consume them by living in them but also stand to gain by selling them, home mortgage interest is not easily categorized as personal or investment related. In our mobile society, many never acquire significant equity in a house, and the interest they pay on home mortgages feels like and functions as a surrogate for rent.

F   A   Q

Q: Isn't home ownership just a form of tax-exempt consumption?

A: The owner-occupier of a home does enjoy its use rent free, while holding an asset that may be sold at a gain. Renters must usually pay for their housing with already-taxed dollars and cannot deduct their rent payments. But the owner-occupier gets to exclude the rental value of the home, which is like getting to deduct the cost of renting it. Hence the owner-occupier is both an investor and a consumer, and enjoys the consumption aspect of homeownership tax free.

---

[1]See Robert Hall & Alvin Rabushka, *The Flat Tax* (1982).

Differences in the tax treatment of interest, however, do not translate into differences in the tax treatment of the principal obligations on which the interest is paid, so we may now return to the latter, the main topic of this chapter, without being concerned about interest.

C. Relief from Liability

In general, getting into debt does not make one better off. But escaping from an existing obligation usually does. A person has income when an obligation is shifted to another who thereafter has exclusive responsibility for it. As *Old Colony Trust* says, "The discharge by a third person of an obligation [of the taxpayer] is equivalent to receipt [of income]. . . ."[2] We have seen that there are exceptions, such as for certain recoveries that discharge obligations. Otherwise, the Court's pronouncement wears rather well.

It is useful to see that this also holds for any *assumption* of a taxpayer's debt by another party. No matter how or why the taxpayer incurred the liability, if someone else assumes it, the taxpayer's net worth is increased *pro tanto*, that is, a dollar of gross income for every dollar of debt shifted away. This can take place as a freestanding transaction, when only the obligation is transferred from one person to another, or in connection with a sale of property or of an entire business.

Example 8.4: Susan borrows $3,000 from a bank to buy a used car from her brother for $3,500. The car doesn't run well and Susan asks for the money back. Her brother can come up with only $500 in cash, but Susan, her brother, and the bank agree that he alone will be liable for payments on the loan. Susan realizes $3,500 on the deal. Fortunately, she has a basis of $3,500 in the car, and so there is no gain or loss. Note that the amount realized consists of the $500 she receives in cash *plus* $3,000 in debt relief. (We do not discuss here the character of Susan's income for the moment.)

Example 8.5: Susan borrows $3,000 from a bank to buy a used car from her brother for $3,500. She wrecks the car and takes a $1,000 net casualty loss deduction on a loss of $1,100. (She had other casualty losses for the year to get her over the 10 percent of AGI threshold for claiming such losses; see Chapter 13.C.) Her basis in the car fell from $3,500 to $2,400. She then sells the car for $100 to her brother, who assumes the obligation of repaying the bank, leaving Susan with no further liability on the debt. Susan realizes $3,100 on the sale and has a gain of $700 ($3,100 amount realized minus $2,400 basis). (We do not discuss here the character of Susan's income.)

The character of the amount included in income — ordinary income or capital gain — depends on the extent of the creditor's rights against the debtor. This refinement of the analysis is taken up in Section E of this chapter.

---

[2] 279 U.S. 716, at 729 (1929).

D. Cancellation of Debt

When the taxpayer is forgiven the balance of a loan, that amount is gross income in the year the loan is forgiven. Partial forgiveness of a debt results in gross income to the extent that the obligation goes away; that is, for each dollar of debt discharged, the debtor has a dollar of ordinary income. The phrases "cancellation of debt" and "forgiveness of indebtedness" are used interchangeably for this category of tax event.

F   A   Q

Q: Why should a debtor have income when a debt is canceled if the transaction in which the debt arose is also canceled?

A: When the reason for a debt's cancellation is the debtor's restitution of property purchased or the rendering of other consideration for exoneration from the debt, the debt cancellation income is reduced by the deduction of the consideration given. Under section 108(e)(5), the discharge of the obligation may be treated as a price reduction rather than as cancellation of a debt. On the other hand, when a taxpayer agrees to pay for another's performance and neither party performs its side of the contract, no debt arises and cancellation of the contract need not be analyzed under cancellation of debt rules.

Example 8.6: Frances runs up a bill of $3,000 at the friendly corner grocery store. When she loses her job, the store owner agrees to cancel her entire bill. Unless Frances is insolvent, she has gross income of $3,000, not for the year when she bought the groceries but for the year in which her debt was forgiven.

In *United States v. Kirby Lumber Co.* a corporation bought back its own bonds at a drastic discount. The Supreme Court held the difference was income because there was no "shrinkage of assets."[3] Outside bankruptcy, the amount of discharged debt is not included in gross income to the extent that the taxpayer is insolvent. In *Lakeland Grocery Co. v. Commissioner,*[4] the taxpayer entered into a settlement with its creditors, paying $15,000 for the discharge of $104,710 in debt. Before the settlement, the taxpayer was insolvent; after the settlement, the taxpayer had net assets of $39,597, which "were freed from the claims of creditors as a result of the [discharge of indebtedness]."[5] The Board of Tax Appeals held that the taxpayer realized gain to the extent it had assets that ceased to be offset by any liability.

Sidebar

RELATED PARTIES

Regulation section 1.108-2 defines cancellation of debt as the acquisition of a taxpayer's obligation by the taxpayer or someone related to the taxpayer from someone not related to the taxpayer. This definition technically applies only to the limitation on COD income that Code section 108 provides, but the idea is applicable more broadly.

---

[3] 284 U.S. 1 (1931).
[4] 36 B.T.A. 289 (1937).
[5] *Id.* at 291.

The Tax Court has held that the "net assets" or "freeing of the assets" test applied in *Lakeland Grocery Co.* is the test Congress had in mind in enacting section 108. In *Carlson v. Commissioner*,[6] a commercial fisherman and his wife bought a fishing boat with a loan from a bank. As security for the loan, the couple granted the bank a mortgage on the boat. When they fell behind in loan payments, the bank foreclosed, sold the boat, and used the sale proceeds to reduce their loan balance. It forgave a total of $53,000 consisting of the rest of this and other loans the couple owed. The bank then mistakenly issued them a Form 1099-A, stating that the loan forgiven was not income to them because they were insolvent. When the IRS disagreed, the taxpayers went to Tax Court, arguing that section 108(a)(1)(B) applied because immediately before the foreclosure sale, their total liabilities exceeded the total fair market value of their assets.

It should be noted that section 108(a)(1) appears to say that insolvency bars any inclusion of COD income, without restricting this to the insolvency amount. The Tax Court rejected this interpretation and recomputed the taxpayers' assets, counting a commercial fishing permit worth $393,000 that was exempt from creditors' claims under Alaska law. The court's disagreement with the taxpayers' interpretation of section 108(a)(1)(B) was perhaps dictum, because it found them not to have been insolvent to any extent, but the court discussed pre- and post-section 108 precedent at length, affirming that *Lakeland Grocery Co.* had "crystallized" an approach that is still good law.

> **Sidebar**
>
> **STUDENT DEBT FORGIVENESS**
>
> Section 108(f) provides an exclusion from gross income for what would otherwise be income on the forgiveness of certain student debts. The debt agreements, however, must contemplate the forgiveness in cases in which student borrowers agree to work "in certain professions for any of a broad class of employers," and the lender must be any of certain governmental or tax-exempt entities.

If a property seller partially forgives the buyer's debt on a particular property purchase, section 108(e)(5) treats the reduction as a price reduction, and hence not as COD income, even if the buyer is not in bankruptcy or insolvent. Legislative history indicates that this rule is intended to avoid factual inquiries into the shadowy distinction between price reductions and discharge of indebtedness in particular cases. If the purchase money obligation or the property has passed into the hands of a third party, the debtor would still have gross income on the discharge of all or part of the purchase money obligation.

E. Recourse and Nonrecourse Debt

It may seem that lenders and other creditors will always rely on and exploit the full credit of a debtor to make sure they get paid. In the commercial context, however, when lenders are impatient to lend or sellers feel pressure to sell, they often depend on a security interest in specific property of the debtor more than on other assets of the debtor. By taking a security interest in one or more very good assets, the creditor can gain priority with respect to them over other creditors. Identified collateral can make the debt itself easier to sell or to vaunt when the creditor must prove his own creditworthiness to banks, investors, and others. Moreover, some borrowers have no

---

[6]116 T.C. 87 (2001).

assets other than the property they will buy with the borrowing to be secured by the property; it simplifies matters both for the parties and for other creditors and investors for the collateral to be clearly identified and for the creditor to waive other recourse against the borrower, which would at best be of negligible value. The law provides no affirmative reason for a creditor to give up his or her claim against other assets of a debtor, but in practice this is often done, perhaps because it also makes the debtor more comfortable in granting the creditor a security interest in a very important asset to think that other assets are free and clear of the creditor's claims.

At any rate, reliance on specific collateral to the exclusion of other property of a debtor is typical of **nonrecourse financing**. Where real estate is concerned, nonrecourse financing customarily requires the borrower to mortgage the property to the lender but does not require the borrower to promise to repay the debt, even if the value of the collateral proves insufficient to cover the obligation. Hence, a nonrecourse borrower is not personally liable to satisfy any deficiency if, after default, the property subject to the obligation does not cover the balance of the obligation.

By contrast, a recourse debt subjects the debtor's full credit to the claims of the creditor. This is the type of obligation most commonly encountered in a noncommercial setting. When you use a credit card, for example, the issuer has recourse against your salary and all of your possessions, present and future. When you buy a house, the lender or its assignee has a mortgage on the house, allowing the loan to be satisfied by the foreclosure of the mortgage and sale of the house, but also has your promissory note on which the lender can sue if the proceeds of the sale of the house do not satisfy the full obligation.

F   **A**   **Q**

Q: Does a recourse borrower have COD income on the disposition of mortgaged property when the borrower has continuing personal liability on the mortgage note?

A: Because the borrower is still liable for repaying the debt, there is no cancellation of debt, even if the buyer of the property agrees with the creditor to be liable on the debt as well.

To review these elements: (1) A recourse obligation may give the obligee the right alongside other obligees to attempt to squeeze the principal out of the obligor; (2) a recourse obligation may give the obligee this claim *plus* a security interest in particular property; but (3) a nonrecourse obligation gives the obligee *only* a security interest in particular property.

F. The Basis of Nonrecourse-Financed Property

A borrower's basis in property acquired with nonrecourse loan proceeds includes the acquisition cost plus the cost of any improvements, just as if the debt were recourse. This rule is not dictated by economic reality or conceptual elegance. It does, however, tend to satisfy one of the overarching goals of tax design: It treats economically similar transactions alike, here the recourse and nonrecourse approaches to acquisition cost borrowing. Why does anyone care if the tax law is neutral as between these two kinds of borrowing? The basis of property acquired with loan proceeds is especially important in the business context, because property used in a trade or business can be depreciated—a little of the basis can be deducted each year— thereby reducing the tax burden on the enterprise. If two comparable businesses used recourse and nonrecourse financing, respectively, to acquire their business assets, and the recourse borrower was able to claim much larger depreciation deductions each year because its business property had a higher basis, and the nonrecourse borrower got lower deductions, not having been allowed to use the cost of the property as its basis for depreciation, then tax consequences would give the recourse borrower a competitive advantage. Tax consequences would affect and possibly alter the decisions of economic agents as they decided what businesses to go into and what kind of financing to use. The tax law might kill the golden goose.

The government itself came up with the idea of treating recourse and nonrecourse financing alike as regards the basis of financed property. The government also advocated, and the Supreme Court accepted, that the artificial basis attributed to non-recourse-financed property requires subsequent treatment of the nonrecourse liability as a real liability, so that escaping that liability has some, if not all, of the consequences of cancellation of indebtedness. We will study this rule both from the perspective of its policy justification and the purely mechanical perspective, making sure that we can apply it accurately without having to reinvent the wheel each time. Getting the policy behind the rule straight actually proves helpful with the mechanics.

First, the mechanics. When property subject to one or more nonrecourse liabilities is disposed of, section 7701(g) provides that the amount realized includes the balance of the nonrecourse liabilities plus any actual consideration received. Note that this applies to all nonrecourse liabilities, not only to those added to the basis of the property as acquisition or improvement costs; we will come back to this. First, recall that section 1001 defines "amount realized" as roughly what in a nontax context we would call "sale proceeds." Do not confuse "amount realized" with "gain realized." Section 1001(b) states the general rule that the difference between the amount realized and basis is gain realized, if the difference is positive, or loss realized, if the difference is negative. The special rule for nonrecourse liability stated in the first sentence of this paragraph is *not* found in section 1001, but in section 7701(g) and in the judicial and administrative interpretation of section 1001.

Three basic topics about nonrecourse liabilities deserve special attention: (1) *debtor forfeiture*, (2) *nondefault disposition of nonrecourse-financed property*, and (3) *any disposition of property subject to nonrecourse equity loan debt*. Some of these terms deserve elaboration. Debtor forfeiture occurs when the person responsible defaults on the repayment obligation, such as by not making payments that fall due, and the creditor exercises its right to seize the property. Sales and exchanges by the owner without default are common nondefault dispositions. Finally, an equity

Sidebar

BORROWERS' REASONS FOR PREFERRING NONRECOURSE FINANCING

Some may think that the nonrecourse borrower is not as virtuous as the recourse borrower because they face different levels of risk. There is, in fact, some danger that less risky nonrecourse financing will be used for transactions that have favorable tax consequences, though they have no realistic prospect of being profitable. But this danger should provide its own cure, because nonrecourse lenders will soon put themselves out of business if they lend to borrowers with specious business plans. So the market—assuming minimal rationality on the part of the players—offers some assurance that the use of nonrecourse financing will have a business purpose.

loan taps the unencumbered value of the property offered as collateral. Home equity loans are familiar, of course, but taxpayers often borrow against business or investment property as well. Most equity loans are with recourse against the borrower's other assets, but some equity loans are nonrecourse.

Here are examples of (1) and (2), respectively.

Example 8.7: Beverly bought a building for her consulting business, putting down no money of her own but obtaining a mortgage loan of $390,000, for which she did not have to give a promissory note. After three years, she had taken depreciation deductions (technically, ACRS deductions under §168)[7] totaling $30,000, which saved her $8,400 in federal taxes. These deductions reduced her basis in the building from $390,000 to $360,000. She paid interest on the mortgage during these years but paid no principal. Early in year four she defaulted on the loan and the bank obtained foreclosure on the mortgage, receiving only $200,000 in net proceeds after a judicial sale. On disposing of the building Beverly had a gain of $30,000, the difference between the balance of the mortgage debt that was deemed to be the amount realized, $390,000, and her remaining basis in the property, $360,000.

Example 8.8: Same facts, except that Beverly sold the building to a friend who assumed the mortgage, so that Beverly did not have to default on it. The friend paid $3,000 for the property subject to the mortgage. On the sale Beverly had a gain of $33,000, the difference between $393,000, which is the sum of the $3,000 she received from the friend and the $390,000 balance of the mortgage, and $360,000, her remaining basis.

Here is an example of disposition of property subject to nonrecourse equity loan debt — item (3) in our list of topics deserving special attention:

Example 8.9: Evelyn buys property worth $200,000 for $100,000 out of her own pocket and $100,000 in nonrecourse loan proceeds from a bank. When the property has appreciated to $300,000, she refinances the loan, now borrowing $200,000 nonrecourse, receiving $100,000 in additional loan proceeds and satisfying the earlier $100,000 mortgage with the remaining $100,000. By refinancing, she effectively obtains an equity loan, that is, a loan equal to the difference between the $300,000 value of the property and the original $100,000 mortgage. She does not, however, invest the $100,000 equity loan in the property. Her basis in the property remains $200,000. If she defaults on the new mortgage or sells the property, her amount realized will include the new $200,000 nonrecourse liability. Thus, she will have to report gross income of $200,000 if she defaults, more if the terms of the mortgage allow her to transfer the property to a third party and the third party pays Evelyn something of value in addition to taking the property subject to the mortgage.

In approaching nonrecourse liability problems, remember to keep separate: the fair market *value* of the property, the *balance of the nonrecourse debt*, and adjusted *basis*. Each can fluctuate over time without affecting the other two. As the property rises and falls in value, basis is not affected, and the property's changing value is also

---

[7]To simplify the numbers, I ignore the midmonth convention applicable to ACRS deductions for nonresidential real property. See I.R.C. §168(d)(2)(A).

independent of the balance of the debt, which depends exclusively on whether the borrower pays down the principal or the creditor discharges it. Basis, equal at the outset to fair market value, changes as the owner takes deductions (depreciation, casualty loss) and for certain other tax-sensitive events, but not as a result of changes in the property's value or in the level of the remaining debt.

Example 8.10: Easy Car Rental Co. buys a car for $25,000, financing the entire purchase with a nonrecourse loan from Global Bank. The value of the car is $25,000, Easy's initial basis is $25,000, and the debt is $25,000. After a year of renting the car, its value has fallen to $22,000; that is what the car would fetch on the used-car market. Easy has paid $7,000 on the nonrecourse debt, so that the amount owed is now $18,000. Easy has also claimed $5,000 in depreciation for tax purposes, so that the car's basis is now $20,000. If Easy sells the car now at fair market value, the gain is $2,000, the difference between the value $22,000 and the basis $20,000.

Example 8.11: Easy Car keeps the car two years longer. After three years, the fair market value is $13,000 and the basis has been reduced to $10,000 by tax depreciation. By special arrangement with the lender, Easy has delayed principal payments on the nonrecourse loan so that the balance is still $18,000. If Easy defaults on the loan and the lender seizes the car, Easy's amount realized is $18,000 — not the fair market value $13,000 (do you see why?). The difference between amount realized and basis is $8,000, Easy's gain on the disposition.

When a taxpayer puts his or her own money into a purchase and finances the rest with nonrecourse loan proceeds, the "cost" for tax purposes is ambiguous. The taxpayer is not personally responsible for the loan, so it is arguably not part of the cost he or she pays. On the other hand, the price paid for the property includes the taxpayer's and the lender's money. In effect, the case law (to be discussed below) equates "cost" with the full purchase price, resolving the ambiguity of the term in favor of the taxpayer. Once established in this way, however, the basis of the property can change in light of other events, such as depreciation and casualty loss deductions.

TABLE 8.1	Comparison of Recourse and Nonrecourse Encumbrances of Property	
	Recourse Encumbrance	**Nonrecourse Encumbrance**
Liability included in basis of collateral	Yes	Yes
Debtor escapes liability on transferring collateral to their party	Not always	Yes, unless debt is converted to recourse
Amount realized includes balance of debt on transfer of collateral	No	Yes
Debtor has COD income if creditor releases debt when collateral is transferred	Yes	No

Examples 8-8 through 8-11 illustrate the holdings in *Tufts v. Commissioner* and *Crane v. Commissioner*,[8] the Supreme Court's two principal decisions on the tax consequences of nonrecourse-financed property dispositions. In *Crane*, the taxpayer had acquired an apartment building at the death of her husband, when the mortgagee of the building offered it to her on generous terms. She took the property subject to a low-interest mortgage at the property's value at the time, but she only had to turn over the rentals net of operating expenses and a reserve for local taxes. She would pay nothing if the building's revenue were too low. For seven years she reported the gross rentals as income and took lots of deductions—property taxes, operating expenses, mortgage interest, and depreciation. Under the agreement she was not required to pay all of the interest as it accrued. Her basis in the building following the government's already standard treatment of nonrecourse debt was $262,000, the building's appraised value when she acquired it. Of this, the building's portion of the basis was $207,000. Over the seven years, she had taken depreciation deductions of $28,000, so that at the time of sale the adjusted basis was $179,000. There was $15,000 in unpaid interest when, with the bank threatening foreclosure, Mrs. Crane sold the building to a third party for $3,000 cash, subject to the mortgage, and paid $500 in sale expenses. The deal was obviously a cozy one, but nothing in the Court's analysis turned on this.

Mrs. Crane argued that she had realized only $2,500 and that even this was taxable at capital gain rates. The Court rejected her argument and agreed with the government that the amount Mrs. Crane realized comprised the unpaid nonrecourse debt of $262,000 together with the net payment of $2,500 that she received on the sale. The government had not argued that the accrued but unpaid interest of $15,000 was also to be included in the amount realized, noting that Mrs. Crane would have been able to deduct this amount if she had paid it.[9] Presumably she would have been deemed to pay the interest if it was deemed forgiven in addition to that of the mortgage principal. The only issue over which the Court hesitated was whether the result would have been different if the value of the property had fallen below the debt balance.[10] The bottom line was that only the balance of the mortgage should be treated as part of the amount realized on the disposition.

The Court's reasoning was not as clear. Mrs. Crane had argued that she should not have been allowed to claim tax depreciation based on the mortgaged value of the building, though she had in fact done so, and that she received no economic benefit on being relieved of the mortgage. The Court blithely combined these points in rebutting her. "The crux of this case, really, is whether the law permits her to exclude allowable deductions from consideration in computing gain."[11] Mrs. Crane's point had been that a nonrecourse borrower stands to lose only the "equity" in the mortgaged property purchased with nonrecourse funds, because this is all the borrower stands to lose in the event of a default on the obligation. This is obviously true, and the borrower has no further economic benefit from a clean slate, because the slate was clean to begin with. But the administrative practice that extended to her the treatment given to recourse borrowers had a downside as well. She must in effect

---

[8]331 U.S. 1 (1947).
[9]*Id.* at 4 n.6.
[10]*Id.* at 14 n.37.
[11]*Id.* at 15.

repay the depreciation deductions to the extent that they came out of the nonrecourse basis.[12]

The Court indirectly acknowledged part of Mrs. Crane's point about her lack of economic benefit by its famous refusal to decide whether the outcome would have been different if the building had fallen to a value less than the balance of the mortgage. You might think of her as trading the building, at least in part for relief from the nonrecourse liability, on selling it to a third party for a small cash payment. The exchange would be taxable, of course, and equal value would be deemed to have been given and received on each side of the exchange.[13] By calling attention to a case in which the fair market value of the property securing a mortgage is undeniably lower than the balance of the nonrecourse liability it secures, the Court recognized the difficulty of maintaining the deemed equality of these two figures. Naturally, such a qualm is already high in the stratosphere, not so much of tax theory as of tax convention, because it is the convention of treating nonrecourse borrowers like recourse borrowers that is the source of the supposed problem.

That is essentially the view taken by the Court when it finally put the qualm to rest in *Tufts v. Commissioner*.[14] To preserve nonrecourse borrowers' parity with real borrowers, the former must be treated as being relieved of a liability when they dispose of the property whose basis depends on it, and hence as having gain measured by the difference between the balance of that liability and the basis of the property surrendered. This is patently a convention, without support from any fundamental analysis of the concept of income; ability to pay, objective economic power, and economic benefit are all powerless to explain it. The Court speaks of the convention as one that avoids tax complexity and is grounded in long-standing administrative interpretation. The Court does *not* say that the purpose of treating the nonrecourse borrower as a debtor is to preserve tax neutrality between transactions that would not differ in a world without income tax, but that is the best explanation for the administrative view.

Is it constitutional? *Crane* apparently said yes, if we are to take the Court's passing reference to the Sixteenth Amendment as framing the issue in constitutional terms, but *Tufts* did not comment on this. Tufts, however, is certainly a strong reassertion of the theme also touched upon in *Taft v. Bowers*,[15] where the Court held that taxing the appreciation of an inter vivos gift to the donee is constitutional, even though the appreciation occurred before the gift was made. There, as here, the Court emphasized that basis rules confer benefits on taxpayers at the same time that they preserve possible gain for later recognition (where gifts are concerned, even recognition by a different taxpayer).

G. Original Issue Discount and Other Elusive Forms of Interest

A parent transfers money to a child as an "interest-free loan," never intending to demand repayment. An employer lends a key employee money for a home mortgage

---

[12]Deductions attributable to nonrecourse basis are actually called "nonrecourse deductions" in the partnership tax regulations. Treas. Reg. §1.704-2.
[13]This fundamental principle is applied universally in the tax law. *See Philadelphia Park Amusement Co. v. U.S.*, 126 F.2d 184 (Ct. Cl. 1954) ("the cost basis of the property received in a taxable exchange is the fair market value of the property *received* in the exchange" [emphasis in original]).
[14]461 U.S. 300 (1983).
[15]278 U.S. 470 (1929).

at a substantially below-market rate of interest. Many taxpayers are able to come up with similar, not very sophisticated tax-saving strategies. Whether an arrangement of payments on an obligation includes interest, how much interest, and when the interest is recognized are sensitive questions for the income tax.

Until 1982,[16] especially during periods of high inflation, loan-based tax stratagems were usually successful. It took Congress and the courts a long time to react. But for 25 years now, the Code has offered tougher rules that are unambiguous in their application to many transactions and do a reasonable job of wiping out this type of creative tax planning. To keep the rules specific enough that they cannot be avoided, Congress chose to enact a unified but sprawling number of Code sections. What follows is a survey of these sections and their main features.

Section 1274 deals with debts for property. If money is lent for the purchase of property, this section sometimes characterizes the debt instrument as providing for more interest than it actually does. The additional interest is sometimes called "tax interest" to commemorate its imaginary status. Suppose that I want to sell you my apartment complex over time. It would be nice to postpone the tax on the gain while having immediate access to the gain in economic reality. To that end we agree that all you pay in the early years is principal and schedule the interest payments for late in the installment sequence.

Blocking this strategy for very large principal instruments,[17] section 1274 recomputes the interest amount at semiannually compounded rates and requires that this interest be reported annually by both the borrower and the lender. Whether this recharacterization process must take place depends on two things: first, whether the interest stated in the agreement is abnormally low, and second, on whether the interest is payable at the end of the loan. An insufficient interest rate is any rate below the "applicable federal rate," which depends on whether the term of the agreement is short (three years or less), midterm (between three and nine years), or long (over nine years). The rates vary with the rates at which the government pays interest on its obligations, and the IRS announces changes in these rates at frequent intervals. Having the borrower pay all of the interest at the end of the loan period, even if at a sufficient rate, would also postpone the tax consequences for the lender, so this too can trigger recharacterization.

Just to make things interesting, an older section applies to most sales of property not covered by section 1274 if payments are not all made within the year of the sale. Section 483 deems any difference between the issue and redemption prices of bonds (original issue discount or OID) to be interest, but lets the consequences depend on the taxpayer's accounting method. It uses the same amounts of interest and safe harbor rule as section 1274, and caps the imputed interest at 6 percent and 9 percent in certain cases.

Sections 1272 and 1273, dealing with debts for cash, now treat OID as interest accruing annually for both income and deduction purposes. But several types of debts for cash are exempt, including tax-exempt obligations, U.S. savings bonds, short-term (one year or less) obligations, and nonbusiness loans between individuals that do not exceed $10,000.

---

[16]Just to be clear: The big statutory overhaul to be described in this section resulted from major new legislation in both 1982 (the current original issue discount rules) and 1984 (rules for gift and other non-gift loans).

[17]Section 1274 applies only to debt instruments given for property, other than certain new business property, for which the stated principal amount is $2,800,000 or more. I.R.C. §1274A(b).

Sections 1276 to 1278 treat the discount from face value at which a bond is sold as interest prorated over the life of the bond, with de minimis exceptions. Cash method taxpayers pay tax only on the interest when they dispose of the bond, and the same is true for nonconventional interest attributable to the original issue discount on loans used to buy such bonds. Sections 1281 to 1283 require the accrual of interest on some short-term (less than one-year maturity) bonds to the extent of any discount on purchase. Interest on a loan incurred to buy short-term bonds not subject to this rule is not deductible to the extent of the amount of interest that would otherwise have been taxed under section 1281.

Section 1286 is a quaint rule that blocks an old loophole. It used to be clever to sell a bond without the "coupons" that would otherwise entitle the holder to interest payments. Although the bond sells at a discount, both for deferred payment of principal and for being stripped of its interest-paying component, the discount may also disguise the conversion of interest into apparent capital gain. This part of the discount is taxed under section 1286 as interest, based on applicable federal interest rates and the length of time to maturity of the bond. By characterizing the discount as interest, the section makes it subject to the original issue discount rules of sections 1272 and 1273.

Sidebar

ORIGINAL ISSUE DISCOUNT

Section 483 addresses a problem that gives its name to the entire configuration of imputed interest rules. "Original issue discount" (OID) refers to the still common practice of issuing a debt instrument for less than its redemption price — the price to be paid by the issuer when the instrument matures and the holder can demand a liquidation of the obligation. The difference between the issue price and the redemption price often represents both interest and an adjustment for anticipated inflation in the currency in which the obligation is to be paid. Because section 483 deprives original issue discounting of its tax advantages, many tax experts refer to the imputed interest provisions of the Code as OID rules.

Another cluster of Code sections is primarily aimed at tax-sensitive interest games between related parties such as parents and children or employer and employee.[18] If the Code selects a loan for special treatment under these provisions, it is because the relationship between the parties suggests the possibility that interest on a loan will not be set neutrally.

Section 7872 singles out "gift" and "demand" loans at abnormally low interest rates. The "forgone interest" — the interest these loans would call for if they were made at market rates of interest — is added to the principal of the loan and the borrower is deemed to pay it to the lender as interest. (The section defines a number of terms, including those in quotes above. A "gift loan" is one whose purpose is to make a gift of the interest forgone. A "demand" loan is one on which the lender can demand full payment at any time, in contrast with a "term" loan, any loan on which the lender accelerates repayment.) Of course, the forgone interest is only implicit in the low rate of interest actually charged. It does not actually pass between the parties. This fiction is just needed to keep things straight. In some cases, the borrower can deduct the fictitious interest, but the lender must in all cases report it as gross

---

[18]Other Code provisions are designed to prevent tax planning based on the similarity or community of interest of related parties. Section 267(a)(1) disallows the recognition of losses on sales of property between certain related parties. On the other hand, taxpayer manipulation of the timing of losses is a broadly different topic, not usually involving implicit interest. Sections 1091 on wash sales and 1092 on stock straddles are closer in purpose to section 267(a)(1), and neither is limited to transactions between related parties.

income. When? To achieve accuracy for situations involving big-figure loans and during times of high market interest rates, section 7872 deems interest at the previously mentioned applicable federal rates to be transferred between the parties at the beginning of the loan, and then treated as earned and paid ratably over the duration of the loan as under section 1272, discussed earlier.

Section 7872(c)(2)(B) restricts this recharacterization of gift loans, for loans between individuals, to those *days* on which the aggregate loans between them exceed $10,000, unless the gift loan is used to buy income-producing assets. For smaller gift loans, the amount of imputed interest is limited to the borrower's net investment income (roughly the excess of investment income over investment-related expenses) for the year, with a complete exemption if this is $1,000 or less. Employee and shareholder gift loans have the same exemptions, but other non-gift loans do not. Congress just could not bring itself to go easy on the few loans within the sweep of section 7872 that are *not* customarily used for creative tax planning.

In summary, the regime of sections dealing with implicit interest recharacterizes some transactions so as to impute interest as being paid, without changing the timing for inclusion and deduction, and recharacterizes others with elaborate timing and compounding rules that may require early inclusion of implicit interest in the lender's income and allow early deduction by the borrower. These interest provisions are obviously directed at large transactions involving sophisticated tax planning and are designed to achieve neutrality in the tax treatment of financing transactions.

SUMMARY

■ Loan proceeds are not gross income as long as the borrower is legally bound to repay the loan, because that obligation offsets what would otherwise be the increase in the borrower's net worth. These are recourse loans, because the creditor can obtain full satisfaction of the debt from all of the borrower's present or future assets.

■ If the obligation to repay a loan or other payment obligation is extinguished by the creditor's voluntary cancellation of the debt or by operation of law, the amount of the debt canceled is ordinary income to a solvent borrower.

■ Some loans, however, are nonrecourse; that is, the creditor can take specified loan collateral but has no claim against the borrower for any deficiency between the value of the collateral and the balance of the loan.

■ Interest paid on a debt is normally deductible if it relates to a trade or business other than that of being an employee.

■ Interest paid to finance investments or for the activity of investing is only deductible if it does not exceed the investment income of the taxpayer for the year.

■ Interest paid other than for business or investment purposes is not deductible, with a few important exceptions.

■ First-home mortgage interest of up to $1 million in principal loan amount and home equity loan interest up to $100,000 are deductible; regulatory tracing rules determine which of these limits applies to a loan.

- Gross income does not include any amount for debts discharged when the taxpayer is in bankruptcy, or to the extent that the taxpayer's liabilities exceeded assets immediately before the discharge.

- The Code treats the reduction of a taxpayer's debt on a particular property purchase as a price reduction, not as cancellation-of-debt income, even if the purchaser is not insolvent or in bankruptcy.

- In some respects, the obligation to pay a debt in order to safeguard debt collateral against seizure by the creditor is treated like debt on which the creditor has full recourse against the debtor's credit.

- In particular, the amount of the debt is initially included in the borrower's basis for the property if the debt proceeds were used to acquire or improve the property.

- When the borrower disposes of property subject to such nonrecourse debt, the amount realized is deemed to include the unpaid portion of the nonrecourse debt in addition to any other consideration actually received.

- Large debts at lower-than-market interest rates are treated as if market interest were being paid annually, so that a business borrower becomes entitled to deduct the fictitious interest and the lender must report it as ordinary income, both currently. Interest is imputed on certain other debts but the interest is not treated as accruing annually.

CONNECTIONS

Satisfaction of a Debt by a Third Party

Although a third party's satisfaction of a debtor's obligation has the same economic effect as forgiveness of the debt by the lender, section 108 does not apply to the former.

Loans to Employees

The rules that recharacterize certain "demand" loans are aimed at situations in which employers lend money on below-market terms to favored employees as a form of additional compensation. The preferential aspect of these loans is not one of the fringe benefits the Code allows employees to exclude from income. See Chapter 3.E.

Net Gifts

When a gift of property in kind is conditioned on the donee's agreement to pay the donor's gift tax liability, the gift is subject to this liability of the donor. The case law, however, holds that satisfaction of the donor's liability by the donee is not cancellation of indebtedness that results in gross income to the donor. See Chapter 5.G.

Depreciation Deductions Using Nonrecourse Basis

Inclusion of nonrecourse debt amounts in the basis of collateral used in a trade or business permits the business taxpayer to claim deductions equal to those that would be taken if the financing were with full recourse against the borrower's credit. See Chapters 7.H and 15.B.

Like-Kind Exchanges

Any liability escaped in a nonrecognition like-kind property exchange under section 1031 is treated as money received, with the consequences that the basis of the like-kind property received in the transaction is reduced by the amount. See Chapter 9.E.2(a).

Deductible vs. Nondeductible Interest

Interest on home mortgage loans is the only interest that can be deducted despite the obligations' lack of a profit-seeking purpose. See Chapter 13.D.

Realization and Recognition 9

People spend more when they think their houses and portfolios have appreciated, but tax law ignores this wealth effect. Gross income usually

O V E R V I E W

includes an upward change in asset value only when the asset's owner realizes the gain. Realization occurs when an asset is sold or exchanged, and with so much riding on these tripwire events, whether they have occurred is not always straightforward. The Code indeed suggests that other dispositions can be realization events. What then constitutes a disposition? The lawyer's task is to draw guidance from the Code, precedent, and theory.

Realized gains and losses are normally recognized, or taken into account, right away. Yet realization does not always trigger recognition. The Code delays this usual consequence in certain circumstances, such as the replacement of property with property of like kind for business use. Nonrecognition rules promote tax neutrality by permitting taxpayers to make certain basic economic decisions without considering tax burdens. Permanent nonrecognition of realized gain or loss, however, would also often violate tax neutrality. Accordingly, nonrecognition is in most cases just a postponement of tax consequences. The Code uses the same clever, if tricky, mechanism in several settings to prevent nonrecognition from turning into exemption. This magic is achieved by adjusting the basis of assets involved in nonrecognition transactions, so that realized gain is preserved for later recognition or to reduce a later loss.

A. The Structure of Section 1001 and Nonrecognition Provisions

Three cardinal concepts — disposition, basis, and amount realized — are closely linked in the grand scheme of the Code. Section 1001 provides that "gain from the sale or other disposition of property shall be the excess of the amount realized therefrom over the adjusted basis . . . , and the loss shall be the excess of the adjusted basis . . . over the amount realized." Chapter 6 noted that amount realized and basis are technical refinements of everyday notions used in describing property transactions. Amount realized stands in for proceeds, as basis does for cost, to ensure that all tax-relevant aspects of an owner's relationship with property are taken into account.

Example 9.1: Arnold renovates his house replacing old windows with new, energy-efficient windows. The project cost of $20,000 is part of his investment in the house and would be considered part of his "cost" in measuring his gain or loss for financial purposes when he sells the house. He is entitled to a $500 tax credit under Code §25C, and the credit is subtracted from the $20,000 cost that would normally be added to his adjusted basis in the house. Arnold's cost or investment in the house now diverges from his basis by $500. He will have $500 more in taxable gain on selling the house than he will have in economic terms.

B. What Constitutes a Disposition?

(1) Securities and Similar Instruments

Section 1001(a) says gain or loss is realized upon "[a] sale or other disposition of property." The interpretational canon *ejusdem generis* tells us that "other disposition" indicates the genus or class of events to which sales belong. Section 1001(c) assumes that exchanges of property belong to the class as well. What is the common element that makes them dispositions?

The Supreme Court first addressed the question in *Eisner v. Macomber*,[1] when it decided that the distribution of a pure or bona fide stock dividend is not a realization event. Mrs. Macomber held 2,200 shares of Standard Oil stock and received 1,100 more, of which 18 percent had a par value of $20,000, and the government determined that this part of the dividend represented income accrued by the corporation after enactment of the income tax. Correctly applying the statute, which expressly included stock dividends in gross income, the government concluded that Mrs. Macomber therefore had $20,000 in ordinary income. The Court disagreed, finding that the dividend had not enriched the taxpayer, there being no evidence that the value of her stock in the company had changed, even though their number was increased. On the basis of this finding, the Court held that (1) the issuance of stock dividends to shareholders does not always cause them to realize gain, and (2) it would be unconstitutional to tax Mrs. Macomber or any taxpayer on unrealized gain. We set aside the constitutional holding for the moment and focus only on the holding that clarifies what a realization is.

To understand this, we must closely examine the corporate action it deals with. A stock dividend is in part the distribution to shareholders of additional shares, usually of the same class, in some proportion to those already held. In this respect, a stock dividend resembles a stock split, which also changes the number of shares in the hands of each shareholder, usually multiplying them by the same factor, without distributing any of the corporation's assets or changing shareholders' rights in any other respect. A stock split may enable shareholders to sell shares more easily, by reducing per-share value without diluting their aggregate value.

A stock dividend does this but also ties the corporation's hands in a way that a stock split does not. With or without changing the number of outstanding shares, a corporation can transfer earnings from earned surplus to stated capital on its books. To declare the stock dividend, the corporation *must* increase its stated capital—the amount of capital shown on its books—by the par value of the total stock dividend. This obliges it to keep separate from its working capital a part of its asset value equal to the increased par value of the stock and take no step that would make this new "stated capital" amount vulnerable to its creditors' claims, say, by borrowing so much that its working capital will not cover the liability.

The *Macomber* Court paid close attention to the rights underlying Mrs. Macomber's shares, having concluded that their number alone was not dispositive, any more

---

[1] 252 U.S. 189 (1920).

than the number of shares involved in a mere stock split would be. The shift of focus from number of shares to underlying rights had important consequences for later cases.

One such case held that when a corporation organized under one state's laws "moves" to another state by getting itself recognized as a corporation of the second state, subject to its different corporation laws, every share of stock of the corporation has suffered an identity change, because the rights of the shareholders have all been altered.[2] In another case, a similar corporate move not only brought the surviving corporation under a different organizational statute, but also changed the dividend percentage rate of reissued preferred shares; again the Court considered the new corporation "essentially different" from the old and treated the substitution of shares in the new corporation for shares in the old corporation as a realization event.[3] Only when a corporation was replaced with another organized in the same jurisdiction did the Court find no difference in corporate identity and therefore no change signaling realization: "[T]he corporate identity was . . . substantially maintained because the new corporation was organized under the laws of the same state, with presumably the same powers as the old . . . [and there] was also no change in the character of securities issued."[4] In each instance, the Court looked through the identity of corporate names and other similarities to ascertain whether shareholders' rights to the underlying corporate assets had changed.

These later cases may have had a constitutional dimension, given their close temporal relationship with *Eisner v. Macomber*, but if so, the constitutional element was not so interwoven with the realization analysis as to make them clearly interdependent. The most recent Supreme Court decision on the nature of realization made the difference between constitutional and statutory interpretation of the realization doctrine fully explicit.[5]

Cottage Savings Association v. Commissioner[6] found that a taxpayer's exchange of one bundle of mortgages for a similar but different bundle of mortgages was a realization event, because the mortgage terms and underlying real estate were materially different. The Court agreed with a Treasury Regulation stating that, as used in Code Section 1001, an exchange is a "disposition of property" only if the properties exchanged are "materially different."[7] As the opinion made clear, the case arose only under the Code and did not implicate the constitutional limits on congressional power to tax income. The Court stressed, however, that the regulation is "consistent with our land mark precedents on realization."[8] Although the transaction at issue was far removed from the financial concerns of everyday citizens, it bore a close resemblance to those in the corporate restructuring precedents discussed above. In each instance, instruments representing a financial interest were formally exchanged. In each, the interests in

---

[2] *U.S. v. Phellis*, 257 U.S. 156 (1921).
[3] *U.S. v. Marr*, 268 U.S. 536 (1925).
[4] *Weiss v. Stearn*, 265 U.S. 242 (1924).
[5] 252 U.S. at 219. Justice Holmes had insisted that the statutory meaning of realization under the 1913 Revenue Act was narrower than its meaning in the Sixteenth Amendment, but no one has since agreed with him.
[6] 499 U.S. 554 (1991).
[7] Treas. Reg. §1.1001-1(a).
[8] 499 U.S. at 561.

the property the instruments represented may have been fungible from the tax-payer's perspective as an investor. The Court chose *not* to link the concept of realization to notions of functional economic similarity, but instead to exalt form over substance — at least where realization is concerned.

F   A   Q

Q: Does a debt, or any creditor's interest in a debt-like obligation, have a basis?

A: Borrowed money or property has a basis in the hands of the borrower equal to its fair market value at the time when the obligation arises. We sometimes also speak of the *lender's* basis in the right to repayment, and the amount of this basis is the lender's basis in the property loaned plus any further amount the lender has invested in preserving or collecting the debt. If a loan is in cash, the amount of cash plus further amounts spent to preserve or collect the debt equal the creditor's basis in the obligation.

The taxpayer in *Cottage Savings Association* was a savings and loan (S&L) asso-ciation. It carried out the mortgage exchange with the conscious goal of recognizing a tax loss. The rates of return on the mortgages had fallen below the market rate of interest for new mortgages. The federal regulatory agency for S&Ls was prepared to allow them to make the swaps without showing *financial* losses on their books; thus, the plan would allow S&Ls to recover past taxes paid by allowing them to incur tax losses without acknowledging to potential lenders and investors that the value of their assets had fallen. Although the financial regulator wanted S&Ls to be bailed out at taxpayers' expense, the IRS saw things differently. It argued that the investments were not "materially different" for purposes of section 1001, because the packages of mortgages were "economic substitutes" for each other. The Tax Court agreed with the IRS, embracing the idea that the swaps did not occasion tax realization of losses any more than they did financial realization under the relaxed accounting standards.

The Supreme Court rejected the government's "economic substitute" gloss on the "material difference" standard as unacceptably vague and potentially arbitrary. It would have required an inquiry into "the relevant market [for the securities in question], [into] whether there is a regulatory agency whose views should be taken into account, and [into] how the relevant market participants and the agency would view the transaction."[9] The Court did not see how this inquiry could be "principled," an obvious swipe at the discord between the IRS and the financial regulator. Instead, it held that "an exchange of property gives rise to a realization event so long as the exchanged properties are 'materially different' — that is, so long as they embody legally distinct entitlements."[10] Focusing on the lack of identity in the mortgage

---

[9]*Id.* at 565-566.
[10]*Id.* at 566.

interest rates and in the identity of the parcels mortgaged, the Court easily concluded that "legally distinct entitlements" had been involved.

Example 9.2: George lends Alice $2,000 in exchange for Alice's promissory note, which requires her to repay the principal with interest at 5 percent compounded annually, over 60 months. After one year, George and Alice agree to change the promissory note to lower the payments and require full payment of the balance of principal and interest only in 60 months from that time. George and Alice also agree to change the interest rate for the extended term of the note. George's rights under the promissory note change, although he is partly compensated by the interest he will receive. If the interest rate is higher than before, George is better off; if it is lower, he is worse off. Which of these it is depends on the interest rate alone. Since George has legally distinct rights and entitlements with the modified note, he is treated as having exchanged the original note for a new one. This is a realization event. George recognizes a gain or loss measured by the difference between his basis in the original note, $2,000, and the market value of the substituted note.

Example 9.3: Same facts, except that George and Alice agree only to postpone three payments of principal and interest. The interest rate remains the same, but three months are added to the original 60-month payout period and George is compensated for the delay in final repayment of the debt by additional interest. Since the interest rate and obligor remain the same, George's entitlements are arguably not distinct from those of the original note. No realization occurs, and George need not recognize gain or loss by virtue of his leniency.

Regulations promulgated since *Cottage Savings* continue to take a position that is not quite that of the Court's hair-trigger test for realization. But there is no mention of the "economic substitute" test the Court rejected. The regulations instead classify some alterations of the terms of a debt instrument, including changes in interest rate and obligor, as insignificant and therefore not realizations.[11] A taxpayer is free to choose: rely on the regulations when they favor you (that is, when you would have a taxable gain on the modification of a debt instrument you own) or rely on *Cottage Savings* when the Court's more sensitive test of realization favors you (that is, when you would have a deductible loss on the modification of a debt instrument you own).

(2) Real Estate Interests

The Supreme Court's tax jurisprudence sometimes fails to harmonize one narrowly decided case with another, despite their shared subject matter. Decisions on modifications and swaps of instruments evidencing interests in other property blithely ignore the Court's principal decision concerning the "modification" of a directly held real property interest.

The Supreme Court in *Helvering v. Bruun*[12] decided that the regulations could legitimately classify a landlord's untimely recovery of the leasehold enhanced by the

---

[11]Treas. Reg. §1.1001-3.
[12]309 U.S. 461 (1940).

tenant's improvements as a realization of gain. Under the common law, when a leasehold is surrendered, improvements made by the lessee revert to the landlord with the land unless the lease specifically gives the tenant the right to remove them. Improvements are part of the land itself. Reversion of the leasehold with new improvements, however, can definitely enrich the landlord. *Bruun* held that the government violated no constitutional norm by treating such gain as realized by virtue of the reversion alone.

Bruun cast doubt on the constitutional dimension of the realization requirement because it allowed the IRS to decide which of severally legally distinct events should be treated as a realization. Such deference to administrative discretion seems foreign to the "material difference" standard clarified by *Cottage Savings*. Perhaps the *Bruun* Court was so preoccupied with *Macomber* that it overlooked the issue of how much deference is appropriate. Not surprisingly, Congress moved quickly to restore certainty, enacting section 109, which excludes the value of improvements returned to a landlord, unless they were in lieu of rent. Section 1019 denies the landlord any basis adjustment for excluded improvement value, subtly acknowledging that the recovery may yet be a realization.

F   A   Q

Q: Did *Bruun* overrule *Macomber*?

A: *Bruun* declares the *Macomber* severance test irrelevant to the problem of determining whether the leasehold forfeiture was a realization event. We may infer from the tone of the Court's reference to *Macomber* that it had little sympathy with the breadth of *Macomber*'s reasoning. Technically, *Bruun* did not overrule *Macomber*.

(3) Other Types of Property Modification or Improvement

The courts or the IRS may eventually identify other patterns of realization besides those involved in the cases and regulations thus far. Code section 1235 addresses a peculiar feature of patent right transactions, laying down a bright-line rule that the sale of a patent must transfer all rights associated with the patent. Congress or the courts may some day address the analogous problem of the licensing of know-how and other intangibles. Clever tax planning in other areas may also raise realization issues.

Example 9.4: Tax shelters often involve transfers of appreciated property from U.S. taxpayers to nonresident juridical persons that pay neither U.S. nor foreign income taxes. The goal is to avoid tax on gains that have foreseeably "built up" during the tax-favored exploitation of business assets in the United States. The government persuades courts in many instances to disregard these transactions as lacking in economic substance, but a court might also find that the U.S. taxpayer has gross income on making such a transfer to a foreign entity, on the grounds that the transfer is a realization of the built-in gain, which is easily valued and will not foreseeably be reduced by subsequent events.

TABLE 9.1	Realization and Nonrealization Events: A Nonexhaustive List	
	Reason for Realization Treatment	Eligible for Nonrecognition Treatment Under §1031 as Like-Kind Exchange
Sale or exchange of personal property	§1001 classifies sales and exchanges as realization events.	Yes
Sale or exchange of noninventory business property	Same	Yes
Sale or exchange of business inventory	Same	No. §1031(a)(2)(A).
Barter of personal services for property	Not a realization event. §1001 does not apply because property is not disposed of, but Treas. Reg. §1.61-2(d)(1) interprets §61 as including barter income in gross income.	No. §1031 only applies to exchanges of "property." §1031(a).
Refinancing of mortgaged real property	Realization of gain on original investment (down payment plus borrowed funds) only if the identity of the mortgaged property changes.	No
Swap of securities of different issuers	Identity of property changes.	No
Swap of securities of same issuer (in most cases)	Change of entitlements of security holder.	No
Swap of securities of same issuer in stock split	Not a realization event.	No
Swap of securities of same issuer in a bona fide stock dividend	Not a realization event.	No

C. The Effect of Encumbrances and Liabilities on Amount Realized

Section 1001(b), as we have seen, defines "amount realized from the sale or exchange of property" as "the sum of any money received plus the fair market value of the property (other than money) received." To ensure that the amount realized includes all aspects of consideration for a disposition that may affect the measurement of the disposing taxpayer's gross income, the regulations make it clear that amount realized includes "the amount of any liabilities from which the transferor is discharged as a result of the sale or disposition."[13]

Example 9.5: Scott buys land for $30,000, paying $20,000 in cash and giving the seller a mortgage and mortgage note at market interest for $10,000. After a year, Penelope buys the land from Scott for $25,000 in cash, subject to the mortgage, and Penelope assumes Scott's obligation on the mortgage note with the original seller's consent. Scott's amount realized is $35,000, the sum of the $25,000 received in cash and the $10,000 in relief from liability on the mortgage note. Scott has a gain of $5,000, the difference between the amount realized ($35,000) and his basis ($30,000).

Think of the shifting of the purchase-money liability as a payment of money equal to that liability, coming to the seller/obligor from the buyer. The result is the same as if such a payment had occurred.

Example 9.6: Penelope buys land from Scott, who holds it subject to a $10,000 mortgage and has personal liability for the $10,000 on a mortgage note. Penelope pays Scott $35,000, enabling Scott to discharge the $10,000 liability, retire the mortgage, and still have $25,000 in net proceeds. Scott has a gain of $5,000.

Obviously, the seller of mortgaged property cannot expect as much for the property as if the property were free and clear of encumbrances. Whether the buyer takes on the liability or gives money that the seller uses to remove the liability, the result is economically the same. Fortunately for tax lawyers, the tax result is also the same.

Example 9.7: Scott buys land for $30,000, paying $20,000 in cash and giving the seller a mortgage and mortgage note at market interest for $10,000. Penelope agrees to pay Scott $25,000, and Scott remains solely liable on the mortgage note. Scott's amount realized is $25,000. He has a loss of $5,000, the difference between the amount realized ($25,000) and his basis ($30,000). Now he actually has $5,000 more in his pocket than before he first bought the land, but he is liable for $10,000 to the original seller.

Sellers of property subject to nonrecourse debt, as Chapter 8.F explained, face different consequences. In essence, the seller of nonrecourse-financed property is treated as if receiving cash in the amount of the nonrecourse liability. Thus the balance of the nonrecourse liability is included in the seller's amount realized.

Example 9.8: Scott buys land for $30,000, giving the seller a mortgage for $10,000 but no mortgage note. The absence of a mortgage note means that the seller can only take the property if Scott defaults and cannot proceed to take other assets belonging to Scott if the property value has fallen below the balance of the liability. Scott sells the land, subject to the mortgage, to Jane for $25,000. Scott's amount realized is the sum of the $25,000 received in cash and $10,000 in nonrecourse liability shifted to Jane.

---

[13]Treas. Reg. §1.1001-2(a).

Scott's gain is therefore $5,000, the difference between the amount realized ($35,000) and Scott's basis in the land ($30,000).

D. Nonrecognition and the Preservation of Tax Consequences

We have noted already that a realized gain or loss is normally recognized when realized. When you sell property with a basis different from its sale price and no special rule alters the usual course of things, you realize and recognize a gain or loss. The gain or loss belongs to the year when the sale is final under state law, and you report the gain or loss on your tax return for that year. This is the norm established by section 1001. Several Code sections, however, create exceptions. They permit the taxpayer to postpone recognition of a realized gain or require the taxpayer to postpone recognition of a realized loss. The gain or loss is still realized, and several rules are formulated with this in mind.

Nonrecognition alone would of course induce people to shape their affairs with tax advantages in mind, demoralizing less clever tax planners, and grossly distorting market forces. But nonrecognition is usually intended to have just the opposite effect, alleviating the influence of taxation on economic decisions. So, to prevent nonneutrality and unfairness, the Code preserves the tax consequences of nonrecognition transactions for a later day. To achieve this, special rules fix the basis of the property received, and sometimes also of property surrendered, in the nonrecognition exchange.

(1) Section 1031

(a) The Mechanics of Like-Kind Exchanges

Far from simple, section 1031 is nevertheless the least complex Code provision that preserves tax consequences by manipulating basis. Section 1031(a) provides that the gain or loss shall not be recognized when business property other than inventory or investment property other than stocks and bonds is exchanged for property of "like kind." This is chiefly a boon to real estate investors and developers, because real estate transactions are more generously classified as like-kind exchanges than transactions involving other property.

In a section 1031 transaction, the basis of the property traded away becomes the basis of the property taken in exchange. The attachment of the old basis to the new property leaves the taxpayer poised to recognize the gain avoided by nonrecognition if that gain survives until the taxpayer disposes of the new property. If the new property loses value, the taxpayer may avoid the gain altogether, but it will be as if the property had never been traded and the original property had lost value.

Example 9.9: Global Corp. holds land for investment with a basis of $100,000. The land appreciates to $150,000. In the course of its business, Global finds property of equal value it thinks will serve its investment goals better and trades the old for the new. Later, Global sells the new property for $175,000. Global's basis is $100,000 — the same as the basis of the original land Global held — and so Global's gain is $75,000.

Part of this gain had accrued before the exchange, because Global's original property would have sold for a gain of $50,000 before it was traded. Part of the net gain accrued after the exchange. Pre- and post-exchange gain are not distinguished when the $75,000 of gain is included in Global's income.

Things are more complicated if the taxpayer receives both like-kind and other property in an otherwise qualifying exchange. Then the nonqualifying property or "boot" (something given "to boot") takes a basis equal to its fair market value (face value in the case of U.S. currency), and the like-kind property gets what is left, the remaining available basis. Section 1031(d) puts this very obscurely, though you can always refer to it if you have the patience and don't care to remember the underlying idea. But the underlying idea is easier to work with. We find a sort of conservation-of-basis principle at work. The taxpayer goes into the transaction with a certain basis in the property to be surrendered and must come out again with the same basis spread between the like-kind property and the boot. The purpose is to make exchange of property for like-kind property painless and to treat the like-kind property as a proxy for its predecessor. To accomplish that, the like-kind property should not get a cost basis, but a basis that reflects the unrealized gain or loss on the property it replaces. When there is no boot involved, the new property just has the same basis as the old. With boot involved, the goal is to let none of the unrealized gain or loss become attached to the boot. Hence, the boot gets a basis equal to its fair market value, essentially a cost basis, and the like-kind property gets the leftover basis.

Example 9.10: Global Corp. holds land for investment with a basis of $200,000, which has depreciated to $150,000. Global exchanges the land for like-kind property worth $120,000 plus $30,000 in cash. The cash is not of like kind with the land, of course. Hence, as nonqualifying property or boot, the cash attracts $30,000 of Global's available basis, $200,000, leaving only $170,000 as the basis for the land received in the exchange. If Global sold the land immediately, while it still had a value of $120,000, Global would have a loss of $50,000, equal to the loss inherent in the property it had previously held.

In general, this sharing of basis between like-kind property and boot requires little thought, unless liabilities are also involved, a wrinkle we consider next.

Section 1031 exchanges are more complex if the property exchanged is encumbered with debt. The debt may stay with the transferor, so that the transferee takes the property free and clear. If so, the debt does not affect the analysis: The like-kind property received has a basis equal to that of the property given up, subject to adjustment for boot. But if the transferor is relieved of debt in the transaction, the transferor is treated as having received additional cash to pay off the debt, and that cash is, of course, boot. So the amount of the liability taken off the transferor's shoulders is treated as money received in addition to the boot for purposes of the basis allocation. Again, section 1031(b) says this, but in exceptionally difficult terms to grasp unless you already get the point. The formula should really be:

Basis of Like-Kind Property = Basis of Old Property
$$\hspace{6em} - \text{Total Value of Boot and Liabilities Avoided}$$

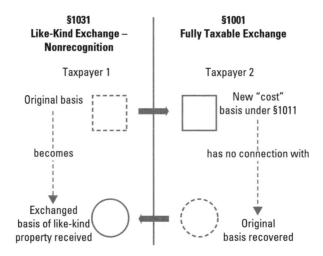

FIGURE 9.1   PURE LIKE-KIND EXCHANGE WHERE ONE PARTY DOES NOT HOLD THE PROPERTIES FOR PROFIT

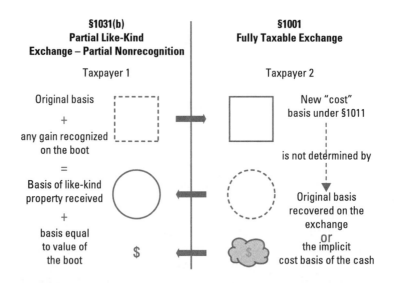

FIGURE 9.2   PARTIAL LIKE-KIND EXCHANGE BETWEEN THE SAME PARTIES

Example 9.11: Global holds land for investment with an FMV of $150,000, a basis of $200,000, and a mortgage of $20,000. (The net value of the land subject to the mortgage is only $130,000.) Global trades the land subject to the liability for like-kind property and no explicit boot. Global's basis in the new property is $180,000, the basis of the old property ($200,000) minus the liability avoided ($20,000).

Example 9.12: Same, except that Global trades the land subject to the liability for like-kind property worth only $110,000 and a yacht worth $20,000 (non-like-kind property). Global's basis in the yacht is $20,000—boot always gets an FMV basis. Global's basis in the land is $160,000, the basis of the old property ($200,000) minus the combined value of the boot and amount of the liability avoided ($40,000 = $20,000 yacht + 20,000 liability).

Leaving the best for last, section 1031 taxes the fair market value of boot received in a like-kind exchange to the extent of the transferor's gain realized on the exchange. Wait a minute! Gain realized? Remember that section 1031 is a nonrecognition rule, not a nonrealization rule. Yes, gain and loss can still be realized on a nonrecognition exchange. As section 1031(b) puts it, "the gain, if any, to the recipient shall be recognized, but in an amount not in excess of the sum of such money and the fair market value of such other property." The amount of gain recognized is added to the basis of the original like-kind property, and this new total basis is allocated between boot (including liabilities expunged and the like-kind property received). The boot attracts its fair market value in basis, and the remaining basis attaches to the new property.

F A Q

Q: Is the treatment of partial like-kind exchanges in section 1031(b), (c), and (d) like that of transactions that are bifurcated, such as bargain sales?

A: No. Section 1031 does not treat partial like-kind exchanges as taxable to the extent of the boot received in every instance. Thus, the involvement of boot in the exchange does not trigger a simple bifurcation of the transaction. If there is no gain realized on the exchange of the like-kind property surrendered, none is recognized even in the presence of boot.

In *Jordan Marsh v. Commissioner*,[14] a holding company sold the physical premises of a department store and land to an unrelated third party, taking back a long-term lease of the same premises. The sale's purpose had apparently been to give the holding company a loss on the property, which had declined in value. The government argued that the event was an exchange of all rights in the property for a modified version of those rights and invoked section 1031. This would have postponed recognition of the loss claimed by the taxpayer. Interestingly, in the present connection, the court decided ultimately that the transaction was a real sale and not an exchange at all, but its analysis proceeded as if the issue were whether the purported sale had been a realization event. In the end, the court concluded that the sale-leaseback was not a *disposition* of the property, and of course, without a disposition, no loss could be realized.

Example 9.13: Dad agrees to sell an old family car to Son for a high price. Dad has no gain because his basis in the car is his original purchase price. Son pays with a promissory note on which he never pays any principal. Son uses the car in a courier business, depreciating the high cost basis of the car for ample tax savings. Later, Son terminates the courier business and goes to law school. At this point he sells the car back to Dad, reporting a gain on which he is taxed at a low tax rate, because he no longer has much income.

Sidebar

SALE-LEASEBACKS

Jordan Marsh also illustrates how the government and the courts test sale-leasebacks, a common tax-planning strategy, for their reality. A purported sale-leaseback may be only a loan to the would-be seller/lessee from the would-be buyer/lessor or the purchase of a subordinate equity interest in the property. If a sale is either of these, it is not a disposition by the seller.

---

[14]269 F.2d 453 (1st Cir. 1959).

Dad pays for the car by canceling the promissory note. The entire transaction may be deemed to have been a sham, in which case neither the sale from Dad to Son nor the sale from Son to Dad was a realization event, because neither was a disposition.

Example 9.14: A rental car company sets up a trust to borrow money from banks that will purchase cars for the company's rental fleet. The trust will nominally buy the cars and lease them to the company. One advantage of this arrangement for the company is that it keeps the cost of purchasing the cars off the company's balance sheet (think Enron!). Is the trust the true owner of the cars? When the cars have been rented out for a few years, they are sold. There is consistently gain on these sales, because the cars are subject to accelerated depreciation. Does the trust or the company take the depreciation deductions while the cars are in service? Which of them recognizes the gain or loss? The company will want to be the owner for both of these tax purposes.

(b) What Is "Like Kind"?

You need only know that virtually any real estate is considered of like kind with any other, even if the interests are of different "grade"[15] (improved versus unimproved), quantum (fee simple versus 30 or longer leasehold[16]), or business versus passive investment status.[17] This administrative position has turned section 1031 into a sweeping nonrecognition rule for real estate. Entire firms exist only to facilitate tax-free real estate swaps. Other kinds of property are more narrowly classified, primarily according to a system of asset classes created just for this purpose.[18] For example, office furniture and computer equipment used in an office belong to different asset classes and are not of like kind.

(2) Nonrecognition Contributions to Entity Capital

Most introductory tax courses illustrate the workings of nonrecognition rules with section 1031 alone. In fact, nonrecognition plays a fundamental role in the taxation of corporations, partnerships, and trusts. The contribution of most capital to a corporation or partnership follows the nonrecognition pattern of section 1031. Distributions from partnerships to partners are nonrecognition events as well, though with important exceptions. Finally, distributions in liquidation of a partnership can qualify for nonrecognition on both sides, again with important exceptions; liquidating distributions from corporations are usually fully taxable.

E. Overriding Recognition Rules

(1) Recapture

More specific or narrowly stated provisions of a statute normally take precedence over more general or broadly stated provisions. Certain highly specific Code

---

[15]Treas. Reg. §1.1031(a)-1(b) (definition of "like kind").
[16]*Id.* at §1.1031(a)-1(c).
[17]*Id.* at §1.1031(a)-1(b) & (c) (non-dealer-owned real estate is "investment" and apparently of like kind with any other such real estate).
[18]*Id.* at §1031(a)-2(b)(2).

provisions threaten to override the broad nonrecognition accorded to contributions to the capital of corporations or partnership, by requiring that certain realized gains or losses must be recognized after all. But there are a few. Sections 1245 and 1250 classify some of the gain on dispositions of depreciable property as ordinary income. Once upon a time, these two sections made no exception to this "recapture" of depreciation deductions previously taken, even if the property were contributed to the capital of a continuing enterprise in corporate or partnership form. Today, section 1245(b)(3) and section 1250(d)(3) expressly exempt such nonrecognition contributions from the burden of recapture. On the other hand, the acceleration of gain required by section 453B when the holder of a tax-deferred section 453 installment obligation disposes of that obligation is granted only a qualified exemption from recognition if the disposition takes the form of a contribution to corporate or partnership capital.[19]

(2) Short Sales and "Short Against the Box" Transactions

Securities traders often engage in "short sales." The traditional short sale consisted of three transactional steps: (1) Trader borrows securities from Lender, expecting them to decline in value over the period for which they were borrowed; (2) Trader immediately sells the borrowed securities at their then market value; (3) Trader buys the same number of these securities at the end of the loan period and returns them to Lender. If the securities' price has fallen, Trader gains the difference between the earlier and later prices, because Trader sold the shares at the earlier price and meets the obligation to Lender at the low price of the later purchase. If the securities appreciated, the gambit would fail and Trader would lose the difference between the two prices. (There are also "naked" short sales, in which Trader does not bother to borrow the shares in the first place but only promises to transfer shares of a given kind to another party on a future date for a predetermined price; if the shares can be bought at the future date for less than the fixed price, Trader has a gain, etc.)

The tax consequences of a short sale are straightforward. The completion of the contract either leaves the short seller better off or worse off, and there is a taxable gain or loss equal to the financial gain or loss. The result mimics what would occur if the obligation to "repay" the loan in kind were compromised by the parties after the fact, with the securities' lender agreeing to accept a smaller sum in discharge of that obligation; this would give Trader cancellation-of-debt income if the transaction were profitable for Trader.

Section 1259 is designed to frustrate a gambit by means of which the owners of appreciated shares were once able to avoid loss in the market value of their shares without facing the realization of built-in gains. The owner of appreciated shares borrows shares like those she already owns, sells them, and then restores them with cheaper shares at the end of the loan — a normal short-sale pattern. But if the shares have fallen in value, so has the value of the shares the owner had to begin with. The economic gain on the short sale equals the economic loss on the retained shares, although this economic loss has not been realized. At worst, the owner of the appreciated shares has gained access to some of that appreciation — and has paid tax on it — but the market decline has not denied her the benefit of the appreciation altogether.

---

[19]Treas. Reg. §1.453-9(c)(2).

Selling "short against the box," as this is called, has the effect of a realization without the usual tax consequences. Section 1259 treats the short sale as a "constructive sale" of the underlying market position, with an adjustment if the short seller must later sell the original shares to meet the obligation of restoring the lender's shares.

Example 9.15: Mary has 1,000 shares of stock that she bought for $20 per share and that are now worth $100 per share. She borrows 1,000 shares of the same corporation's stock and must return them a year later. She sells the shares right away for $100,000, realizing and recognizing no gain because she had a $100,000 basis in the shares (property borrowed in kind has a basis equal to its fair market value just as borrowed money does). The shares decline in value to $80 per share by the end of the year. She must pay only $80,000 to restore the borrowed shares. Her $20,000 gain, however, is equal to her unrealized $20,000 loss, because her original shares have gone from $100,000 to $80,000 in value. Under section 1259, she recognized $80,000 in gain when she borrowed the shares that protect her from the economic loss, but the gain is reduced to zero if she sells all 1,000 of her original shares to raise the cash to cover the short-sale obligation.

Example 9.16: Mary again sells short against the box, but the stock does not lose any of its value. She is still treated as having constructively sold the entire block of $100,000 in share value, for a gain of $80,000, in the year in which she borrowed the shares for the short sale.

F. Loss Recognition — Sections 165 and 267(a)(1)

Code section 1001 is the clearinghouse for the realization and recognition of gains and losses, but it does not require gains to be included in gross income — the definition of gross income in section 61 does that — nor does it permit losses to be deducted. Realized and recognized losses are sometimes *not* deductible.

Section 165 provides, "There shall be allowed as a deduction any loss sustained during the taxable year and not compensated for by insurance or otherwise." For business and profit-oriented investment activities, the broad rule of loss deductibility has few exceptions. Section 165(b), however, disallows the deduction of other losses by individuals unless they are from fire, theft, or other casualty.[20] We usually refer to other losses of individuals as "personal" losses, borrowing the term from section 262, which disallows deductions "for personal, living, or family expenses," except as expressly provided elsewhere in the Code.

Together, sections 165 and 1001 authorize taxpayers other than individuals to deduct losses when they are realized, unless a nonrecognition rule intervenes. Section 1001 makes recognition of a loss the normal consequence of the realization of the loss, and section 165 makes a recognized loss deductible for these taxpayers. The two sections authorize individuals to deduct recognized losses unless they are personal losses.[21]

In one notable instance, the Code makes certain losses nondeductible in order to prevent taxpayers from contriving to recognize losses without facing economic

---

[20]See Chapter 13.C.
[21]Chapter 4.C(2) and D explain that recovery exclusion and loss deductibility are regulated by different standards.

consequences. Section 267(a)(1) disallows the deduction of a loss realized in a sale or exchange of property with a party related to the taxpayer. Section 267(b) contains a long list of relationships that trigger the loss disallowance, such as that of family members (brothers and sisters, spouse, ancestors, and lineal descendants). If one spouse sells property at a loss to the other spouse, even though the sale was at fair market value, the loss is not deductible. Section 267(d), however, grants the transferee some relief from the recognition of gain on a subsequent sale or exchange of the property: The gain is reduced by the previously disallowed loss. Obviously, this is a nonrecognition rule, but of a novel sort. The disallowed loss is recognized on the later transfer, and no deduction is allowed; on the later sale, technically, part of any gain is not recognized. Nonrecognition in this situation does not postpone the gain; it exempts it entirely.

G. Realization and Receipt

Be careful not to confuse realization and receipt. As Chapter 9.A(1) explains, mere receipt of something valuable will not support a finding that the recipient has gross income. Money received by an agent on behalf of his or her principal (the person for whom the agent has the power to act) is not income to the agent. It does not belong to the agent, does not increase the agent's wealth, and cannot lawfully benefit the agent.

Even when receipt of a valuable item is income to the recipient, we do not say the recipient has realized the value of the item, unless the receipt was triggered by the recipient's disposition of property. Recall that section 1001, discussed in Chapter 8.A, is only about dispositions of property and speaks only of realization with respect to such events.

SUMMARY

- Gains and losses in the value of property are taken into account for tax purposes only when they are realized; economic gain or loss may accrue, and may even be easily ascertained as in the case of securities traded on public exchanges, but still not be realized.

- Realization is the normal, but sometimes not the only, requirement for recognition, or taking into account, of gain or loss.

- Numerous Code sections provide for the nonrecognition of gain or loss in specified circumstances, usually when a realized gain or loss, if recognized, might change a taxpayer's non-tax-motivated decision whether to follow through with the transaction that causes realization. Remember that we still speak of a gain or loss as having been realized even if it is not recognized.

- Nonrecognition would create destructive inequalities between taxpayers if the tax consequences of the disposition that causes realization without recognition were not somehow preserved to be taken into account later. Adjustments to the basis of the property received in a nonrecognition disposition preserve these tax consequences.

- Liabilities encumbering property at the time of a disposition either remain the responsibility of the taxpayer who disposes of the property or are discharged, removing a burden from the previously liable taxpayer's shoulders. If discharged, the amount of the liability is treated as money received by the taxpayer, or, if the transaction qualifies for nonrecognition, reduces the basis of the property that replaces the transferred property.

■ Section 1031 is a typical nonrecognition provision in several respects: (1) It allows complete nonrecognition of realized gain or loss if property is disposed of exclusively in exchange for like-kind property; (2) it allows partial nonrecognition if property is disposed of in exchange for like-kind property and boot, that is, money or other non-like-kind property; and (3) it requires that the basis of the boot equal its fair market value, while adjusting the basis of the like-kind property to adjust for this and for any gain recognized by the transferor.

■ If a more broadly stated nonrecognition rule conflicts with a more narrowly stated rule that expressly requires recognition of a realized gain, the latter controls. Several express recognition provisions, however, contain exceptions for broader nonrecognition rules; for example, section 1245(c) provides an exception from recognition of recapture income when a contribution to the capital of a corporation or a partnership otherwise qualifies for nonrecognition.

■ A semantic point: It may be tempting to use "realize" and "receive" interchangeably, but the two terms have very different meanings in tax law; be sure to keep them distinct.

CONNECTIONS

Basis, Realization, and Gain or Loss

Section 1001 establishes this basic relationship between the property's basis, the realization of some or all of the property's value, and the measurement of gain or loss on realization. The tax consequences of property dealings, especially of property dispositions, turn on this relationship throughout the Code. See Chapter 6.A.

Recovery of Basis on Recognition of Gain or Loss

The owner of property gets the full benefit of his or her basis in the property only at disposition of the property. This is because gain or loss on the property is only realized and, usually, recognized then. The close relationship between realization, recognition, and basis thus determines when basis is recovered—that is, taken into account in a final manner—for tax purposes. Realization is a prerequisite for claiming the benefit of property's basis as shelter against the recognition of gain, although this is because it is also the prerequisite for gain and loss recognition.

Gifts and Realization

The making of a gift is not a realization event to the extent that it qualifies as nothing but a gift for purposes of section 102. When in the same transaction a donor gets back from the donee something of value less than the gift property, the transaction is partly a gift and partly not a gift. The non-gift aspect of the transaction can and normally does involve realization of gain or loss by the donor. See Chapter 5.F and G.

Cancellation of Debt

If the obligation to repay a loan or other payment obligation is extinguished by the creditor's voluntary cancellation of the debt or by operation of law, the borrower realizes the amount of the cancelled debt as ordinary income. But note that price reductions are not treated as realization events. On both points, see Chapter 8.C.

Disposition of Encumbered Property

When a taxpayer disposes of property subject to nonrecourse debt, the amount realized is deemed to include the unpaid portion of the nonrecourse debt in addition to any other consideration actually received. See Chapter 8.F and G.

Timing and Transactional Parity

10

The courts have devised several broad tax principles that override statutory rules of narrower application. Among these are rules concerning

OVERVIEW

claims of right, economic benefit, constructive receipt, and tax benefit. Each exists to solve problems of income classification or timing. Some appear to serve both purposes, and collectively they sometimes appear to yield conflicting answers to the same questions. Although the fog can be cleared away, uncertainty as to the scope and content of these rules remains, despite the best efforts of courts and commentators.

A. THE JUDICIAL DOCTRINES

1. Constructive Receipt
2. Economic Benefit
3. Claim of Right
4. Tax Benefit Rule

B. COMPARISON OF CLAIM OF RIGHT AND TAX BENEFIT ADJUSTMENTS

C. OVERLAPPING APPLICATION OF THE JUDICIAL DOCTRINES

A. The Judicial Doctrines

Transactions sometimes do not fall naturally into well-worn tax categories. The courts have responded by formulating special rules for these awkward cases. This chapter groups four such rules into pairs for ease of exposition. The rules of each pair occasionally seem to get in each other's way. On closer examination, the apparent rivalries fade away, but it must be admitted that there are fact patterns in which more than one rule may still seem relevant.

(1) Constructive Receipt

Constructive equivalents for legally significant acts are familiar features of other areas of the law. For example, everyone has constructive notice of recorded deeds, even though few have actual knowledge of their content. The owner of land may be said, for certain purposes, to have constructive possession of everything that is found on the land. A landlord constructively evicts a tenant if he has the right to control happenings that substantially disturb the tenant's enjoyment of the lease-hold but does not control them. The concept of **constructive receipt** is closely akin to these.

Items of potential income that are already at the disposal of the taxpayer but not actually received are deemed to have been received. In most cases, a taxpayer has constructive receipt of a payment owed or a benefit to be conferred by another person when the taxpayer is aware that she can, at her option, take possession of it. Your boss offers to pay your regular wages just before the end of a year, but you choose not to accept the offer in order to push the income into the following tax year and thereby (you hope) delay the tax liability. The scheme does not work. A taxpayer is in constructive receipt of the wages made available for receipt, and the income must be reported for the year in which it was made available.

F   A   Q

Q: When an employee picks up a paycheck but has not cashed it, is there constructive receipt?

A: Yes, if the check would not have bounced. Thus, even before the bank honors the check, the payee has constructive receipt of any income it represents. Not all checks represent possible income to the payee; some are loans, refunds, etc. But paychecks do represent income to the person being paid for services. A paycheck delivered to an employee on December 31 but not cashed until January 1 is income for the previous year.

When all that stands between a taxpayer and income realization is receipt, constructive receipt settles the income issue. Note that when receipt is *not* the only unresolved issue or when even actual receipt would not justify attributing income to the taxpayer in question, constructive receipt is not sufficient.

Example 10.1: A real estate broker is the agent for Jones, who owns land she would like to sell. By phone, a prospective buyer offers the broker a deposit for the purchase of the land. Although the broker could have taken the deposit, the deposit is not income to the broker because an agent who receives something of value for his or her principal does not have income.

The rule is sometimes inaccurately paraphrased as treating anyone in constructive receipt of an item of economic value as having income in that amount. This leaves out the important qualification that receipt must be the deciding factor.

Receipt is the deciding factor when the taxpayer has a right to the item of value *and* the taxpayer's accounting method makes receipt necessary for inclusion of an item in income. To grasp this more fully, we must briefly explore tax accounting methods. An **accounting method** is a set of rules mainly used to determine to which tax year an item of income and deduction belongs. It is beyond doubt that the rent paid to lease business premises is deductible, but some businesses properly deduct rent when it is paid and others when it is accrued, whether paid or not. Their tax accounting methods differ. The underlying goal of tax accounting is that the income, deductions, and losses of a taxpayer should be assigned to the period to which they relate most closely in the income-earning process. This goal is expressed in Code section 446(b) and the regulations as clear reflection of income.

The two most important accounting methods assure the clear reflection of income differently. Some businesses collect payments from clients or customers in a flexible manner or allow returns of merchandise of a generous return period; for them it is best to consider the income from a particular transaction as earned "when all the events have occurred that fix the right to receive the income and the amount of the income can be determined with reasonable accuracy,"[1] whether actual payment has been received or not. For smaller sellers of inventory and service providers, the lapse of time before bills to clients or customers are collected may vary widely and may have serious economic significance because of the small volume and greater fluctuation of the key items of revenue and outlay. Their standard accounting method is the cash receipts and disbursements method, a more skeptical approach toward expenses that also gives the proprietor the benefit of the doubt and delays the recognition of revenue when payment due does not arrive on time. On the cash method, a taxpayer has income when she receives something of value to which she is entitled.[2] Constructive receipt clinches a cash-method taxpayer's having income if the constructively received item also belongs to her.

As this brief look at accounting methods indicates, constructive receipt is not sufficient to make an item income. It is only a twist on an accounting rule that attaches basic, if not exclusive, significance to receipt. We will soon discuss how it could be relevant to accounting methods other than the cash method, but it is primarily a refinement of the cash method.

> **Sidebar**
>
> **TAX ACCOUNTING METHODS**
>
> Any workable income tax system must measure income and impose tax liability at frequent intervals. The division of a taxpayer's economic life into separate taxable years is the first step in the process. Not all economic events, however, have unambiguous or natural connections with a particular year. "Accounting methods" are rules that arbitrarily but consistently assign economic events among the years of a taxpayer's life. The cash receipts and disbursements method and the accrual method are the most commonly used, but the IRS is willing to consider alternatives proposed by taxpayers. The burden of proving an alternative method to be reasonable is substantial.

---

[1]Treas. Reg. §1.446-1(c)(ii).
[2]*Id.* §1.446-1(c)(i).

(2) Economic Benefit

By contrast, the **economic benefit** doctrine is a fundamental litmus test for income. If action of a third party makes a taxpayer *better off economically* without granting the taxpayer access to the funds or property (such as an entry made by a bank in the taxpayer's favor, subject to some temporary withdrawal restriction) and *no one else can lay claim to the funds or property*, the taxpayer has gross income.

An employer's contribution of money to a retirement arrangement for an employee, beyond the employer's or its creditors' reach, is the paradigm. In *United States v. Drescher*,[3] a corporation purchased two annuities for an officer and director of the corporation. The contracts obligated the annuity company to begin to make installment payments to this taxpayer when he reached the age of 65, and until that time the corporation kept possession of the originals of the contracts, effectively preventing the taxpayer from assigning them to a third party. This was obviously a scheme of deferred compensation. The annuity contracts, which declared that all annuity payments "shall be free from the claims of all creditors to the fullest extent permitted by law," underscored the separateness of the annuity rights from other interests of the corporation. The court held that the taxpayer had income as soon as his employer purchased the annuity contracts for him, reasoning that the ownership of the annuities was a "present economic benefit" to him.[4] Whether the taxpayer would live long enough for the annuity benefits to be paid did not figure in the court's reasoning. Once the taxpayer had the economic benefit, constructive or actual receipt of the money was irrelevant.

The Second Circuit in *Drescher* did not spell out how economic benefit is to be determined. Meals and lodging provided to an employee for the convenience of the employer are an economic benefit, as we ordinarily speak of such things, yet both the courts and the IRS considered them not to be income long before section 119 was added to the Code.[5] Events beyond a taxpayer's control may also confer an economic benefit that no one would consider to be income. The development of neighboring land can greatly increase the value of a taxpayer's land. A celebrity's favorable comment on a restaurant can enrich the owner. In these cases the economic benefit is even at the immediate disposal of the taxpayer, unlike retirement fund contributions, yet they are not considered income.

F   A   Q

Q: When money is placed in trust for an employee, but other employees and the employer's creditors have rights against the entire trust corpus, does the employee have income under economic benefit analysis?

A: No. As *Minor v. United States*[6] illustrates, if the employer can benefit from the satisfaction of others' claims out of the trust corpus, the economic benefit of the trust has does not yet belong to the employee. Apparently, that others are not likely to assert

---

[3]179 F.2d 863 (2d Cir.), *cert. denied*, 340 U.S. 821 (1950).
[4]*Id.* at 865. The court refused to say the value of that benefit was the purchase price of the annuities because it quibbled over whether to subtract some value for the right to assign, which the company retained. *Id.*
[5]Judge Arnold, who dissented in *Benaglia*, specifically made the point that the taxpayer's meal and lodging in that case were an economic benefit to him. *Benaglia v. Comm'r*, 36 B.T.A. 838, 841 (1937).
[6]772 F.2d 1472 (9th Cir. 1985).

any claim against the trust corpus does not reverse the answer. Thus, some employers deliberately create trusts for key employees that are vulnerable to others' claims in order to delay the attribution of income to the intended beneficiary.

Other cases on economic benefit do little to sharpen the doctrine's boundaries. *Pulsifer v. Commissioner* relied on a finding of economic benefit in deciding that children who had won a prize in the government-run Irish Sweepstakes had income right away, even though the money had not been released to their legal representative. The children were minors and so could only have claimed the money for themselves when they came of age. The Tax Court held that, because their right to the winnings was absolute and nonforfeitable, it constituted income without regard to their access, control, or receipt. Although *Pulsifer* applies the economic benefit doctrine outside the deferred compensation context, the opinion does not explain why receipt of the income in dispute was optional.

Agency principles suggest a common element in *Drescher* and *Pulsifer*. The *Pulsifer* prize money *was* in the hands of an agent of sorts, the Irish court acting on the taxpayers' behalf. Ordinarily, an agent's receipt of potential income on a taxpayer's behalf is classified as actual receipt. If that were so here, this would explain why the court did not consider constructive receipt. Yet the court also did not find actual receipt, which would have triggered income inclusion for the minor cash-method taxpayers. Moreover, the taxpayers in *Pulsifer* and *Drescher* had no legal right to immediate release of what they "owned" from the party holding it for them, whereas an agent's principal can always dissolve the agency relationship and demand that the agent turn over the property.

> ### Sidebar
>
> **BENEFIT AND INCOME**
>
> It may seem that whenever a taxpayer enjoys a new economic benefit, she has income. But as Chapter 3 illustrates, employees enjoy a variety of job-related benefits that both the IRS and the courts agreed should not be counted as income. In the case of pensions, however, well-grounded expectation alone seems again to persuade the courts to attribute income to the beneficiaries. Commentators have not yet bridged the theoretical chasm between these two areas.

In *United States v. Basye*,[7] the Supreme Court decided an issue like that in *Drescher* without mentioning economic benefit. A large limited partnership of physicians benefited from contributions made by a health maintenance organization to a retirement trust for the partnership's members. The Court found that neither the HMO nor its creditors could reach the contributions under any circumstances. Instead of relying on economic benefit, the Court held that the taxpayers had assigned part of their salaries prospectively to the trust, but that such anticipatory assignment of income is ineffective for tax purposes. (We examine this *assignment of income* doctrine in Chapter 16.) The Court did not explain how the holding relates to constructive receipt or economic benefit.

Economic benefit is an exception to the receipt requirement of the cash method and to the requirement of the accrual method that income accrues when all events have occurred to fix the right to receive it. The courts, however, have not characterized the doctrine as an accounting rule.

---

[7] 410 U.S. 441 (1973).

(3) Claim of Right

Claim of right, the next judicial doctrine we consider, classifies as income the value of property or cash that a taxpayer controls and claims as of right even if the law may later require the taxpayer to surrender it. The doctrine resembles constructive receipt and economic benefit because all three are about timing, at least in part. Like economic benefit, claim of right is an exception to the cash and accrual methods of accounting. Like constructive receipt, it creates an exception to the cash method. But claim of right is fundamentally an accounting rule, and in this respect belongs to the same sphere as constructive receipt, whereas economic benefit governs both whether and when an item is income.

"If a taxpayer receives earnings under a claim of right and without restriction as to its disposition, he has received income which he is required to return, even though it may still be claimed that he is not entitled to retain the money, and even though he may still be adjudged liable to restore its equivalent." So the Supreme Court held in *North American Oil Consolidated v. Barnet*,[8] emphasizing that this rule applies to both cash and accrual method taxpayers. Thus, actual receipt becomes relevant for accrual method taxpayers, to which it is otherwise irrelevant, and something less than receipt with an absolute right to retain becomes relevant to cash method taxpayers. But the origins and purpose of claim of right are narrow, and we will see that this may guide us in applying it. An oil company extracted oil from public land under a contract with the United States. When the government sued the company for the profits, these were turned over to a receiver for a number of years. The company prevailed at trial, and the court ordered the receiver to pay over the profits to it with interest. The government appealed. Three years later the appeals court recognized the company's right to the money, removing any further legal uncertainty. The company asserted that the income arose either in an earlier or later year than its trial court victory, either of which results would have lowered its tax liability. The Supreme Court found that the company's claim of right and dominion over the funds after their disbursement by the trial court resolved the timing issue against the company.

F   A   Q

Q: Why does claim of right apply to accrual taxpayers?

A: The obvious justification for this deviation from the accrual method is that appealable judicial and administrative judgments *become* final retroactively, when appeal rights expire or if the appellant does not vigorously pursue them. To give them immediate effect for accounting purposes avoids a waste of administrative effort. Normally, the accrual taxpayer's definite legal right to payment from a debtor or definite legal obligation to pay a creditor are the thresholds for assigning economic events to a particular taxable year. Claim of right weakens that requirement but only does so when the taxpayer's dominion over funds or property provides an objective touchstone for early income attribution.

---

[8]286 U.S. 417 (1932).

The timing problem the doctrine addresses can still arise in litigation, although today a court is less likely to release disputed funds before an appeal is resolved. Nevertheless, the claim of right doctrine has its clearest and most helpful application in resolving the status of appealable money judgments. When a court awards a money judgment, the plaintiff's right to any disputed funds already under the plaintiff's control is no longer contingent in the ordinary sense. If the defendant does not appeal, the plaintiff's right will become absolute without more. The courts' standard statement on claims of right, however, could apply to other cases of disputed possession.

Example 10.2: James received a deposit of $5,000 from a client for services to be provided. Smith thought he deserved full payment of that amount after doing some work, but he chose not to send the client a bill right away. He holds the money under a claim of right, even though the client may dispute his claim upon receiving a bill. Smith should report the income for the year in which he completed the legal work. True, the government is not likely to discover the facts on which this application of the doctrine rest.

Example 10.3: Frank borrows $500,000 from a bank. Frank has a legal right to the loan proceeds from the outset because the loan agreement is valid and he received the money under that agreement. His use of the loan proceeds is "unrestricted" in a certain sense, because he can use the money however he likes. He does not have to include the loan proceeds in his income for the year in which he received them, because loans are not income unless the obligation to repay them is released, but we only know that the claim of right doctrine does not apply because we know this is not the kind of situation the doctrine should cover. (What we know about the income tax treatment of loans trumps the potential application of claim of right.)

The Supreme Court found yet another fact situation, having nothing to do with court cash awards, sufficiently like them to justify a modification of the doctrine. In *James v. United States*,[9] it overruled its own earlier holding in *Commissioner v. Wilcox*,[10] now deciding that an embezzler had sufficient dominion over wrongfully taken money to be required to include the embezzled funds in his income. Citing *North American Oil Consolidated*, the Court altered its formulation of the claim of right doctrine to say: "When a taxpayer acquires earnings, lawfully or unlawfully, without the consensual recognition, express or implied, of an obligation to repay and without restriction as to their disposition," the taxpayer must report the money as income for that year.[11] It is now assumed that this extension of the claim of right doctrine applies to all final illegal acts of property misappropriation.[12]

Extension of the doctrine to wrongful acts seems inconsistent with the requirement that the taxpayer have a claim of right. The essence of the doctrine, however, is that the claim, even if specious, must be "of right" in that it contradicts all other claims to the same property, just as an adverse possessor must claim the disputed property against all other claimants. In neither case need the right be well grounded.

---

[9]366 U.S. 213 (1961).
[10]327 U.S. 404 (1946).
[11]*Id.* at 219.
[12]*See, e.g., Wood v. U.S.*, 863 F.2d 417 (5th Cir. 1989) (drug-smuggling proceeds were subject to claim of right doctrine). The possibility that claim of right might be used to pile further criminal sanctions on primary sanctions already imposed persuaded the Court to limit Montana's application of claim of right. *Dep't of Rev. v. Kurth Ranch*, 511 U.S. 767 (1994).

The extension of claim of right to the proceeds of wrongful acts is not extravagant. It is merely the recognition that a taxpayer should not be allowed to act as if something were income without facing tax consequences.

There is one important statutory difference between lawful and unlawful claims of right. For the former, the Code provides relief if the putative income must later be "restored" to another. The term "restore" is used as a term of art in this context to avoid making it a requirement that the restoration be ordered by a court or otherwise legally compelled. The restoration can be voluntary, as when the taxpayer simply acknowledges that he or she is under a legal or moral obligation to disgorge the previously claimed income. Section 165 allows the lawful claimant of right to deduct the value of what is restored as a loss. Section 1341 ensures that in these cases the taxpayer will not suffer a net tax detriment if his or her marginal rate is lower in the year of restoration than it was in the year for which the income was reported.

Example 10.4: Walter's pension administrator miscalculated his benefits, overpaying him for the first year of his retirement by $100,000. He, of course, included the amount received, believing them to be properly paid. Technically, he complied with the claim of right doctrine, though he was unaware of doing so. In the fourth year, the pension administrator demanded the money back, and Walter agreed to repay it. His marginal tax rate has declined by then because he made less in retirement than he did while employed. In the year of payment, his marginal tax rate was 28 percent, and the additional tax he paid was $28,000. A deduction of $100,000 for year four, however, saves him only $15,000 in taxes, because his marginal rate was then 15 percent. To alleviate this serendipitous burden, Code section 1341 provides that the tax benefit for the year the loss is claimed shall not be less than the additional tax paid for the year of inclusion if the amount to be deducted is more than $3,000. As the cereal boxes say, some restrictions apply, but these are beyond the scope of this book.[13]

Recall that the cancellation of debt is generally income to the debtor.[14] This originally judge-made rule is now codified in sections 61(a)(12) and 108. The reason for recalling it at this point is that, like the other doctrines studied in this chapter, it is also partly about timing. Whereas claim of right assigns an early year for reporting an item of potential income, the standard income tax treatment of debt waits patiently to see whether the debt will become income by cancellation. A taxpayer does not have any claim of right to borrowed funds as such, but inevitably some debts go unpaid and lenders write some off. All in all, the ownership of borrowed funds is not uncertain enough to be covered by the claim of right doctrine. A borrower does not have or assert a claim of right to the borrowed funds. Embezzlers have no cognizable right to the money they steal, but they behave as if it were theirs, and the courts have decided to treat this as close enough for claim of right to be controlling in criminal contexts.

(4) Tax Benefit Rule

Another type of uncertainty plagues the division of the taxpayer's life into annual accounting periods. On recovering an item properly deducted in an earlier year, a taxpayer is normally taxed on the item unless the prior deduction did not reduce his

---

[13]Code §1341(b) provides special rules and limitations.
[14]See Chapter 8.D.

or her tax liability. This "tax benefit rule" (TBR) also applies to credits: To the extent that an item for which a credit was claimed in an earlier year is recovered, the taxpayer must normally pay additional tax for the current year, unless that part of the credit gave the taxpayer no tax benefit. (A credit simply comes off your tax bill as a dollar-for-dollar reduction, so that to undo the effect of a credit that is no longer deserved, we add the amount of the credit to the current tax liability.) Below we will consider a broader formulation of the rule, but this will do for now.

The rule is both inclusionary and exclusionary. Previously deducted or credited items must be reported as income when they are recovered (inclusionary), but only to the extent that the deduction or credit yielded a tax benefit (exclusionary). The tax benefit of a deduction is usually equal to the amount of the deduction multiplied by the taxpayer's marginal tax rate. Hence, a deduction of $100 for a taxpayer in the 31 percent marginal tax bracket produces a tax saving of $31. When a taxpayer's taxable income is zero, however, a deduction offers no benefit, because taxable income cannot go below zero. Similarly, if a taxpayer's income is low but above zero, a deduction may serve only to "zero out" his or her taxable income, thereby producing a tax benefit equal to the tax rate applicable multiplied by the taxpayer's taxable income, computed without the deduction. If before taking a deduction of $100, the taxpayer would only have had taxable income of $50, and only $50 of the deduction can result in a tax saving — that is, the tax due on an income of $50. For credits, the rule is similar. If an outlay by the taxpayer resulted in a credit for a given year, and there is a "price adjustment" in a subsequent year, reducing the net amount of that earlier outlay, the taxpayer's total income tax for the year of the adjustment increases by whatever part of the credit could not have been taken for the adjusted price in the earlier year. (The foreign tax credit and certain environmental credits are not subject to the TBR at all.[15])

F   A   Q

Q: Given that a taxpayer can amend an earlier year's tax return, is the TBR necessary?

A: There is no official policy statement from the courts or the IRS. The following explanation, however, makes sense. Mere passage of time does not affect the application of the TBR. Deductions and credits that prove to have been inappropriate are corrected in the year when the fundamental inconsistency is discovered, no matter how many years have passed since these deductions and credits were claimed. By contrast, taxpayers can only amend earlier years' returns until the statute of limitations on amending a return and on the government's assertion of a deficiency for the return year has run. Under section 6501(a), the limitations period for most returns begins on the date the return is filed and runs for three years from that date. Decoupling the TBR from the statute of limitations is an evenhanded approach. It does not penalize justified reporting, for which the justification is later undermined, and it does not reward those for whom time bars the amendment of an earlier year's return.

---

[15]I.R.C. §111(b)(3).

The reduced benefit of deductions for taxpayers with low taxable income is balanced by a lighter burden in the event that the item deducted is recovered. Code section 111(a) succinctly states this exclusionary aspect of the rule: "Gross income does not include income attributable to the recovery during the taxable year of any amount deducted in any prior taxable year to the extent such amount did not reduce the amount of tax imposed. . . ." Section 111(b)(2) relieves the taxpayer from including income in the later year to the extent that a credit taken in an earlier year did not lower the taxpayer's tax liability in that year. Note that section 111 does not codify the *inclusionary* aspect of the TBR but takes it for granted. Congress thus left it to the courts, in dialogue with the IRS, to develop this aspect of the rule. The judicial version of the TBR, left standing by section 111, ignores the time value of money and fluctuations in applicable tax rates, neither requiring nor allowing any later adjustment of the taxpayer's income to compensate for them. If events that trigger the TBR are genuinely unpredictable, as they should be, neither taxpayers nor the government stands to gain or lose by them on average. The legislative response to the TBR contrasts with the legislative response to the claim of right doctrine. When later events justify the deduction of $3,000 or more with respect to income included under claim of right in an earlier year, section 1341 corrects for any change in the tax rate (but not the time value of money) that would be to the taxpayer's disadvantage.

To continue the comparison with claim of right, it is useful to delve further into the rationale of the TBR. One early court explained the TBR by postulating a rather abstract conversion of deductions into capital assets that are reconverted into income if contradictory events later occurred.[16] A less strained explanation merely supposes that the Great Bookkeeper in the Sky would want to balance the entry of a deduction in one year with an entry of income in another so that the taxpayer's actual amount of income over the period that includes both years will be accurately measured.[17] Both views contain the same thought in kernel — that the TBR is a corrective measure intended to protect the integrity of income measurement against a shortcoming of the annual accounting convention. What neither fully specifies is the kind or kinds of new information that should justify such a correction. In this connection, a brief comparison of the TBR with the claim of right doctrine will shed light on both.

The TBR is akin to the claim of right doctrine in its concern for getting income measurement right over multiple accounting periods. Claim of right responds to the danger that temporally ambiguous items of income will be taxed too late or not at all if we wait for the ambiguity to be resolved. The TBR is not concerned with the risk of the underreporting because it is about taxpayers' deductions and credits, not income, and there is an obvious incentive to claim *them* when one can. Instead, the TBR deals with uncertainty that may exist when all knowable facts support the claim of a deduction or credit, and only new information or changed circumstances in a later year undermine the previously justified reporting position. Unlike the claim of right doctrine, the TBR leaves much to the ingenuity of the courts and the IRS, because the type of uncertainty it addresses is less well circumscribed.

Before we come to that, it is important to note that the TBR is not intended to cover the mere correction of mistakes of fact or arithmetic. Sometimes a taxpayer has a good but mistaken reason for claiming a deduction or credit when filing an annual return, but later events reveal that mistake. We must be careful here. There is

---

[16]*Nat'l Bank of Comm. v. Comm'r,* 115 F.2d 875 (9th Cir. 1940).
[17]*S. Dakota Concrete Prods. Co. v. Comm'r,* 26 B.T.A. 1429, 1431 (1932).

a crucial difference between (1) later discovery that the factual assumptions for the filing position were already mistaken at the time of the return and (2) later discovery of facts that are inconsistent with a reasonable view of the facts known at the time. A few illustrations will quickly make this clear.

Example 10.5: Janet correctly enters all the relevant information on her Form 1040, but makes an arithmetic error in subtracting her allowable deductions from her adjusted gross income, resulting in an understatement of her taxable income. If she or the IRS finds the error, inevitably in a year later than that to which the error pertains, the proper correction is for her to file an amended return to replace the erroneous one, and not for her to include the untaxed income on her return for the year in which the error is discovered. If the error is discovered after the statute of limitations for filing an amended return has run, Janet need not report or pay tax on the untaxed income at all.

Example 10.6: Jacob reports a loss of $1,500 on the sale of a share of stock when he should have reported a gain. It was an innocent but tax-saving mistake. If Jacob or the IRS finds the error before the statute of limitations for filing an amended return has run, the correct procedure is again for Jacob to file an amended return showing the loss as a gain, and of course paying the additional tax due.

Both factual and arithmetic mistakes are properly dealt with, not by application of the TBR, by reporting income in a later year to balance an unwarranted deduction or credit, but by amending the mistaken return.

Errors by their nature need no justification. If the TBR applied to mere mistakes as well as to justified incorrect reporting positions, anyone could claim a deduction without justification and then own up to the "mistake" later, thereby postponing the need to pay tax on the corresponding amount of income — an easy way to make money at the government's expense, at least if the same tax rate applies to the taxpayer in both years.

Example 10.7: In year one, Mary falsely claims a deduction for business expenses of $100,000 that she has not actually incurred or paid. This saves her $36,000 in taxes for year one, because her marginal tax rate is 36 percent. If the TBR applied, she could later report $100,000 in income to offset the earlier "mistake" and pay $36,000 in additional tax if her rate is the same for the later year. If ten years have passed, and the inflation rate has been 3 percent per annum, she has made (at least) $9,213, because the present value of a payment of $36,000 after ten years, discounted at 3 percent, is $26,787.

Mistakes as such should not qualify for an approach like that of the TBR that does not adjust a taxpayer's liability for the time value of money or for fluctuations in tax rates.[18]

The distinction between errors and justified reporting positions that deteriorate in the light of later information or events is not always easy to apply in practice, but

---

[18]There was once a parallel problem for conscious overpayments of tax by corporations with the purpose of earning the handsome interest rate the government was once obliged to pay on such overpayments. The law now sets the overpayment interest rate lower for all corporations, and lower still if the overpayment exceeds $10,000. I.R.C. §6621(a)(1)(B).

the idea is straightforward. We must now come to grips with how that can happen. The Supreme Court addressed this puzzle most exhaustively in *Hillsboro National Bank v. Commissioner*,[19] dealing with two consolidated cases in which the government argued that the TBR should apply despite the absence of a recovery by the taxpayer of a previously deducted amount.

In the first of the consolidated cases, a bank paid and deducted from its income a state property tax on behalf of its shareholders. The state's highest court later held that tax to have been unconstitutional, and the state refunded the tax to the shareholders rather than to the bank. The government thought the refund of the deducted amount to parties related to the taxpayer triggered the TBR. In the second, an incorporated dairy deducted the cost of cattle feed for a taxable year, but liquidated two days after that year ended and distributed the feed to the shareholders without recognizing gain; the shareholders continued to run the dairy and, under then-current liquidation rules, took the feed with a basis equal to that of their stock and deducted this basis on giving the feed to the dairy cattle. Note that in both cases shareholders of the taxpayers *obtained the economic benefit* of the taxpayers' deducted outlays. Neither situation involved a *recovery* of a deducted item by the taxpayer that took the deduction. The traditional formulation of the TBR in terms of recovery did not literally, or even metaphorically, apply to either case.

The Court held that the TBR (1) did not require the bank to include the refunded state taxes in its income, but (2) did require the dairy to include the value of the feed in its income for the year of liquidation. Most important, however, the Court announced a new, broader standard for events that trigger application of the TBR's inclusionary side: Rejecting the idea that only recoveries call for inclusion, the Court said that any event that is "fundamentally inconsistent" with a previously claimed deduction does so. "The basic purpose of the tax benefit rule is to achieve rough transactional parity in tax . . . and to protect the Government and the taxpayer from the adverse effects of reporting a transaction on the basis of assumptions that an event in a subsequent year proves to have been erroneous." Transactional parity may be in the eye of the beholder. "Not every unforeseen event will require the taxpayer to report income in the amount of his earlier deduction. On the contrary, the tax benefit rule will 'cancel out' an earlier deduction only when a careful examination shows that the later event is indeed fundamentally inconsistent with the premise on which the deduction was initially based."[20] Justices Stevens and Marshall thought the TBR should not apply in either case. Justices Blackmun and Brennan agreed that it should be applied in both cases. Thus, only five justices formed the majority.

Note the following peculiarities of the *Hillsboro* and *Bliss* fact patterns. In *Hillsboro*, the "recovery" of tax by the bank's shareholders did not cause any change in the combined income of the bank and its shareholders. The "recovery" in *Hillsboro* turned out to be harmless because Code section 164(e) allows a corporation to deduct a tax

---

[19]*Hillsboro Nat'l Bank v. Comm'r*, 460 U.S. 370 (1983).
[20]*Id.* at 383.

it pays on behalf of shareholders.[21] It also denies the shareholders any deduction for payment of the tax, which of course they do not themselves pay. There is a further twist: Treas. Reg. §1.164-7 says the shareholders need *not* include the amount of a tax paid on their behalf by the corporation as a constructive dividend. (*Old Colony Trust*, lest we forget, stands for treating such tax payments as income to the beneficiaries.) Thus, it was not necessary to include the refunded amount in the bank's income in order to achieve transactional parity. In *Bliss*, by contrast, a rule for corporate liquidations, since repealed, allowed the same business expense—the cost of cattle feed—to be deducted by closely related taxpayers, first by the incorporated dairy and then by its shareholders. The Court evidently thought that the liquidation rules haphazardly allowed the dairy operation functionally to deduct the same business expense twice, and so the Court concluded that the TBR must apply.

F   A   Q

Q: How would the "fundamental inconsistency" test apply to the refund *to the corporation* of a non-tax payment obligation on behalf of shareholders?

A: The corporation that pays a debt for its shareholder, unlike the employer that pays a work-related obligation for its employee, is not entitled to a deduction, and so on the refund of the payment to the corporation there is no problem of transactional parity—the payment was a nonevent in the corporation's tax history, and the refund is another such nonevent. When an employer pays an obligation of an employee, however, the employer will almost certainly claim a business expense deduction for the outlay, just as it does for the payment of wages; indeed, the employer usually intends such payments as additional compensation. The refund of the payment to the employer would therefore be inconsistent with the earlier deduction, and the TBR requires that the refund be included in the employer's gross income.

A final word: As the *Hillsboro* majority noted, the TBR takes a "transactional" approach to income measurement to reach different conclusions in some instances than would follow if annual accounting periods were respected. This makes the TBR akin to the preservation of net operating losses (NOLs) under section 172 and to various judicial and statutory exceptions to piecemeal basis recovery. The "closed transaction" approach we trace to *Burnet v. Logan*,[22] which permitted a taxpayer to recover her basis before recognizing any gain from the sale of a working mineral interest for a contingent price. Regulations permit partners whose partnership interests are liquidated to elect to use a similar method of basis recovery.[23] The difference between the TBR and these kindred transactional approaches is that the TBR is about clawing back the benefit of tax deductions and credits, and the latter extend benefits to taxpayers by deferring recognition of gain.

---

[21]This generous provision dates back to 1921, when Congress adopted it on the recommendation of the government's own expert T.S. Adams, without expressing a rationale beyond sympathy for corporations that felt it their duty to pay shareholders' taxes. *Id*. at 393-394.
[22]283 U.S. 404 (1931).
[23]Treas. Reg. §1.736-1(b)(5)(ii) & (iii).

B. Comparison of Claim of Right and Tax Benefit Adjustments

Although it is possible to confuse claim of right and the TBR, they are opposites in one important respect. Claim of right requires early inclusion of putative income, with possible later deduction as a correction if the included amount must be restored to a third party. Tax benefit requires a later adjustment if an earlier deduction or credit, fully justified when taken, is fundamentally inconsistent with facts that occur or become known in a later year. In brief, the first of the two rules is about early inclusion and later "backing out" (claim of right), while the second is about early deduction or crediting of an item and later "backing out" when fundamentally inconsistent events come to light. Both rules serve the goal of assuring the accurate measurement of transactions that cross boundaries separating tax years. This relationship to annual accounting is important, because it reminds us that neither doctrine has anything new to say about what constitutes income or about when a deduction or credit is justified in the first place.

C. Overlapping Application of the Judicial Doctrines

The types of inclusion or adjustment discussed in this chapter all concern how a taxpayer's income should be reflected over several years. We will now consider cases and examples that force us to choose, sometimes with difficulty, among the rules we have been studying. Recall that constructive receipt is only relevant where actual receipt would be relevant. That is primarily for cash method taxpayers, because receipt is the critical event in fixing the taxable year to which an item of income belongs, but no more than that—not everything of value that a person receives is income to him or her.

Example 10.8: Soda Co. bottles and distributes a certain brand of soft drink. It forms an alliance with other distributors of the same beverage to mount an advertising campaign. Soda Co. is chosen to represent the others in hiring an advertising firm and paying for media services. It takes in a substantial sum from each of the others to fund this project. Soda Co. is not entitled to receive any compensation for its efforts and returns a proportionate share to each of the other distributors of the funds not spent on the project. Because Soda Co. is an agent for the others, its receipt of the project funds does support a determination that the funds were income to it.[24]

Example 10.9: Same facts, except that the other distributors allow Soda Co. to make no contribution in exchange for its efforts in heading up the project. Soda Co.'s receipt of the funds is still not what will decide whether it has income from the arrangement, but receipt may be a crucial event if it is determined that the firm is otherwise entitled from that moment to share in the benefits of the advertising campaign without

---

[24]*Seven-Up Co. v. Comm'r*, 14 T.C. 965 (1950). The Tax Court did not discuss constructive receipt, but expressly refused to apply claim of right to the bottling company's receipt of the funds for the project on the grounds that the company was only a conduit for relaying money contributed by others to the advertising campaign.

paying for them. In any case, this is not a situation in which receipt plays its usual role in determining the timing of income under the cash method of accounting.

Example 10.10: Same facts, except that the other distributors send Soda Co. separate payment for its services, pursuant to a contract among them for Soda Co.'s conduct of the advertising campaign. If Soda Co. is a cash-method taxpayer, then its receipt of the payment is the last straw in determining that it has income in the amount of the payment for the taxable year when it receives the payment.

Example 10.11: Same facts, except that the other distributors do not send Soda Co. the payment it is due for its services in running the advertising campaign, pursuant to the contract. Instead, they let Soda Co. know that they are prepared to pay for its services whenever its CEO informs them payment is to be made. Although the CEO may refrain for a year or more from claiming the payment, it has been constructively received as soon as receipt was practically possible. Here constructive receipt determines the timing of the income to be that taxable year in which Soda Co. could have received payment if the CEO had immediately given notice.

Notice how the question of receipt is front and center in the last two examples, but marginal in the first two. The shifting focus is due to the importance in the first two examples of whether there is a *right* to income and when that right existed. Cases and commentators rarely stress the distinction between the right-to-income issue and the accounting issue of receipt. Moreover, receipt is normally important only for cash-method taxpayers. As the last four examples illustrate, there are issues in the first two, whether the taxpayer is on the cash method or not.

Now let's turn to a more specific version of the rivalry between pure income determination and accounting convention.

Example 10.12: Dr. McGee is the employee of a health network, which pays him a regular salary. After being employed for some time, McGee has an implied contract under state law to be paid at his normal salary for his services. At this point, he asks the payroll officer of the network to deposit 10 percent of each of his paychecks into a retirement account for his benefit. The account is not a qualified plan within the meaning of Code §401 et seq., and it is subject to the claims of the employer's creditors. Does this arrangement reduce McGee's income? Because he would have received immediate payment of the 10 percent of his salary that was withheld, were it not for this arrangement over which he had complete control, McGee *constructively received* this portion of his salary and actually received the rest. It is all income to him as soon as the employer would normally have paid it to him, absent the special arrangement. If this were not so, however, the withheld portion of his salary would not be of *economic benefit* to him and would not be included in his income under the doctrine of that name.

This example is on all fours with *Minor v. United States*,[25] in which the Ninth Circuit held that the withheld salary was not income to the doctor. In *Minor*, however, the government conceded that the taxpayer was *not* in constructive receipt of the money withheld, and so the court did not consider the issue. In the example, given that the

---

[25]772 F.2d 1472 (9th Cir. 1985).

doctor was entitled to his full salary under an existing employment contract, there would be constructive receipt.

The government in *Minor* may have declined to press this issue because it feared that the court might find the employment contract to be essentially a new contract for each year or each time the employee requested and was granted a change in the terms of the contract. Such a holding was possible but unlikely. In *Amend v. Commissioner*,[26] the Tax Court decided that a wheat farmer who sold wheat to a grain operator under a contract that delayed his right to receive payment to another calendar year had not constructively received payment when the contract was formed (that is, in an earlier taxable year). But the court in that case noted conspicuously that the farmer regularly asked those who bought his wheat to agree to pay him later, even when there was no tax advantage for him in doing so; he simply preferred to receive payment around the same time that he had to pay for ground rent and farming supplies.

Another variation on the theme of receipt and right to income: Here claim of right is also relevant. Recall that a claim of right can exist even when the taxpayer's right is not fully and finally established.

Example 10.13: Barbara was a plaintiff in a class action against a credit card issuer. When the court resolved the liability issue in favor of the plaintiffs, it set up a procedure for parceling out the cash damages award among them. Each plaintiff must submit proof of his or her identity and of having had one of the issuer's credit cards during the time with which the action was concerned. Barbara received the notice in year one, but managed to provide the proof of her identity and issuer account only in year two, when she could have received $300 in damages, but did not go to the office of the lawyer for the class to pick up her check. The issuer prevailed in appealing the judgment in year three, and Barbara never got her share of the damages. She had constructive receipt of the money in year two once she completed the procedure for making the claim and had been notified of the check's availability. Her failure to pick up the check does not matter. She still might not have had to report the $300 on her year two return, unless the claim of right doctrine applies. She had constructive receipt, which counts as receipt, and she had a claim of right to the money, so the combination of constructive receipt and claim of right apparently makes the money reportable as income for year two. If this is correct, she can deduct a loss of $300 for year three.

Constructive receipt is a surrogate for receipt and probably triggers all the same tax consequences as receipt, but no case or ruling confirms this for the fact pattern in the example. For claim of right, it should make no difference whether receipt is actual or constructive, because this would permit collusive deferral of the obligation to report and pay the tax due. Another reason for applying claim of right here is that the lawyer who holds the check for the client is also the client's agent, and what an agent receives on behalf of the principal is received by the principal.

---

[26]13 T.C. 178 (1949), *acq.*, 1950-1 C.B. 1.

SUMMARY

■ Courts have formulated rules of uncertain scope that override the Code on some income and timing issues. (1) Constructive receipt, (2) economic benefit, (3) claim of right, and (4) tax benefit rules sometimes seem to apply to the same tax determinations.

■ Courts have recognized *constructive receipt* as dispositive when receipt will settle whether a taxpayer has gross income with respect to a potential income item. Money or property placed at the taxpayer's disposal, though not actually received, is constructively received.

■ Under the *economic benefit* doctrine, if another person's action (such as an entry made by a bank in the taxpayer's favor, subject to some temporary withdrawal restriction) makes a taxpayer economically better off and *no one else has any claim to the wealth in question*, the taxpayer has gross income, even if the taxpayer does not have immediate access to or control of the item of value.

■ When a taxpayer acquires unrestricted dominion over something of value under a *claim of right*, the taxpayer must report gross income in that amount; the taxpayer can deduct the amount previously included on being required to restore it in a later year, but cannot amend the earlier year's return to remove the item. An employee's deduction in the later year would be itemized and restricted.

■ When a taxpayer has deducted or claimed a tax credit for an item in an earlier year, and in a later year some fundamentally inconsistent event occurs or fundamentally inconsistent information comes to light, the taxpayer must report as income the amount deducted or restore the tax benefit of the credit, except to the extent that the deduction or credit did not reduce the taxpayer's tax liability for the earlier year.

■ If the taxpayer's marginal tax rate is lower for the year in which the claim of right doctrine allows the taxpayer to deduct an item previously included in income, section 1341 increases the taxpayer's tax reduction for the year of deduction to equal the increase in tax that resulted from inclusion in the earlier year if the deduction exceeds $3,000.

■ If the taxpayer's marginal tax rate is different for the year in which the tax benefit rule requires the taxpayer to include an item deducted in a previous year, section 111 reduces the additional income for the later year to the amount that produced a tax benefit but does not correct for the tax rate difference.

■ Constructive receipt is of narrower scope than economic benefit, because receipt is relevant only for cash method taxpayers. Economic benefit is relevant for all taxpayers, without regard to their method of accounting.

■ Claim of right can require an earlier reporting of income than either the cash method or the accrual method would require of taxpayers using those methods.

■ Both claim of right and tax benefit rules advance transactional parity—uniform taxation of transactions that spread over more than one taxable year—by requiring that taxpayers adjust their tax reporting for different years.

■ Neither constructive receipt nor economic benefit serves transactional parity, but claim of right resembles them both in one respect: All three can require an item to be reported in an earlier year than the basic rules of the cash and accrual methods of accounting would.

CONNECTIONS

Income — Whether and When?

Of the judicial doctrines surveyed in this chapter, only economic benefit can support a determination that a taxpayer has income without receipt or immediate control over that income. Although a taxpayer who thus acquires a remote economic benefit will in most cases gain access to that benefit at some time in the future, failure of that outcome does not entitle the taxpayer to a later adjustment of tax liability as it would under claim of right. Economic benefit answers a question akin to whether a given fringe benefit is income to an employee, but the other judicial doctrines covered in this chapter do not. See Chapter 3.J. On the other hand, economic benefit, like constructive receipt and claim of right, answers the question "when?" differently than ordinary accounting rules do, compelling a taxpayer to recognize income before the applicable accounting method ordinarily would.

Overlap of Constructive Receipt and Economic Benefit

An event signals income on grounds of economic benefit only when the event is *not* the receipt of a valuable thing by the taxpayer. In this respect, economic benefit appears to enlarge the range of income items without regard to receipt, making constructive receipt seem irrelevant. Economic benefit, however, deals with a narrower range of events than constructive receipt. Along similar lines, the Code deems some taxpayers to have income when interest accrues in the taxpayers' favor, even though not received. See Chapter 8.H (original issue discount and related rules).

Accounting Methods

Individual taxpayers, as the main users of the cash method of tax accounting, are those primarily affected by the constructive receipt doctrine. Compare Chapter 13.C (individuals' control over personal losses).

Net Operating Losses (NOLs)

An obvious parallel links the judicial doctrines that promote transactional parity — the claim of right and tax benefit rules — with section 172, which allows net operating losses to be carried to earlier and later taxable years of the taxpayer. The carryover of NOLs denies the usual separateness of taxable years by allowing losses from one year to offset income from another year. Unlike the two rules surveyed in this chapter, however, section 172 is mainly for the taxpayer's advantage. See Chapter 6.D.

Fitting Families In

11

OVERVIEW

The income tax is more at ease with individuals than with families. Members of households have both selfish and unselfish motives in dealing with each another, which blurs the contrast between investment and consumption. What can the income tax, which tries to make that contrast absolute, make of this? It deals piecemeal with basic family transfers related to divorce and child support. Other rules apply to ongoing family life. Taxpayers can deduct medical expenses as well as standard allowances for dependent relatives. Parents can deduct childcare or elder-care expenses, or pay them tax free through a complicated withholding and reimbursement mechanism. Parents and others can also save for their children's higher education in tax-preferred arrangements. We have already seen that the rules for gifts are especially relevant to families because gifts between related individuals are so common. Putting all of this together, the income tax still falls short of horizontal equity in dealing with households of different configurations and leaves some issues unresolved.

A. **KEY TAX ISSUES RAISED BY GROUPS OF RELATED INDIVIDUALS**

B. **TAXPAYERS' EXPENSES FOR CHILDREN AND ELDERLY DEPENDENTS**

    1. Medical Expenses
    2. Section 152

C. **THE JOINT RETURN AND THE MARRIAGE PENALTY**

D. SEPARATION AND DIVORCE

1. Property Settlements
2. Alimony
3. Child Support
4. Medical Expenses Paid for a Nondependent Child
5. Survey of Divorce and Separation Payments

E. JOINT AND SURVIVOR BENEFITS FROM QUALIFIED PLANS

F. RESTRICTIONS ON TAX ITEMS RELATED TO INTRAFAMILY TRANSACTIONS

G. UNRESOLVED FAMILY AND HOUSEHOLD TAX ISSUES

1. Work in the Home
2. Transfers Within Households and Among Relatives

A. Key Tax Issues Raised by Groups of Related Individuals

People who share a common bond do not typically relate to each other as self-interested economic agents. They use things in common without caring who owes what to whom. As we saw in Chapter 4 on gifts, families share resources, costs, and opportunities all the time. Of course, not all families are alike — children sometimes share households with elderly parents, couples (of the same or different sexes, married or unmarried) form households with each other, grandparents bring grandchildren into their households. Non-tax law generally does not interfere in the group relationship by prescribing rights and obligations except upon the dissolution of the group — divorce law, the law of concurrent ownership, and the law of employment are a few examples of this wary approach. Tax law impinges on families in many respects, facing more challenges as a result.

The income tax *does* take a modular approach to some groupings of individuals. First, it allows married couples[1] to file a **joint return**, subject to a lower tax rate than would apply to two single filers, but a higher rate than would apply to the couple's total income if each were allowed to file a single return for just half

Sidebar

BUSINESS ARRANGEMENTS AMONG FAMILY MEMBERS

Brother and sister may be employer and employee, and deal with each other in these roles as unrelated people would, while caring for elderly parents without counting costs. The tax law recognizes the possibility of "family partnerships" in which relatives by blood, marriage, or civil union hold capital interests in an enterprise just as they would if they were not related. Even when family members have no profit-oriented motives with respect to each other, their economic relations may be altruistic in some respects and self-centered in others. A parent may lend money to a child with the intention of treating her as an ordinary debtor and then later decide to forgive the obligation. Each of these patterns calls for slightly different tax treatment.

---

[1]Section 3 of the Defense of Marriage Act, Pub. L. No. 104-199, 110 Stat. 2419 (1996) ("DOMA") defines "marriage" as "a legal union between one man and one woman as husband and wife," and the definition has been codified as a general rule of construction for federal statutes in 1 U.S.C. §7. The IRS has so far ruled only privately that this precludes same-sex married couples from filing a joint return. See, e.g., Tech. Ad. Mem. 9850011. Couples married under the law of states that permit same-sex marriage may file state joint returns, of course, as may couples in common law marriages in those states that recognize common law marriage. Before DOMA, the IRS followed state law in determining who is married for joint return purposes.

their combined income;[2] we examine this feature of the income tax rate structure further in Section C below. But more basically, the Code recognizes relationships between taxpayers and their **dependents**, providing a definition of that term that extends to certain nonrelatives as well as to children, both when young and when somewhat older and almost emancipated, and relatives such as elderly or disabled individuals for whom the taxpayer provides support. A taxpayer can claim an **exemption**, a special above-the-line deduction from gross income, for herself and for each dependent. The joint return and dependent exemptions are direct responses to the two main features of families and similar "collectives," that is, the sharing of income and the sharing of expenses. We saw in Chapter 5 that the exclusion for gifts received is also primarily of benefit to families and other related individuals when they transfer property out of benevolence, goodwill, or for other unselfish reasons. Other special rules, to be examined in detail in this chapter, single out the expenses and savings arrangements of groups of related individuals for special treatment.

F   A   Q

Q: Who should claim a dependent child's exemption if both parent and child have income to report?

A: Just as the Code allows spouses to file singly, section 152(c)(4) allows parents and dependent children to decide who will claim the dependent's exemption. Spouses never face a lower combined tax rate by filing separately. The combined tax burden of parents and dependent children with their own income will be less only when the former face a lower joint or single filer rate than a dependent, and then it is unlikely the child will meet the test of dependency. For example, a 20-year-old full-time student who is still a member of a single parent's household will benefit from claiming a personal exemption on her tax return only if the parent makes less money or has considerably more business and personal deductions. The reason for this is that the value of the exemption, like the value of any other deduction, is equal to the taxpayer's marginal tax rate times the current exemption amount. It is even less likely that joint filers and dependents could gain by shifting the exemption to the child because of the higher marginal joint tax rate.

Joint returns and dependent exemptions, however, are one-size-fits-all solutions that give the wrong result in many cases. Notoriously, the joint return lives up to expectations only for married individuals whose separate incomes are not roughly equal. For those couples, the joint return imposes a marriage penalty, because the spouses would pay lower rates of tax if they were single. Joint rates are not as low as the rates that would apply if each spouse were allowed to pay tax at single-filer's rates on half of the couple's combined income. We examine the marriage penalty and related issues in Section C.

---

[2]I.R.C. §1(a).

B. Taxpayers' Expenses for Children and Elderly Dependents

(1) Medical Expenses

When the Code allows a payment of a specified kind to be deducted, the taxpayer who claims the deduction must be the person both who makes the payment and for whom the payment is of the kind in question. For example, your parents cannot deduct a mortgage interest payment they make on your behalf, if not signatories of the mortgage note, but you can deduct the payment if, as is overwhelmingly likely, they intended to make you a gift of the amount in question. On this principle, however, parents should not be allowed to deduct medical and dental expenses they pay for their children. Although the deduction now reduces one's tax liability only if out-of-pocket payments exceed the high threshold of 7.5 percent of AGI (see Chapter 12.B), an express provision in Code section 213 permits parents to deduct payments on behalf of their children, whether dependent or not. To grasp the extent of this family-oriented extension of the deduction, have a look at the definition of "dependent."

(2) Section 152

Broadly speaking, a **dependent** is a child or a close relative supported by the taxpayer. The statutory definition of the term is more specific, and we examine it in the next paragraph. Section 63 allows taxpayers to **claim a personal exemption** for each dependent as well as for herself and a spouse. The amount varies with filing status and is adjusted for inflation; the personal exemption, an inflation-adjusted amount, was $3,650 for 2010.

The idea of personal exemptions for dependents has deep roots in the history of the income tax. From the outset, a central goal of the tax was to adjust tax burdens to personal means. At first, most countries chose simply to exempt a subsistence level of income from the tax. Back in 1894, the U.S. income tax set the personal exemption at $4,000, a realistic estimate of a subsistence income. Earlier European income tax laws had exempted comparable income levels. The amount of the personal exemption is now much smaller in real dollars (currently $3,650), but other deductions and adjustments for families also reduce the burden of the income tax, arguably protecting subsistence adequately. Taxpayers filing a joint return are each allowed one personal exemption, as well as one for each dependent.

Example 11.1: Jack and Jill, who file a joint return, have $50,000 AGI for 2009. They have a dependent daughter. For the year, their itemized deductions would have been less than $11,400. Their taxable income is $27,650 = $50,000 AGI − (3 × $3,650 personal exemptions and dependency allowance) − $11,400 standard deduction. The standard deduction, personal exemptions, and dependency allowance reduce their taxable income by almost half.

Section 152 defines dependent differently for **qualifying children** and other **qualifying relatives**. Children include the taxpayer's descendants (children, grandchildren, etc.), siblings, and stepbrothers and sisters and their descendants. Those children who qualify must (1) have the same "principal place of abode" as the taxpayer for more than half of the taxable year; (2) be under 19 or, if a student, 24; and (3) not have provided over half of his or her own support for the year. Qualifying relatives include children as defined above, but also parents, other ancestors, step-parents, nieces and nephews, aunts and uncles, in-laws, and unrelated members of the taxpayer's household. The further qualifications then come thick and fast. For example, children include foster children (with tedious further specifications), and siblings include brothers and sisters "by the half blood." A recently added humanitarian extension of the support rule allows parents to claim as a dependent a missing child presumed by the police to have been kidnapped by someone other than a family member.[3] There are further complex rules for children who can be claimed by more than one person, as is often the case for divorced parents. Which divorced parent gets the exemption is usually determined by agreement between them (now it must be evidenced by the correct IRS form), but can also be decided by complex triage prescribed in the regulations. (None of this is likely to be taken up in an introductory tax course.)

F A Q

Q: Are a taxpayer's dependents treated as his or her agents, so that the taxpayer stands in the shoes of the dependents for tax and other purposes?

A: No, a dependent may have gross income, deductions, credits, and losses of her own, unrelated to those of the taxpayer whose dependent she is; she may also be required to file a separate tax return and be solely liable for income tax. (It is beyond the scope of this discussion, but dependents can have separate legal identity in all respects from those whose dependents they are. Children are sometimes but not always dependents of their parents, and parents sometimes have legal responsibility for the acts of their children, but there is no simple correspondence between these relationships.)

Here we should note as well that section 1(g) subjects the "unearned income" (roughly, what we ordinarily call investment income) of children under 18 to the same tax rate as their parents' income, allowing the parent of under-18 children whose income is less than ten times the personal exemption amount for the year to elect to report the children's income on their own return.

Back to the big picture: The Code obviously struggles to find the right patchwork analysis of who should be grouped with a taxpayer as an exception from the rugged individualism of the income tax law. Although the standard is never clearly stated, it is something like this: Anyone is a taxpayer's dependent whom the taxpayer supports and lives with—recall that completely unrelated individuals may be dependents if

---

[3]I.R.C. §152(f)(6).

members of the taxpayer's household. Yes, there are lots of limitations, but that's the general idea. How seriously does it depart from strict treatment of all individuals as separate, profit-oriented atoms?

Not that much. The low level of the personal exemption, far less than a subsistence wage, is not a serious substitute for deducting what dependents actually cost. Medical expenses for a dependent are deductible, but the current high threshold for medical expense deductibility, 7.5 percent of AGI, confines this tax benefit to extreme illness scenarios. So what is going on?

C. The Joint Return and the Marriage Penalty

As noted in Section B above, the Code provides a special regime for married couples, allowing them to file joint returns that permit spouses to pool income and deductions so that the net figure is as low as possible, and then applies a special in-between set of marginal rates to the resulting taxable income. The history of this institution is useful background for understanding how and why the joint return is tied to special rates. Before World War II, few working families filed income tax returns at all, because the incomes of any modest wage earner would be reduced to zero taxable income by the high standard deduction, and because employers were not required to withhold taxes on wages, so that a modest income earner need not file a return to claim a refund of taxes withheld. Withholding by employers of taxes on employees' wages was introduced in 1943, and in 1948 the joint return was introduced.

Initially, joint filers' shared total income was "split" and taxed as if each spouse had earned half of it. The Code set the tax on the couple at twice the tax a single filer would pay on half of their combined net taxable income. This approach treated each spouse as a co-earner of any income earned by the other spouse outside the home. But it ignored the fact that work in the home yields the equivalent of income that should also be taxed, in order to preserve equity with spouses who both work outside the home and must pay third parties to do housework income on which they pay tax. Congress modified the joint filers' rate structure so that it imposed a tax equal to roughly one and one-half that imposed on a single filer. By raising the tax on couples with one cash income above the level of the tax that would result from income splitting, the new joint-filer rate structure implicitly imposes a low but substantial level of tax on the benefit of housework.

As more and more families included two working spouses, the mandatory joint filing requirement for spouses subjected some of them to a higher joint rate of tax than they would have faced if not married: The so-called "marriage penalty" became conspicuous. Although the higher income of one spouse would have benefited from a lower rate if it had been the only income of the couple, by stacking the earnings of the spouse whose income was lower on top of that of the other spouse, this second income faced a higher rate of tax than it would have if earned by a single filer. Couples with only one high income, depending on how high it is and how low the other income, receive a "marriage bonus," in comparison with couples who pay more than they would as separate single filers.

Example 11.2: Jack and Jill each earn $100,000 a year as lawyers. The difference in their tax liabilities as a married couple and their aggregate tax liabilities as single filers is as follows:

	Married Couple	Individual	Individual × 2
AGI	$200,000	$100,000	
Minus exemptions and standard deduction	−18,700	−9,350	
Taxable income	$181,300	$90,650	
Federal income tax	$39,028	$19,102	$38,204
Marriage penalty	$1,102		

Sections 1(f)(8) and 63(b) now go some way toward removing the marriage penalty for some joint filers. They increase the standard deduction for joint filers to twice the standard deduction for single filers and increase the size of the 15 percent tax rate bracket for joint filers to twice the size of the 15 percent bracket for single filers. These adjustments to the rate structure reduce taxes of married couples who would otherwise pay a marriage penalty as well as those of married couples that enjoy the marriage bonus.

F   A   Q

Q: Is it possible to both eliminate the marriage penalty and retain the benefits of the joint-filer rate structure for couples with only one income earned outside the home?

A: Yes, by imputing a specific value to work done in the home, perhaps doing so by reference to objective indicia like the number of children below school age who are not in full-time daycare, whether the couple pays anything for professional housecleaning or lawn work, etc. This would be intrusive and hard to audit. It would, however, make it possible to treat all taxpayers alike, whether they work outside the home or not, by applying the same single-filer rates to everyone.

D. Separation and Divorce

That marriages often fail is a sad fact of life. Family law is largely about the extinction of marital ties. Tax consequences aggravate the difficulties of separation and divorce, although the current tax rules affecting the principal financial items are both flexible and reasonably predictable.

(1) Property Settlements

Property settlements related to separation or divorce usually involve the transfer of property from one spouse to the other; for example, one gets the house and the other gets the muscle car. The transfers are not gifts, because there is consideration for them, consisting of the release of claims or actual transfers of other property. Accordingly, without special provision in the Code, these transfers could have whopping tax consequences. For example, if the wife gets the house, she could have gain measured by the difference between her basis, if any, in her interest in the house (she may be a tenant by the entireties or a community property co-owner) and its full fair market value. Not surprisingly, the tax law has found a way around such harsh results.

Until recently, a property settlement could saddle one or both former spouses with taxable gain, but a somewhat obscure doctrine moderated the harshness of the result. In *United States v. Davis*,[4] the Supreme Court confirmed that the transfer of property from one spouse to the other as part of a divorce settlement was a realization event, and thus by default under section 1001 an appropriate occasion for the recognition of gain or loss. In 1954, the taxpayer transferred DuPont stock to his soon-to-be ex-wife in satisfaction of her claims against him (expressly including certain marital rights). The taxpayer's basis in the stock was lower than its fair market value at the time of the transfer. In earlier cases, the Court of Claims had accepted the view of the Sixth Circuit that the value of the marital rights "bought" by the settlement could not be established and that the gain was therefore not taxable. But in other cases, the Second and Third Circuits had disagreed.

The taxpayer had argued that the stock transfer was part of a division of property owned by both spouses, and that the property settlement as a whole was to be analyzed like the division of community property by operation of law in a community property jurisdiction. Delaware, where this couple resided, was and is a common law property state. The Court regarded this "as if" analysis as too much of a stretch because the incidents of the wife's inchoate marital rights under Delaware law did not justify treating *them* as property co-owned by the spouses during the marriage. Since the stock and the marital rights were not part of a common pool, settlement had to be regarded as an exchange. By the way, even the waiver of a co-owner's rights to an undivided interest in co-owned property is typically treated as a taxable exchange. Secondly, the Court held that the Court of Claim's own decision in *Philadelphia Park Amusement Co.*[5] stated the correct general tax principle that the properties exchanged in an arm's-length transaction are presumed to be equal in value. Hence, the result was that the former wife got the stock with a fair market value basis, having recognized no gain in the process, while her ex-husband recognized the gain on the stock he handed over, just as if he had sold it on the market. Just to be cautious, let us note that the Court's holding about the tax treatment of the taxpayer's transfer of stock was unambiguous; there was some vagueness in the Court's comments on the wife's side of the transaction, the full tax treatment of which was not at issue.

In *Farid-Es-Sultaneh v. Commissioner*,[6] the Second Circuit had earlier reached a similar decision concerning the waiver of marital property rights in an antenuptial

---

[4] 370 U.S. 65 (1962).
[5] 130 Ct. Cl. 166, 189 (1954).
[6] 160 F. 2d 812 (2d Cir. 1942).

agreement. The bride-to-be received corporate stock in lieu of other property rights against her prospective husband. After the marriage was over and the stock had appreciated, she sold it, and the IRS claimed that her basis was that of her former husband. The Court held that she had a cost basis in the stock, because she had exchanged rights presumed to be equal in value to the stock at the time of the transfer.

This remained the standard approach until 1984, when Congress enacted section 1041. Technically a nonrecognition provision, section 1041 relieves both parties to a divorce or separation from the burden of recognizing gain or loss on property shifted between them, effectively treating all such transfers as gifts. (To avoid confusion: Not all economic arrangements pursuant to divorce or separation are property transfers for this purpose; alimony and child support are treated differently and are discussed below.) The basis of transferred property in the hands of the transferee is the same as the transferor's — not the usual split basis mandated for inter vivos gifts in section 1015. This extends even to situations in which one spouse partly buys the other's interest in specific property, such as the house, with cash. The recipient of the money does not recognize gain in any amount.

(2) Alimony

In *Gould v. Gould*,[7] the Supreme Court held that alimony could *not* be taxed to the payee as "gains or profits and income derived from any source whatever" under the 1917 Revenue Act. From this holding, an approach developed that treated alimony as a gift as well. Congress eventually reversed this, implicitly treating alimony as a surrogate for compensation on which the recipient should be taxed as if he or she had earned wages or salary. Section 215(a) includes alimony in the recipient's gross income, and sections 62 and 71(a) allow the payor to deduct it. The option of shifting of gross income between divorcing spouses is vitally important in family law, because of its impact on the financial benefits and burdens of divorce settlements.

Distinguishing alimony from other payments could pose a problem, were it not for the narrow definition of the term in section 71. Alimony must be paid in cash to a former spouse who is no longer a member of the same household, must be expressly required by a divorce or separation instrument, and must terminate with the death of the payee. It was formerly required, but no longer is, that alimony be paid pursuant to a state-law obligation of support. To prevent lump-sum payments from being disguised as alimony, a statutory formula requires that certain high payments in early years be recharacterized as nondeductible if later-year payments are disproportionately lower, unless payments cease because of the death of either ex-spouse during a three-year period that includes the higher payments.

Note the contrast in economic function between alimony and property settlements. The former, paid in cash over an indefinite period of time, constitutes an uncertain stream of revenue, whereas the latter are definite in amount and hence have an ascertainable relationship to the wealth of the spouses at the time of the separation or divorce. Property settlements therefore appear to be based on already taxed amounts on hand when the payments are calculated, whereas alimony is contingent on future events and is therefore likely not yet taxed when the agreement requiring alimony is struck.

---

[7] 245 U.S. 151 (1917).

(3) Child Support

While they remain "married with children," amounts spent by either parent for the children are nondeductible "family" expenses.[8] Payments required by a divorce or separation instrument that is payable for the support of a child of the payor spouse are also nondeductible. More specifically, they do not qualify as alimony or separate maintenance payments.[9] Most states do not require the ex-spouse who receives child support payments to keep this money separate from alimony payments or to account for the use of the child support. In some circumstances, payments designated as child support may therefore enrich the recipient rather than the children. The Code follows state law in ignoring this possibility.

It is the ex-spouse, however, and not the children, to whom the right to child support belongs. This can give rise to interesting puzzles. In *Commissioner v. Lester*,[10] a Supreme Court case decided before the current version of section 71 was passed, a written divorce agreement reduced payments to the ex-spouse by a fixed fraction if any of the three children of the former couple should marry, become emancipated, or die. One-half of the payments were therefore indefeasible until the recipient died or remarried. The Supreme Court held nonetheless that the entire payments were alimony, because the agreement did not sufficiently "fix" the amount intended for child support only. Section 71(c) now picks up the language about "fixing" the amount payable as child support, suggesting that the *Lester* holding is still good law.

Sidebar

DUTY OF SUPPORT

All states recognize and occasionally enforce the child's right to parental economic support without regard to whether the parents are divorced or have a separation agreement that requires payment of child support. In one important respect, the treatment of a parent's direct payment of support to a child parallels that of the indirect payment of child support to an ex-spouse. The parent's nondeductible economic support of a child, which in some states includes the right to support for higher education, is probably not to be included in the child's income, but treated instead as a gift.[11] Child support paid to an ex-spouse is also not deductible by the payor and not included in the income of either the recipient ex-spouse or partner and the child for whose benefit the money is paid.

---

[11]See *St. Joseph Bank & Tr. Co. v. U.S.*, 716 F.2d 1180 (7th Cir. 1983) (Posner, J.) (discussion of gift status of divorce-related college support trust).

(4) Medical Expenses Paid for a Nondependent Child

As Section B.2 pointed out, a divorced parent who is not entitled to claim a child as a dependent may nevertheless deduct medical expenses paid for the child.

(5) Survey of Divorce and Separation Payments

There is a coherent scheme in the ensemble of holdings and rules concerning property settlements, alimony, and child support. Note that the treatment of payor and payee is roughly opposite for alimony and child support payments, respectively. Note too that all three types of transfer have some of the characteristics of gifts but are not all treated as such. Why? One reason may be that some but not all of the three involve "payment" for the kind of innate right that you cannot acquire by

---

[8]Code §262(a).
[9]Code §71(c); Treas. Reg. §1.71-1T(c), Q-15 & A-15.
[10]366 U.S. 299 (1961).

purchase and that other taxpayers get to exploit without having to pay tax on its value. This is true of the marital rights exchanged in *Davis* and *Farid*, and that forms an interesting link between the two cases.

E. Joint and Survivor Benefits from Qualified Plans

An important family-oriented tax rule requires the annuitized benefits of tax-preferred employer-sponsored retirement and employment-related savings plans to be "joint and several," that is, paid over the expected lives of the employee and of the employee's spouse, unless the spouse expressly waives this right.[12]

F. Restrictions on Tax Items Related to Intrafamily Transactions

Several Code provisions acknowledge the community of interest among family members by denying deductions and other tax advantages to transactions in which the family relationship may change ordinary economic motivation. For example, section 267(a)(1) does not allow a taxpayer to recognize a loss on disposing of property to a close family member.[13] A number of provisions deny transactions between co-owners of corporations or partnerships their usual consequences, apparently on the grounds that the family members may be acting more or less in each other's interest. For example, section 318 treats a shareholder as owning the shares owned by a spouse, parent, child, or grandchild in determining, among other things, whether a redemption has reduced the shareholder's interest in a corporation. Similarly, section 704(e)(3) treats a partnership interest purchased from a spouse, ancestor, or lineal descendant as if it had been a gift, for the purpose of restrictions on gifted interest.

G. Unresolved Family and Household Tax Issues

(1) Work in the Home

Income tax systems, both ours and those of other countries, ignore what a taxpayer does for herself, even if it enables her to avoid out-of-pocket expense or frees up economic resources for other use. Economists impute income to one who saves

---

[12]Code §§401(a)(11), 417.
[13]See Chapter 9.G.

money in this fashion, and that obviously makes sense. But the tax law turns a blind eye. The exclusion of such imputed income is a matter of administrative common law; no Code section endorses it.

Work in the home is the paradigm case of productive but untaxed personal effort. Note that while consumed in the home, the product enriches the household by the cost avoided. The benign neglect of imputed income is inequitable to those who pay for similar work, because they do not avoid the cost and enjoy no exclusion or deduction for it.[15] It should be noted that work for oneself or for relatives in the home is not explicitly taken into account for Social Security taxes or benefits, although survivor benefits may partly correct this.

(2) Transfers Within Households and Among Relatives

As the overview of this chapter indicated, the Code's piecemeal approach to family-based tax issues does not address pervasive or less frequently encountered differences between individuals and groups acting as collective economic units. Transfers of money and services without consideration are normal among relatives and household members. Most such transfers do not exceed the annual amount that would require a gift tax return, but some do. In practice, the IRS never audits these totals. Estate tax return audits sometimes delve into the decedent's lifetime gifts to children for which tax returns were not filed, but this almost never has income, as opposed to estate, tax consequences for the living or the dead. On the other hand, purported sales over time between parents and children, or between otherwise related parties, for which the buyer claims interest deductions and/or a cost basis in the property transferred risk closer scrutiny. The IRS sometimes challenges such sales as disguised gifts, and the Code treats some as gifts, regardless of the consideration given, in the treatment of family partnerships (Code §704(e)).

SUMMARY

- Family units of various types are treated for certain tax purposes as if transactions among members of these units were not separate taxpayers.

- For each dependent, a taxpayer is allowed an "exemption" that amounts to an above-the-line deduction in an amount that is annually adjusted for inflation.

- Spouses of different sexes are required to file a joint tax return that permits them to pool their deductions, but also subjects their pooled net income to a higher rate of tax than that applicable to single filers. Same-sex spouses are neither required nor allowed to file joint returns.

- The marriage penalty is the higher rate of tax that applies to the incomes of joint filers who both work outside the home.

- Neither the transferor nor the transferee recognizes gains and losses realized on transfers of property pursuant to a divorce or separation agreement.

- Alimony is normally deducted by the payor and included in the payee's gross income, although ex-spouses can waive both aspects of this income-shifting

---

[15]See Chapter 12.D.2(a) on the tax treatment of childcare expense.

treatment; that is, noninclusion in the payee's income is permitted only if the payor cannot deduct the amount paid.

■ Child support cannot be deducted by the payor and is not included in the payee's income.

■ Losses on sales or exchanges of property between persons having certain family relationships are not recognized *and* the transferor's basis does not carry over to the transferee; however, certain gains on later disposition by the transferee are excluded, providing a rough equivalent to the operation of carryover basis.

CONNECTIONS

Gift Exclusion and Family "Transactions"

The income tax disregards many transfers of money or the equivalent within households, especially when some members of the group are dependent on others. The volume of transfers would make it difficult to ascertain which cancel each other out and which go unrequited. The joint return, dependents' exemptions, and the gift exclusion help remove families and other households from the domain of the income tax. See Chapter 5.B(3).

Family Transfers and the Preservation of the Progressive Rate Structure

Some transactions between family members and others with a "community of interest" could threaten the progressive rate structure if higher-bracket taxpayers could freely transfer income to related lower-bracket taxpayers, if lower-bracket taxpayers could freely transfer built-in-loss property to higher-bracket taxpayers, or if higher-bracket taxpayers could sell built-in-loss property to lower-bracket taxpayers to recognize the loss while retaining control of the property. The assignment of income doctrine bars the first, section 1015 the second, and section 267(a)(1) the third of these potential abuses. See Chapters 6.E, 9.G, and 16 passim.

Mortgage Interest and Property Tax Deductions

Although not limited to groups, the mortgage interest and property tax deductions benefit households of related persons more than individuals, because the former need larger houses than the latter and accordingly benefit more from the tax preference for home ownership. See Chapter 13.D.

Assignment of Income

The courts have disapproved a variety of techniques for shifting income from one person to another when the result would be to reduce the parties' collective tax liability at the government's expense. The pro-family provisions discussed in this chapter tend to have the opposite result. Chapter 16 discusses current judicial standards that constrain assignments of income among taxpayers.

Spending Money to Make Money: Business and Investment Deductions

12

Measuring income net of costs is what makes the income tax fairer and less likely to distort economic decisions than gross receipts, wealth, or

O V E R V I E W

transfer taxes. The idea is simple, but as we look into how going concerns actually work, distinguishing profit-driven spending from loose spending or consumption turns out to be less so. The specter of nondeductibility inspires investors and business owners to claim and even believe that everything is profit related. Although a connection with profit exists, matching outlays with revenues that belong to the same time period introduces another layer of difficulty. The time value of money, as we saw in Chapter 7, requires such matching, and the administrative goal of sorting taxable events into annual pigeonholes reinforces the matching imperative. In this chapter, we focus only on distinguishing business or investment expenses from personal, living, or family expenses.

A. **EXPENSES OF SEEKING INCOME VERSUS PERSONAL EXPENSES**

B. **THE BROAD SCHEME OF BUSINESS AND INVESTMENT DEDUCTIONS**

C. **"ORDINARY" AND "NECESSARY"**

D. **PERSONAL EXPENSES DISGUISED AS PROFIT-ORIENTED EXPENSES**

   1. Hobbies
   2. Employee's Expenses for the Trade or Business of Being Employed

3. Housing
4. Travel, Transportation, and Commuting Expenses
5. Entertainment
6. Home Office and Vacation Rentals
7. Litigation Expenses

A. Expenses of Seeking Income Versus Personal Expenses

In order not to be a gross profits tax, the income tax must allow the costs of making a profit to be deducted. The fidelity of income taxation to the goals of horizontal equity and tax neutrality[1] requires this. Not all expenses, of course, *should* be subtracted from gross income. Much of what a person spends is not a cost of earning income but for final consumption. The U.S. income tax makes exceptions for some consumption items: Medical expenses, casualty losses, charitable contributions, home mortgage interest, certain state taxes, and a few miscellaneous kinds of expense are all deductible within various limits.[2] But these personal deductions are not integral to the structure of the income tax; they are not among its defining features. We call them **tax expenditures** because they are implicit government subsidies for the conduct they favor. They are neither neutral nor fair, because the taxpayer's income level affects how much of each is allowed.

Putting these two thoughts together—the overall nondeductibility of personal expenses and the deductibility of profit-oriented expenses—it is obvious that taxpayers have a strong incentive to disguise the former as the latter. In fact, they may honestly consider personal expenses to serve their pursuit of gain, because lives are not easily compartmentalized. Safeguarding the distinction between the two kinds of expense is a major task for the tax law.

B. The Broad Scheme of Business and Investment Deductions

We must get used to a statutory distinction between two broad types of profit-oriented activity: first, those that constitute a **trade or business**, and second, those that relate only to the **production of income**. The boundary between them sometimes governs which deductions are allowed and certain other tax consequences. Like "income" itself, these are terms the Code does not define but that are mainstays of other definitions and rules. Code sections 162-190 and 212 selectively authorize deductions related to trades or businesses and other activities for the production of income, whereas sections 262 through 280F limit deductions authorized by those earlier, less restrictive Code sections.

---

[1]See Chapters 1 and 2.
[2]See Chapter 13 passim.

Although "trade or business" has no statutory definition and not much of a regulatory one, judges, administrators, lawyers, and accountants use precedent and intuition in applying the term. It roughly means quests for profit that involve more than buying low and selling high. Conversely, an endeavor limited to occasional property dealings or collecting the revenue from the use of property is *less* than a business. In brief, the deductibility of costs depends in part on the nature of the profit-seeking conduct.

Note, however, that whether expenses are for a trade or business or for profit-oriented investment, most are deductible only if **ordinary and necessary**. The common law developed by the courts has left the meaning of these terms almost completely inexplicit, yet everyone manages to live with that. Section B will unpack them as well as the case law permits.

> **Sidebar**
>
> **ACTIVELY AND PASSIVELY PROFIT-DIRECTED AFFAIRS**
>
> We speak of the *vitality* of a business, how well the business is *going*, but of *passive income* from investments. The underlying contrast between the need for frequent and concerted effort in business and the comparatively occasional character of investing is reflected in the Code's distinction between a "trade or business" and other "income production."

F   A   Q

Q: Have courts or the IRS managed to make "trade or business" any more definite than "ordinary and necessary"?

A: Most tax lawyers are reasonably sure of their ability to use these terms safely in planning and persuasively in arguments before the IRS or the courts. Their conviction is rooted in frequent experience with uncontroversial usage of the terms, but there is still no touchstone for the meanings of "trade or business" and "ordinary and necessary" that is both authoritative and definite enough to resolve hard cases. The regulations, for example, conspicuously say as little as possible on the topic. *See, e.g.*, Treas. Reg. §1.162-1.

Many specific Code sections allow deductions only for a trade or business, including deductions for:

- the everyday expenses of operating a trade or business (section 162)
- interest properly allocable to a trade or business (section 163)
- state, local, and foreign taxes paid or accrued in carrying on a trade or business (section 164)
- losses incurred in a trade or business (section 165)
- business bad debts (section 166)

Other Code sections allow deductions not for the full amount of a business expense, but for portions of a long-term business investment:

- Sections 167 and 168 make tangible property used in a trade or business, other than land, eligible for depreciation or a modified version thereof called accelerated cost recovery.

■ Section 197 allows goodwill purchased for use in a trade or business to be amortized, which is roughly the equivalent of depreciation for intangibles. These are only highlights of the Code's pervasive allowance of business-related deductions.

Similarly, but not as generously, the Code allows many costs of producing income to be deducted (section 212), although costs and outlays related to holding property for future sale or development are not amortizable or, with few exceptions, deductible. The income-oriented taxpayer who is not engaged in a trade or business can deduct only the "ordinary and necessary" costs of:

■ collecting income—section 212(1)
■ managing, conserving, and maintaining property—section 212(2)
■ expenses in connection with the determination, collection, or refund of any tax—section 212(3)

Note that verbs of activity in this list are relatively narrow. It is the collection of income, not the preparation to do so or the planning that results in an opportunity to collect income, that makes an expense deductible. Similarly, it is the costs of managing, conserving, or maintaining property, like the costs of investigating which property to acquire, or studying the market in which such properties are sold, or cultivating the prospective purchasers of the property one has for sale, that can be deducted. Other day-to-day expenses are not deductible, especially those of continuous places of operations. The language of section 212 quietly draws a distinction between background and foreground activities associated with collecting income or holding property. Section 162 is remarkably less specific about the scope of trade or business expenses.

This is roughly how deductions under sections 162 and 212 are distinguished. Almost anything reasonably closely tied to the kind of ongoing activity that constitutes a trade or business is deductible, while only the more proximate costs of turning property into profit or of collecting the income from an owned source are deductible. In *Moller v. United States*,[3] a couple with extensive and profitable investments sought to deduct home office expenses, financial newspaper and journal expenses, and other similar tangential expenses associated with their way of investing. The IRS did not question the deduction of expenses for subscriptions, office supplies, accounting and legal services, and other similar items,[4] but to qualify to deduct home office expenses under section 280A, the taxpayers needed to show that their investment activity rose to the level of a trade or business. The Federal Circuit held their trading activity was too occasional for this purpose. The considerable amounts of time spent by the taxpayers in their home office did persuade the court otherwise. Since investment activities are relatively passive, it is more difficult for what an investor spends to be clearly ordinary and necessary for the pursuit than it is for the operating costs of a trade or business, typically a more continuous and encompassing activity.

---

[3]721 F.2d 810 (Fed. Cir. 1983).
[4]*Id.* at 812 n.3.

C. "Ordinary" and "Necessary"

Sections 162 and 212 permit only **ordinary and necessary** expenses to be deducted, *even if* clearly related to a profit-seeking activity. The relationship between an expense and the activity it supposedly serves can have many dimensions, but the terms "ordinary" and "necessary" describe the only two that matter here. But their meanings have proved elusive. "Ordinary has the connotation of normal, usual, or customary," and, on the other hand, "an expense may be ordinary though it happen but once in the taxpayer's lifetime." This gloss from *Deputy v. DuPont*[5] tells us that an expense need not be common or frequent to be ordinary. A similar breadth of usage must guide our understanding of what it is for an expense to be necessary to a profit-seeking activity. "Necessary" suggests a causal criterion, but few if any expenses that contribute to an outcome are causally necessary on their own. Thus, the ordinary and necessary standard is not straight-forward.

We learn more, though not a great deal, from *Welch v. Helvering*.[6] To establish his credit in a new occupation, a commissions agent in commodities voluntarily paid off the debts of a bankrupt corporation of which he had been a director and owner. The Supreme Court agreed with the IRS that the taxpayer's repayment of another party's debts could not be deducted right away but must instead be capitalized to (that is, added to the basis of) the taxpayer's new venture. The brief, meandering opinion by Justice Cardozo falls into two parts.

The first addresses the question whether the repayments were ordinary and necessary for *any* trade or business. Discussing only whether the repayments were "ordinary," the opinion considers businesses like that of the taxpayer the touchstone and concludes that the taxpayer's payments were "extraordinary." The inquiry, in other words, was whether the repayments in this case had substantial precedent in the conduct of similar trades or businesses.

The second part, however, suggests that the repayments were not ordinary because they benefited the taxpayer's new enterprise over an indefinitely long period of time. In this part of the opinion, the repayments are found to be neither ordinary *nor* necessary. The Court therefore appears to consider the phrase "ordinary and necessary" to constitute a standard with one rather than two elements. Moreover, the contrast between ordinary and necessary expenses and capitalizable expenditures is taken for granted. In dictum, the Court comments that amounts spent to create goodwill "of an old partnership" are not deductible, and that the same applies to educational expenses. The reference to goodwill suggests that even advertising expenses should be capitalized, rather than expensed. Today, government and courts alike agree that if advertising furthers a business, it is currently deductible.[7] Education costs are neither deductible nor amortizable, unless they merely preserve the taxpayer's qualifications for existing employment.[8]

Welch ultimately concedes that the connection between the taxpayer's repayments and his current business was sufficient to support adding them to the basis of the new venture. This on its face contradicts the Court's earlier conclusion that the

---

[5]308 U.S. 488, 495-496 (1940).
[6]290 U.S. 111 (1930).
[7]*See* Treas. Reg. §1.263A-1(e)(iii)(A) (allowing deduction of "advertising . . . costs").
[8]*Id.* §1.162-5(b)(1).

expenses lacked the requisite relationship with either the old or the new business. But the opinion does not notice the contradiction or explain how the standard for capitalization differs from that for expensing an outlay.

Subsequent cases have allowed taxpayers to deduct amounts paid to satisfy the debts of another, for the benefit of the taxpayer's reputation, for example, when the taxpayer had promoted an incorporated venture that fizzled, leaving disappointed investors clamoring for their money.[9] What *do* we learn from *Welch*? Certainly, a close tie must exist between an expense and a taxpayer's profit-oriented activity to support its deduction as ordinary and necessary. But several other points asserted or assumed in *Welch* are no longer reliable.

Sidebar

OUTLAYS FOR GOODWILL AND THE "ORDINARY AND NECESSARY" REQUIREMENT

Welch relies on the contrast between expenses for current operations and expenses for goodwill in discussing the "ordinary and necessary" requirement for section 162 deductibility. "Goodwill" in the tax context has a broad meaning, possibly broader than any you have encountered before. It is a label not only for the good reputation of a business or the people connected with the business, but also any value the business has over and above the value of its assets. Goodwill is therefore sometimes used in tax discussions interchangeably with "going concern value."

Spending to create goodwill is indeed still neither deductible nor amortizable, but section 197 allows purchased goodwill to be amortized over 15 years. Expenses incurred before a business is underway also constitute a clear exception to "ordinary and necessary" business expenses. Attempts to deduct such "preoperating" expenses used to be routinely denied, with the advice that they must instead be added to the basis of the enterprise itself. Recently enacted, section 195 now permits preoperating or "start-up" expenses to be amortized over 15 years.

Legal expenses for defense against civil and criminal claims arising directly in the taxpayer's conduct of a trade or business are deductible as ordinary and necessary expenses.[10] *Welch* itself supports this, stating that "counsel fees" for a "lawsuit affecting the safety of a business," although such litigation may happen only once in the course of a business, are ordinary and deductible by the same standard.

D. Personal Expenses Disguised as Profit-Oriented Expenses

Jobs and independent commercial ventures are often of personal benefit in indirect ways to the people involved. Because an employee or self-employed person can choose to some extent how to perform these roles, there is a particular danger that personal preference rather than the demands of the enterprise will shape these choices. (We considered aspects of this business/personal overlap in Chapter 2 in connection with the convenience of the employer doctrine.) It is worthwhile to note that section 162, which allows trade or business expenses to be deducted, has a foil in section 262, which denies deductions for "personal, living, or family expenses."

---

[9]*See, e.g., Dunn & McCarthy v. Comm'r*, 139 F.2d 242 (2d Cir. 1943); *M.L. Eakes Co. v. Comm'r*, 686 F.2d 217 (4th Cir. 1982).
[10]*Comm'r v. Tellier*, 383 U.S. 687 (1966); *Clark v. Comm'r*, 30 T.C. 1330 (1958). *But see Gilliam v. Comm'r*, 51 T.C.M. 515 (1986) (legal fees paid to defend taxpayer against criminal charges arising from conduct while temporarily insane on business flight were not deductible).

Thus, despite the inevitable spillover of benefit from the business sphere to the personal, the income tax insists on drawing a sharp line. In some cases, apportioning costs between the deductible and the nondeductible creates that boundary, but in most cases the tax law treats costs that may yield both profit and indirect personal benefit as entirely deductible or not at all.

F   A   Q

Q: If a business activity would not be possible but for a particular expense, is the expense then deductible?

A: "But for" causality is not the litmus test for deductibility. Outlays for everything from the purchase of manufacturing supplies to the not-so-vital purchase of the owner's breakfast are necessary in that sense for a business activity. On the other hand, an outlay that does not meet the "but for" standard may yet be "necessary" for purposes of sections 162 and 212, because it in fact advances the profit-oriented activity. In brief, "necessity" for deductibility under these sections is not causal necessity.

(1) Hobbies

Pursuits that may be profitable or recreational pose this problem acutely. The person with a full-time job who "works" every weekend on a farm that does not quite cover its costs is not rare. The IRS usually recognizes hobbies for what they are. But the line of demarcation is not always clear.

A wealthy horse fancier in *Bessenyey v. Commissioner*[11] was denied deductions for losses incurred in running what she claimed was a breeding operation, the purpose of which was to save a certain breed of horse from extinction in this country. She sold only one horse in eight years. Her plans, however, had evolved. In later years, she bred the horses for their special characteristics as workhorses and trained them for this purpose as well. The Tax Court thought her professed hope of making a profit in future years insincere and disallowed the loss deductions for the previous years. The Second Circuit affirmed, noting that "when certain productive activity is generally regarded as a business," Congress might allow business deductions regardless of profit motive, but it had not done so, and the evidence of the taxpayer's profit motive in this case was weak. The Tax Court's decision was not clearly erroneous.

In contrast, the taxpayers in *Nickerson v. Commissioner*[12] were an advertising executive and his wife, whose project was the slow development of a successful dairy farm. The farmland was a five-hour drive from their urban residence. They rented out some of the land to a tenant farmer who agreed to develop a profitable crop, with the purpose of preparing the land for them to take over later. Meanwhile, they renovated the farmhouse and an abandoned orchard. Mr. Nickerson read agricultural journals and consulted the area extension agent. The farm had no livestock or equipment, but also no recreational facilities. The taxpayers did not invite guests to visit the farm.

---

[11]45 T.C. 261 (1965), 379 F.2d 252 (2d Cir.), *cert. denied*, 389 U.S. 931 (1967).
[12]42 T.C.M. 211 (1981), *rev'd*, 700 F.2d 402 (7th Cir. 1983).

The Tax Court found this was a hobby, because there was no realistic chance of the farm becoming profitable, but the Seventh Circuit disagreed. Reviewing the regulations on profit motive,[13] the court observed that the factors listed there were all related to the inquiry whether the taxpayer's *intent* was to make a profit. Here, the sincerity of the taxpayer's hope that the farm would become profitable was not in question. That the taxpayer may not have been realistic, according to the court, was not dispositive.

Many amateur farmers, horse breeders, and similar hobbyists fail to produce evidence of their unswerving pursuit of profit, especially when the disputed activity runs at a loss year in and year out. Despite the relative ease with which the profit motivation of these activities can be rebutted, Congress has seen fit to provide two generous **safe harbors** for them. A safe harbor is a clearly defined case of a broader type of tax-favored transaction, singled out by the Code or regulations to make it easier for taxpayers to know whether their circumstances merit the tax advantage in question; meeting the conditions of the safe harbor is sufficient but not necessary for obtaining the benefit in question. In this instance, the safe harbor is one that creates a presumption of profit-making intent if the taxpayer actually makes a profit in past years.

First, section 183(b) allows a taxpayer with a hobby to deduct all the usual deductions associated with a profit-oriented activity but only "to the extent that the gross income derived from such activity for the taxable year exceeds the deductions allowable" without regard to the profit-seeking character of the activity. The latter deductions are also allowed. The idea is that the sought-after profit-seeking deductions can shelter only hobby income that would not be sheltered anyway by deductions like those for property taxes and mortgage interest. Section D(5) of this chapter explains that section 280A revokes this generosity for hobby expenses for a residence of the taxpayer.

Second, section 183(d) allows a taxpayer to claim all the usual deductions associated with carrying on a trade or business without separately establishing the intent to make a profit, if the activity is profitable, after items that would be deductible if it is a trade or business have been deducted, for three of the five taxable years ending with the year in question. In other words, the activity can run a loss this year and in one of the previous four years, and there would still be no need to establish the intent to make a profit. Section 183(b) becomes unnecessary when this alternative safe harbor applies, because now a taxpayer can take the deductions of an activity engaged in for profit even if they would produce a loss.

Section 183 may serve administrative convenience by allowing taxpayers who might otherwise claim more aggressive deductions of for-profit activities, to claim a smaller deductible amount without any struggle, thus perhaps persuading them to lower their sights and provoke fewer costly audits. Whether this is shrewd bargaining on the part of the government or not, no one can say.

[13]Treas. Reg. §1.183-2(b)(1)-(9).

A taxpayer can still claim unwarranted deductions in the comfortable knowledge some will be allowed in any case. Section 183 may only raise taxpayers' consciousness of the difficulty the government faces in auditing hobby deductions.

(2) Employee's Expenses for the Trade or Business of Being Employed

Recall that an employee always has a trade or business — not the trade or business of the employer, but that of being an employee of whatever kind it is. Given the routine classification of employment as a trade or business, the full gamut of deductibility extends to those of the employee's expenses that are ordinary and necessary for the employment — more than would be deductible under section 212 for profit-oriented activities that are not trades or businesses. Yet the boundary between personal and profit-oriented (in the case of the employee, business-oriented) expenses is fraught with difficulty, as we shall see.

Some employer-provided benefits made available for the convenience of the employer are not gross income to the employee.[14] This basic proposition is almost but not exactly parallel with the further proposition that an employee should only be allowed to deduct an expense under section 162 if the expense serves the employee's job and not the employee's wants and needs apart from the job. Unfortunately, there is no sharp boundary between business and personal aspects of employee spending. Benefits for the convenience of the employer may not be confined to the workplace. The corner office cannot be taken home, but lunch in the employer's lunchroom may take pressure off the employee's food budget. Thus, what an employee spends in fulfilling the demands of the employment may confer a spillover benefit, and deducting the expense may make a personal, living, or family expense deductible.

> **Sidebar**
>
> **LIMITED DEDUCTIBILITY OF EMPLOYEE BUSINESS EXPENSES**
>
> Deductible employee business expenses may not produce much tax relief, because all such expenses are subject to the threshold for deductibility provided in section 67. Employment-related and other miscellaneous itemized deductions must collectively exceed 2 percent of the taxpayer's or joint filers' AGI to be deductible.

The tax law responds to the blurry line between personal and business aspects of employee spending by arbitrarily making the boundary sharper with bright-line rules. A few of these are statutory (restrictions on deductions for home offices), while others have emerged from case law or administrative practice (the nondeductibility of commuting expenses).

(a) Childcare and Similar Expenses

Childcare, housekeeping, and comparable services are often needed if parents are to work outside the home. This is no longer an exotic idea but it was not always so. After World War II, the government not only assumed that one spouse would stay at home to care for children and do housework, but also actively campaigned to persuade them to do so. Working single parents were rare. It was in this environment

---

[14]See Chapter 2.B.

that the default rule concerning these living or family expenses, for such they are, was first established. In *Smith v. Commissioner*,[15] the married taxpayers, who both worked, claimed deductions for in-home childcare expenses. The court flatly held the expense to be personal and therefore ineligible for deduction, despite the fact that this couple would not have incurred the childcare costs but for the wife's having taken a full-time job. The court's reasoning is remarkable. Noting that a spouse could work in the home without having to declare the value of his or her services as income, it concluded that there could be no deduction if another was paid to do the same work. But the inference might be just the reverse: If not taxing households on self-provided labor is seen as an exclusion from income, then parity requires that others who must pay for the same labor should be allowed to deduct the expense. Exclusion and deduction would here have the same effect on net income.

The *Smith* analysis has not been overruled. Childcare and housekeeping expenses are still not deductible under section 162. But Congress has moved on. Section 21 allows employment-related expenses for both household services and care for qualifying dependents to be credited. The credit is limited. For a taxpayer with adjusted gross income less than $15,000, it is 35 percent of the expenses in question. The percentage is reduced to 20 percent by one percentage point for every $2,000 by which the taxpayer's AGI exceeds $15,000. Hence, a taxpayer with AGI of $45,000 or more is allowed a credit of 20 percent. In addition to these limits, if there is only one qualifying dependent, a maximum of $3,000 in household services and childcare expenses qualify for the credit; that is, the cap is $1,050 for someone with AGI under $15,000 and $600 for someone with AGI above $45,000. If there are two dependents, these amounts double. Overnight camp costs are not creditable. These amounts are small in comparison with the annual cost of childcare in most urban centers. Many taxpayers, however, qualify for more generous treatment through employer-sponsored dependent-care plans.[16] Up to $4,800 can be excluded from income annually for housekeeping and childcare if certain elaborate payment arrangements are followed; in contrast with section 21, the cap on eligible daycare expenses under these plans does not depend on the number of dependents in care.

(b) Business Clothes

Although an employer may require shop assistants to buy and wear designer gowns on the job, the employees cannot deduct the clothing costs under section 162. In *Pevsner v. Commissioner*,[17] the government conceded that the taxpayer never wore her mandatory expensive clothes off the job, but the Fifth Circuit reversed a favorable decision by the Tax Court and held that work clothes were not deductible, acknowledging an exception only for situations in which required clothing is not adaptable for general use. Uniforms are not adaptable for general use, and so an employee can deduct the expense of buying them.

Are a construction worker's tools deductible if required for the job but taken home and perhaps used there for personal purposes? The tools would be deductible, subject only to apportionment of the deduction to the purely nonpersonal use. Again, only a rule of administrative convenience explains the irrebuttable presumption that clothes other than uniforms are a personal expense. Every working person in the

---

[15] 40 B.T.A. 1038 (1939), *aff'd per cur.*, 113 F.2d 114 (2d Cir. 1940).
[16] Code §125. Section 125 authorizes similar arrangements for the indirect exclusion of other employer-provided benefits — so-called "cafeteria plans."
[17] 628 F.2d 427 (5th Cir. 1980).

country might otherwise claim virtually all of his or her clothes as a business expense. What makes the hazard greater in the case of clothes is that everyone must have them, whether they are employed or not. More narrowly, however, section 132(a)(2) excludes qualified employee discounts for clothes and other items sold in the employee's line of work. Chapter 3.E(2)(b) discusses the details.

(3) Housing

Recall that section 119 excludes meals and lodging provided on an employer's premises from the employee's income. The exclusion has the same effect as inclusion of the value in the employee's income coupled with the deduction of that amount as a business expense. But everyday meals, even if taken on the employer's premises, are *not* deductible, by well-settled and easily defended interpretation of section 262, because these are paradigmatic personal or living expenses. If an employer requires an employee to live near her work — as some municipalities require of their employees — again, there is no deduction. The contrast between excludible meals and lodging and ordinary meals and lodging is striking. Yet it too has exceptions, as we learn in the following section, dealing with meals and lodging taken while traveling overnight for employment or self-employment.

(4) Travel, Transportation, and Commuting Expenses

Administrative practice and case law sharply distinguish travel, transportation, and commuting expenses, allowing the costs of the first two but not of the last to be deducted as ordinary and necessary business expenses. In order to understand this approach, it is useful to consider travel at the outset.

Section 162(a)(2) expressly characterizes expenses for travel "away from home" as ordinary and necessary business expenses and indicates that travel expenses include amounts spent on meals and lodging during travel, as long as they are not "lavish or extravagant under the circumstances." Other expenses related to business travel may also be deductible if the facts and circumstances make them so. IRS Publication 463 indicates that in most cases laundry expenses and lodging taxes are ordinary and necessary travel expenses. Section 274(d)(1) conditions the deduction of travel expenses on more-than-usually-detailed documentation.

United States v. Correll[18] upheld the IRS interpretation of travel in this context as *overnight* travel. Correll was a traveling salesman whose normal day began early. He ate breakfast and lunch on the road and returned home for dinner. He claimed a business expense deduction for the meals eaten during the day, asserting that these were "away" from home. The Court held that "away" from home means far enough away to require "sleep or rest," reasoning that the words "away from home" in section 162 would be surplusage if otherwise interpreted.

In *Commissioner v. Flowers*,[19] the taxpayer took up employment as in-house counsel for a railroad. The railroad generally required his services at its nearest headquarters, but allowed him to continue to live some 200 miles away. The taxpayer claimed deductions for the costs of going back and forth between his residence at the headquarters and for meals and hotels while not living at home. The Court denied the

---

[18]389 U.S. 299 (1967).
[19]326 U.S. 465 (1945).

deductions on the grounds that they were not "necessary" to his employment and thus did not satisfy the "ordinary and necessary" requirement for business expense deductibility. The government had argued that the principal issue was whether the taxpayer's "home" was where he resided or where he worked. The frugality of the Court's reasoning in *Flowers* stands in contrast to the elaborate scheme of classification the IRS frequently advocates in litigating travel and similar business expense issues.

Let us turn now to the three-way division of travel, transportation, and commuting. **Commuting** is going from a residence to a usual place of work and returning to the residence at the end of the day, if that is the pattern.[20] Neither an employee nor a self-employed person can deduct the expense of the commute. The courts now regularly accept this initially administrative rule. At bottom, what is at stake is the judgment that commuting costs are generally a function of the employee's decision of where to live. If they were deductible in an unrestricted way, some employees would enjoy a greater subsidy for this lifestyle choice than others would, given the unavoidable inequality in distances to be traveled and available means of transportation. Of course, deductibility of commuting expenses might be limited, and differences in what employees spend might then be properly reflected in the computation of their net income. Some countries with sophisticated tax systems allow a limited deduction for commuting expenses in the name of fairness. Our system does not, however, and all that one need know is how this rule is applied when the commuting pattern is unusual or cannot easily be labeled as commuting at all. Commuting expenses differ markedly from **travel expenses**, as *Correll* and *Flowers* illustrate, which are the expenses of getting to and from a workplace if the trip would normally require sleep or rest. They include otherwise nondeductible personal or living expenses if these happen to be incurred during and for the sake of the travel. **Transportation expenses** are those of getting from one workplace to another in the course of business activity, when this does not constitute commuting or travel. They include only the expenses of public or private means of locomotion, not meals, lodging, telephone, or other incidental expenses.

Given that travel and transportation expenses are deductible and commuting expenses are not, the IRS tries to eliminate the need for difficult factual or policy analysis in classifying them. The agency has long stood by its own detailed classification scheme. A few of the more prominent elements in that scheme depend on the notion of a "tax home," routinely invoked in IRS rulings and determinations. It has not gained the endorsement of the courts.

An employed or self-employed person's **tax home** is one of several places, depending on how the person gains a livelihood. It is her regular place of business or post of duty, which includes the entire city or general area where the place of business or work is and need not be the same as the person's place of residence. If a person has more than one regular place of business, her tax home is the most important of them. If a person does not have a regular place of business, her tax home may be where she resides, but that depends on several other factors. If a person has neither a regular place of business nor a regular place of residence, she is considered a transient or itinerant and her tax home is wherever she works, even if that is not a regular place of business or post of duty. Transients are never away from home and so never have deductible travel expenses. A person whose tax home is his or her actual

---

[20]Reg. §§1.162-2(e), 1.212-1(f), 1.262-1(b)(5).

place of residence can deduct the expenses of any moving around for business purposes, at least as transportation expenses, that is, not including personal expenses for meals and other incidentals.

F   A   Q

Q: What is the tax home of someone with different enterprises in different cities?

A: There is no general answer in the judicial or administrative rulings. If a taxpayer is employed in one city and self-employed in another, the problem is more acute, because two occupations are plainly not a single one for which there just happens to be no principal place of business. In most cases, the temporal demands of one of the occupations will make it more important, and the more important occupation could determine the taxpayer's tax home. But there is no authority to this effect. Members of Congress "generally" have their tax homes in Washington, D.C., but not necessarily. It depends on where most of their working time is spent and where their "business activities are centered."[21]

The notion of a tax home is intended to sharpen the distinction between travel and transportation. If a trip for business purposes does not take a person away from (tax) home overnight, only the transportation expense is deductible (transportation, remember, is understood to exclude commuting). As long as a trip is in the course of employment, the pursuit of a profession, or any other trade or business, it must either be travel or transportation. Commuting, as previously stated, is disqualified as such from counting as in the course of any of the foregoing. Could a trip from the workplace to the taxpayer's home during the course of the day escape the commuting label? Presumably so, if it were for specific business reasons, such as to retrieve work-related items or to pick up personal belongings for an immediate business trip to some other place.

Although the *Correll* court did not embrace the IRS's conception of a tax home, the holding of the case can easily be expressed in terms of it. The taxpayer had no regular place of business, but "traveled" widely during the course of each day, eating meals along the way, and returning home each evening. He wanted to deduct these "travel" costs. Since his tax home was where he resided, the IRS would consider him entitled to deduct the transportation expenses. Transportation, however, does not include meals, which are deductible only while traveling. The taxpayer was not traveling because his trips did not require rest or repose. He was not so far from his residence, which in his case was his tax home, to have to sleep out.

Reliance on tax-home analysis also complements the rule against deducting commuting expenses. For those with a regular place of business or post of duty, there is no business need to get from tax home to work, and so the deductibility of the expense of that trip is a nonissue — this is of course Orwellian newspeak, but it probably warms the hearts of regulation and ruling writers.

---

[21]Rev. Rul. 73-468, 1973-2 C.B. 77.

Despite its virtues, the courts have not warmed to tax-home thinking. In *Hantzis v. Commissioner*,[22] the taxpayer spent a law school summer working for a New York law firm but maintained her residence in Boston. She claimed deductions for travel, as well as for meals and lodging in New York. The Tax Court held for her, but the First Circuit disagreed. The taxpayer's "functional" home, the court found, was New York, because she had no trade or business connection with Boston (despite spousal and law school ties there). The court, however, expressly rejected the administrative notion of tax home and related rules, preferring more flexibility. *Hantzis*, in line with *Flowers*, sounds a call for judicial restraint and a mild refusal to defer to the administrative expertise in this area.

(5) Entertainment

The wheels of commerce are greased with expense-account lunches and nights on the town. Whether business could go on without them is open to doubt, but no empirical test of the issue seems possible. The government's ability to police the boundary between consumption and profit-oriented activity is severely tested by taxpayer claims for the deduction of entertainment expenses. The "ordinary and necessary" standard of section 162 provides vague guidance at best.

Into this void, Congress inserted section 274, which cuts back on arguably valid business expense deductions for entertainment, recreation, group employee activities, and the like. Note that section 274 does not itself authorize the deductions it regulates; its role is exclusively as a backstop to section 162 and other provisions that otherwise authorize business-related deductions. Section 274 deals with problems of substantiation and potential abuse of those other provisions. In particular:

- Deductions for entertainment, including meals, are allowed only if the entertainment was closely linked with doing business, which in the case of meals means business actively conducted before, during, or after the meal.
- Deductions even for most business-related meals are limited to 50 percent of the amount claimed.
- Business gift deductions are limited to $25 per year per donee.
- Substantiation of business deductions for all (overnight) travel, entertainment, gifts, and certain property expenses is an absolute condition of deductibility; the taxpayer must prove the amount spent, as well as when, for what, and with whom.
- The expense of taking a spouse along on business travel cannot be deducted unless the spouse is also an employee, the business purpose is substantial and bona fide, and the spouse could have deducted the expense.
- Exceptions are made for certain group entertainment.

Business entertainment (meals, sports events, Broadway shows, and the like) were a chief target of section 274, and yet the language apparently intended to restrict deductions for these items (which include all sorts of amusement and recreation) is not much clearer than the "ordinary and necessary" standard of section 162. There is one absolute prohibition: Expenses for "facilities" "used in connection with" entertainment cannot be deducted, no matter how close the connection is.

---

[22] 638 F.2d 248 (1st Cir.), *cert. denied*, 452 U.S. 962 (1981).

Meals, shows, etc., on the other hand, *can* be deducted if they are "directly related to . . . the active conduct of a trade or business" or immediately precede or follow discussions "associated with . . . the active conduct," etc. Now, the language about timing is new. It may be understood to mean that meals cannot be deducted at all unless they take place just before or after serious business discussion. Importantly, as well, there is no prohibition against deducting one's own meal if one is allowed to deduct the meal of a client or customer. But everyone agrees that a meal taken without a business associate, client, customer, or the like cannot be deducted.

F   A   Q

Q: Are all deductions under section 162 or section 212 subject to the stringent substantiation requirements of section 274(d)?

A: No. Section 274(d) does require detailed substantiation for quite a few business-related deductions. Travel, entertainment, amusement, recreation, gifts, and expensive cars are all covered. But it does not restrict the deduction of other outlays. The items for which unusual documentation is required are all potential consumption items for the taxpayer or its key employees. To deduct the cost of sheet metal used in the manufacture of dumpsters, a taxpayer would not have to keep the specific records required in section 274(d), but would instead only have to keep ordinary business records that might not record the specific use or cost of particular items.

Section 274 indicates the outer limits of the meal restriction sketchily at best. The regulations bluntly say that entertainment is not limited to the entertainment of people outside the firm, which of course means that the substantiation requirement of section 274 applies to deductions claimed for in-house meals, recreational events, and the like. The affirmative possibility that entertainment involving coworkers alone could support the deduction of expenses has yet to be confirmed in the cases. Nonetheless, *Moss v. Commissioner*[23] goes some way in that direction. In the opinion, Judge Posner says the requirements that a meal should be "a real business necessity . . . is most easily satisfied when a client or customer or supplier or other outsider to the business is a guest,"[24] and Judge Sterrett of the Tax Court below noted in a concurrence that in his view the denial of the deductions in this case did follow from the presence of only coworkers.

The taxpayer was one of several law partners, all litigators, who met to discuss ongoing cases more or less every day at cheap Café Angelo near the courthouse. The partnership claimed a deduction for the meal expenses and passed a share of that deduction through to the taxpayer. The IRS denied the deduction, and the Tax Court and Seventh Circuit agreed. Judge Posner concluded that the lawyers' meals were not deductible under the "ordinary and necessary" standard of section 162 and were now disallowed under the putatively higher standard of section 274(a)(1).

---

[23]758 F.2d 211 (7th Cir. 1985).
[24]*Id.* at 213.

(6) Home Office and Vacation Rentals

You can use your home for profit in many ways, but two of the most common are renting it out and maintaining a home office. These two kinds of use are quite separate, even if you set up an office at home in connection with renting another part of the home. All the same, section 280A cleverly combines the rules for sorting out which expenses should be deductible for either.

For both home office and home rental purposes, a single definition of "residence" applies. A dwelling unit is the taxpayer's residence if he or she spends *the greater of* two weeks of the year *or* 10 percent of the number of days the taxpayer does not use the dwelling for personal purposes and the unit is rented out at a fair rent. When only a home office is at issue, the part of this definition dealing with renting the residence will not apply; a dwelling is a residence if the taxpayer is there at least two weeks in the year. Obviously, the clause concerning the ratio of personal use to rental use matters greatly when the issue is the deductibility of second homes and other vacation property.

Some people conduct their professional lives in their homes: doctors, lawyers, independent sales agents, and other independent contractors. It is both fair and tax neutral to allow these and perhaps other groups to deduct business expenses for the partial use of their residences. Section 280A nonetheless takes a severe approach to their predicament. Deductions beyond those available whether the residence is used for business purposes or not are allowed if space in the residence is:

- used as *the* principal place of business for a trade or business of the taxpayer, *or*
- a place of business (perhaps only one among others) routinely used by the taxpayer to meet with patients, clients, or customers, *or*
- located in a separate structure, like a garage, that is not attached to the living space of the residence.

Home office deductions are not allowed for the nonexclusive use of space as *a* place of business or even *the* principal place of business. But more important, these deductions are denied for profit-oriented activities that do not constitute a trade or business. Recall that *Moller v. United States* denied home office deductions to taxpayers whose investment activity did not rise to the level of a trade or business. A separate provision in section 280A(b)(4) accords special treatment to home daycare arrangements, without requiring these to meet the more stringent requirements for home offices.

In *Popov v. Commissioner,*[25] the taxpayer made her living as a violinist with two regular orchestras and as a studio musician for a large number of motion picture contractors. She was required to sight-read the scores she played for the latter. She claimed she used the living room of the one-bedroom apartment she shared with her husband and child exclusively for violin practice, and claimed a deduction for 40 percent of the annual rent and electricity bill under section 280A, contending that the living room was her principal place of business. The Ninth Circuit agreed, reversing the Tax Court, and held that the amount of time spent in the residence was the only relevant factor under section 280A for a profession like the taxpayer's

---

[25]246 F.3d 1190 (9th Cir. 2001).

(presumably also for certain others), in which a product cannot be delivered where it is produced.

Allowable deductions for home offices, daycare operations, and home rentals, however, are more restricted than they would be under sections 162, 168, etc. alone. The business deductions can only equal the gross income derived from the office, daycare, or rental use for the taxable year less nonbusiness deductions allocable to the use and other business deductions allocable to the trade or business or rental activity of which the use is part. The deductions thus curtailed are not permanently disallowed, but can be carried forward to future years.

Strangely, section 280A(e)(1) permits more business-specific deductions to some taxpayers who rent out dwellings. These taxpayers use the dwellings in question personally, but not enough to trigger "residence" classification. Then the business-specific deductions are prorated on an annual basis by the ratio of the number of days the dwelling is rented out to the total number of days it is used by anyone. Notice that this can be a higher fraction of the total business-specific deductions than is allowed under the more complicated formula of section 280A(b)(5).

Section 280A does not affirmatively grant the right to deduct business-related costs; sections 162-168 and 197 do so. From their relationship to each other in the Code, section 280A appears only to limit deductions otherwise putatively allowable under those sections. It is possible, however, to understand section 280A as clarifying the congressional understanding of what constitutes, say, a section 162 expense for the special cases of home offices and residence rentals. The issue of interpretation is complicated by the fact that section 280A allows an exclusion of income — for the gross income from renting out a residence for less than two weeks in a year — but only personal deductions related to the dwelling are allowed for this period, such as home mortgage interest, property taxes, etc. This is equivalent to allowing more expenses to be deducted than could be justified under sections 162-168 and 197 in every instance. Despite this oddly placed exclusion provision, however, section 280A only limits deductions and does not authorize them.

> ## Sidebar
>
> ### SECTIONS 183 AND 280A ARE MUTUALLY EXCLUSIVE
>
> Recall that section 183, dealing with "hobby" activities that have some business characteristics, allows business deductions for some expenses that are not profit seeking. In contrast, section 280A limits business deductions for expenses that *are* profit seeking to amounts that would be deductible under section 183. Could they conflict in their application to the same fact pattern? Section 280A(f)(3) specifically prevents any such conflict; it provides that if section 280A(a) applies to the use of a residence for a given year, section 183 does not apply. Hence, deductions for the business use of a residence cannot enjoy more favorable treatment under section 183.

(7) Litigation Expenses

In *United States v. Gilmore*,[26] the Supreme Court held that a taxpayer's litigation expenses in resisting his wife's claim to a community property share of his controlling interests in several car dealerships were not deductible under section 212(2) as expenses related to a profit-seeking activity. The Court held that "the availability of [either a section 162 or a section 212] deduction is that the expense item involved

---

[26]372 U.S. 39 (1963).

must be one that has a business origin."[27] Putting it slightly differently, the Court also said that whether litigation costs are deductible "depends on whether or not the claim *arises in connection with* the taxpayer's profit-seeking activities."[28] Earlier cases had said the same thing: In *Lykes v. United States*,[29] legal expenses incurred to resist liability for gift tax were not deductible, even if the tax might have required the taxpayer to liquidate stockholdings that were his main source of income; in *Kornhauser v. United States*,[30] the taxpayer *was* allowed to deduct litigation expenses for his defense against a former partner's claim that certain fees the taxpayer had earned were partnership income rather than his own separate income.

The "origin of the claim" doctrine, as *Gilmore's* holding is sometimes called, is not easy to apply in other situations. We may well wonder how the Court would have come out on a hybrid of the facts of *Gilmore* and *Kornhauser*. Would a taxpayer be allowed to deduct his legal costs for resisting his ex-wife's claims to a greater share of income from their family partnership? As we saw in Chapter 10, family relations are often not profit oriented, but sometimes are.

SUMMARY

■ The income tax law sharply distinguishes profit-seeking expenses from personal expenses, even when the motives for incurring an expense are mixed; the classification of expenses is therefore sometimes arbitrary.

■ Sections 162 and 212 permit taxpayers to deduct the ordinary and necessary expenses of two types of income-producing activity: trade or business activity and investment activity. The Code, however, does not define "trade or business," and provides only an incomplete definition of investment activity to which section 212 applies.

■ Expenses incurred to provide a taxpayer with the necessities of employment are generally deductible under section 162 unless they confer personal or family benefits. Thus, tools to be used on the job are deductible but commuting, clothing, and childcare costs related to employment are not. The Code now makes childcare excludible or creditable by special provision.

■ Section 274 disallows deductions for some gift, travel, and entertainment expenses that section 162 would otherwise allow. It disallows the deduction for business meals unless a business conversation takes place during or just before or after the meal, and even then allows only 50 percent of their cost to be deducted in most cases. The business gift deduction is limited to $25 per donee per year. The cost of travel for an accompanying spouse is deductible only if the spouse is an employee of the business, the business purpose is substantial and bona fide, and the spouse could have deducted the expense.

■ Under section 183, activities that are not regularly profitable are presumed to be for profit if they make money in three out of five years, ending with the year for which the return is filed; otherwise, however, business deductions are allowed

---

[27]*Id.* at 42.
[28]*Id.* at 44 (emphasis in original).
[29]343 U.S. 118 (1952).
[30]276 US. 145 (1928).

even without a profit motive up to the amount of revenue minus other non-business-specific deductions.

■ Business deductions like depreciation and utilities are allowed for home offices only if the taxpayer has her principal place of business there, regularly meets clients or customers in the home office, or is in a separate structure not attached to the living space of the residence. Home daycare is less restricted.

■ Commuting expense is not deductible. Transportation is deductible. Travel, while away from home overnight for business reasons, includes what would otherwise be deductible transportation, but also other personal living expenses of the trip.

■ Litigation expenses are deductible under section 162 only if the claim arises in connection with a business activity.

CONNECTIONS

Business Expenses and Personal Benefit
Judicial and administrative interpretations of sections 162 attempts to distinguish sharply between items for which a business deduction under section 162 can be claimed and items of personal consumption. Nevertheless, the business expenses of employees are subject to the same restrictions as other miscellaneous itemized deductions and can only be claimed on Schedule A. See Chapter 13.G. If an employer provides an employee with a benefit in kind, the cost of which the employee could have deducted as a business expense under section 162 if the employee had paid for it herself, the benefit is excluded from the employee's income as a "working condition" fringe under section 132(a)(3). See Chapter 2.F.

Business Gifts
Case law under section 102 leaves open the possibility that excludible gifts may be given for a business purpose, but section 274 denies the donor taxpayer any deduction under section 162 for gifts aggregating more than $25 per donee in a taxable year, effectively scotching the urge for businesses to grease the wheels of business by making gifts to business associates. See Chapter 4.C. Section 102(b) expressly denies gift status to transfers from an employer to an employee.

Record-Keeping for Business Meals and Entertainment
Section 274 makes the keeping of specific records of names and business conversation topics a prerequisite of section 162 deductions for business meals and entertainment. See Chapter 13.G.

Relationship Between Sections 183 and 280A

Although section 183, dealing with "hobby" activities that have some business characteristics, allows business deductions for some expenses that are not profit seeking, section 280A limits business deductions for residence-related expenses to amounts that would be deductible under section 183, even if the activity were not profit oriented. Section 280A(f)(3), however, provides that section 280A supersedes section 183 when the two sections might otherwise apply to the same fact pattern. Compare this with how sections 1245 and 1250 override section 1231. See Chapter 15.H.

Itemized (Mainly Personal) Deductions

13

OVERVIEW

The income tax falls short of its promises in various ways. There is no better example than the deductibility of personal expenses that are not even remotely profit oriented. Quite a few personal deductions are allowed, and all are now settled features of the tax landscape. We taxpayers love them dearly, of course. The home mortgage interest deduction, which has no direct role in measuring income, is a sacred cow, beyond the reach of any but the most theoretical opposition. Other personal deductions have proved similarly stubborn in their hold on grassroots support. They include deductions for casualty losses, medical expenses, interest paid, certain state taxes, and charitable contributions. A few other miscellaneous expenses, including employee business expenses and individual taxpayers' investment expenses, are also lumped together with itemized deductions, although not all miscellaneous expenses are personal in nature. Collectively, they reduce adjusted gross income after personal exemptions and a variety of exclusions from income are taken into account. Some are subject to specific limitations, such as the limitation of miscellaneous expenses to those in excess of 2 percent of AGI. No single itemized deduction, however, saves a taxpayer money unless their total amount exceeds the standard deduction. If their total is below that threshold, they have no tax effect, because the standard deduction takes their place and would be available regardless of the amount of the taxpayer's personal deductions. See Figure 13.1 for an illustration of the limitations of itemized deductions.

A.   DEDUCTIONS ABOVE AND BELOW THE LINE

B.   MEDICAL EXPENSES

C.   CASUALTY LOSSES

D.   HOME MORTGAGE AND EQUITY LOAN INTEREST

E.   STATE TAXES

F.   CHARITABLE CONTRIBUTIONS

G.   MISCELLANEOUS ITEMIZED EXPENSES

H.   PERSONAL (NON-ITEMIZED) EXEMPTIONS

I.   ALIMONY, CERTAIN RETIREMENT SAVINGS INVESTMENTS

A. Deductions Above and Below the Line

Itemized deductions, unlike those subtracted in calculating AGI, do not invariably lower net taxable income. Several are instead first reduced by an amount equal to a percentage of the taxpayer's AGI. The remaining sum of itemized deductions is then compared with the **standard deduction**, a minimum amount by which AGI is reduced for every taxpayer. Only the greater of the two is deducted. The standard deduction varies from year to year and differs markedly for single and joint filers; the IRS website and page two of the current year's Form 1040 are convenient places to find its current amount.

    Given that everyone is entitled to reduce AGI by the standard deduction, itemized expenses may not reduce the tax to be paid. A deduction of $1,000 for allowable moving expenses reduces the tax owed by a taxpayer in the 10 percent marginal bracket by $100, but a deduction of $1,000 for medical expenses reduces the tax owed by the same taxpayer by less than $100 at most, because medical expenses are deductible only to the extent that they exceed 7.5 percent of the taxpayer's AGI. If the taxpayer's AGI is $20,000, no deduction at all is allowed, because $1,000 is less than $1,500, or 7.5 percent of $20,000. AGI would have to be less than $13,333 for any of the medical expense to be deductible. Even then, the taxpayer would save no taxes by reason of the medical expense deduction unless he or she had other allowable itemized deductions in excess of $5,700 for a single filer or $11,400 for joint filers. Obviously, someone with AGI as low as $13,333 may not be able to spend so much on deductible personal items—food and rent, for example, are not deductible.

    Broadly speaking, taxpayers benefit most from itemizing in the first decade or so after buying a home with a mortgage. Mortgage interest is often substantial, and property taxes are also

Sidebar

TAX EXPENDITURES

Recall that an income tax reduction for a reason other than the correct measurement of income is a tax expenditure. Stanley Surrey and Paul McDaniel coined this term.[1] There are many tax expenditure provisions in the Code. In effect, tax law is used for a purpose that direct government spending could have achieved more directly. The contrast between "the correct measurement of income" and other purposes has proven to be controversial. Nevertheless, Congress requires the presidential budget proposal to include a tax expenditure analysis of all provisions of the Code. Personal deductions are routinely cited as tax expenditures.

---

[1]See Stanley S. Surrey & Paul R. McDaniel, *Tax Expenditures* (1985).

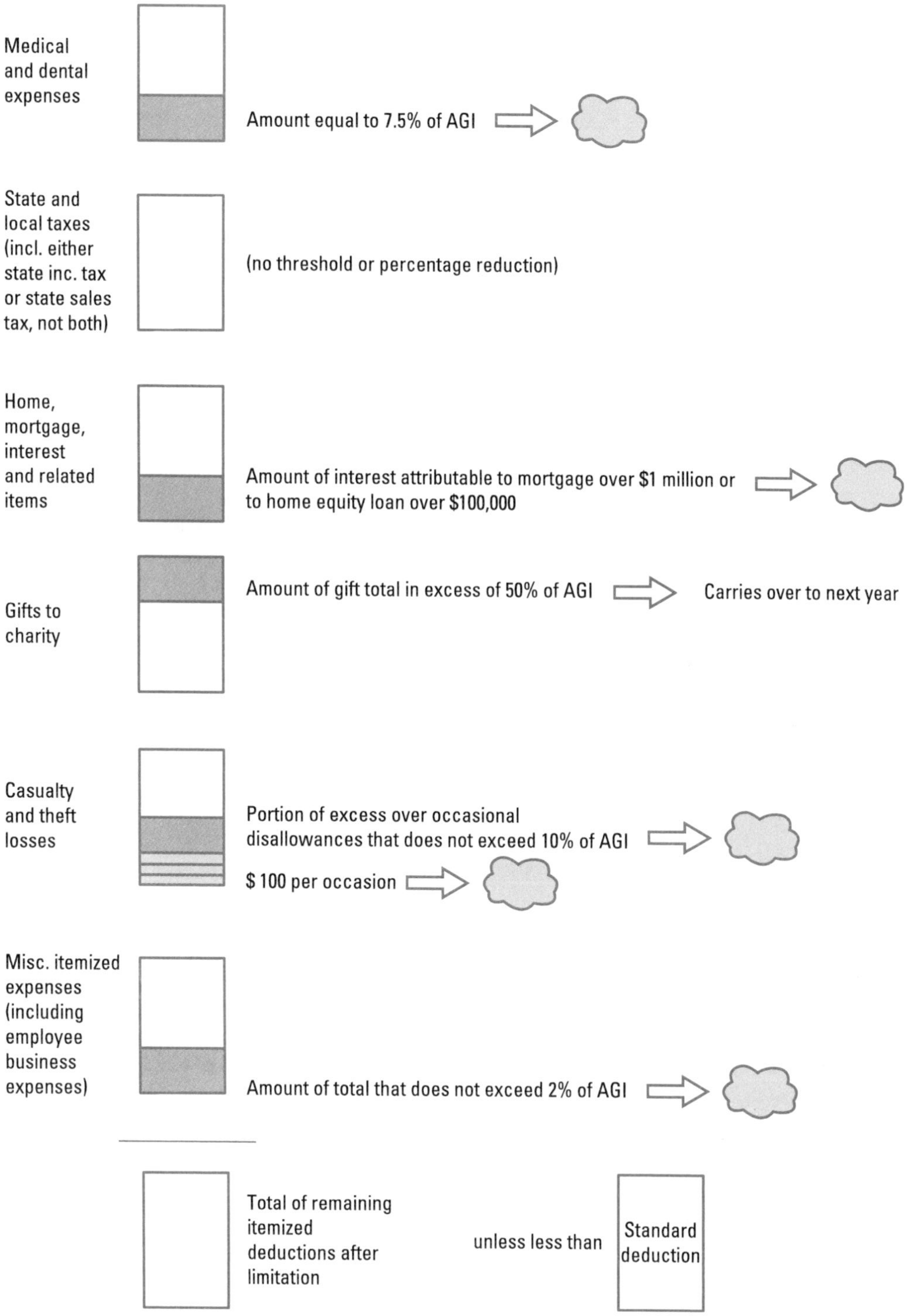

Medical and dental expenses

Amount equal to 7.5% of AGI ⇒

State and local taxes (incl. either state inc. tax or state sales tax, not both)

(no threshold or percentage reduction)

Home, mortgage, interest and related items

Amount of interest attributable to mortgage over $1 million or to home equity loan over $100,000 ⇒

Gifts to charity

Amount of gift total in excess of 50% of AGI ⇒ Carries over to next year

Casualty and theft losses

Portion of excess over occasional disallowances that does not exceed 10% of AGI ⇒

$ 100 per occasion ⇒

Misc. itemized expenses (including employee business expenses)

Amount of total that does not exceed 2% of AGI ⇒

Total of remaining itemized deductions after limitation

unless less than

Standard deduction

FIGURE 13.1 **THE LIMITATIONS OF ITEMIZED DEDUCTIONS, APART FROM SECTION 68 PHASE-OUT**

deductible, so that in most cases, the combined deductions will get the taxpayer over the threshold of the standard deduction.

Example 13.1: A single taxpayer in the 28 percent bracket who pays a combined $30,000 in mortgage interest and property tax on a home can deduct the excess of this amount over the standard deduction (about $5,000). The amount saved in taxes is $7,840.[2]

Since deductions related to home ownership usually exceed the standard deduction, they virtually guarantee that other personal deductions will yield a tax benefit as well. Home ownership is more common in the higher tax brackets. The effect of these deductions is generally to make the nominal tax rates applicable to higher incomes less progressive that they appear. As we have noted elsewhere, the value of a deduction depends on the tax rate, with proportionately more tax being saved, the higher the applicable tax rate.

Example 13.2: A charitable contribution of $1,000 benefits a 10 percent bracket taxpayer by at most $100 in taxes avoided; the same contribution usually can benefit a 28 percent bracket taxpayer by $280 in taxes avoided.

Deductions, unlike credits, operate as upside-down subsidies, benefiting higher-income taxpayer more than lower-income taxpayers. If the deductions are intended to operate as incentives or benefits, it is not clear why they should grow with increasing marginal income. But some of them, arguably, do not or should not incentivize spending. Medical expenses, which we consider next, do not warrant compassionate subsidies that vary with gross income, and they should not require incentive subsidies either.

B. Medical Expenses

Section 213 allows a deduction for medical expenses that are not reimbursed by insurance, to the extent that they exceed 7.5 percent of the taxpayer's AGI. These include expenses for "medical care," defined with some specificity as "amounts paid . . . for the diagnosis, cure, mitigation, treatment, or prevention of disease, or for the purpose of affecting any structure or function of the body," as well as related transportation, prescription drugs, and certain qualified long-term care. Dental expenses come under the rubric of "amounts paid . . . for the purpose of affecting any structure or function of the body." Insurance for medical care, as defined, and for long-term care are also deductible. The 7.5 percent threshold is so high that most medical expenses, though deductible, yield no tax benefit.

The exclusion of the value of employer-provided health and accident insurance (§106) and of the benefits received under such insurance contracts (§104(a)(3)) plays a larger role than the medical expense deduction and costs the government a huge amount in tax revenue forgone.[3]

---

[2]The alternative minimum tax or AMT further limits the tax benefit of itemized deductions for some taxpayers. The taxpayer's income is recalculated without certain itemized deductions and personal exemptions and the new income amount (AMT income) faces a lower but still high tax rate. See Code sections 55-59.
[3]See Chapter 3.C.

Example 13.3: Able and Baker are ill. Able's employer provides comprehensive health insurance as an employment benefit. Baker works for an employer that does not offer this benefit and buys insurance directly for herself and her family. Able is not required to report the health insurance provided by his employer as gross income on his Form 1040. Baker is entitled to deduct the cost of her insurance on Schedule A as a medical expense, but its cost does not exceed 7.5 percent of her AGI, and so she effectively pays tax on her insurance because she buys it with after-tax dollars.

It is often said that the rationale of permitting medical expenses to be deducted is to avoid counting the restoration of health or bodily function as a positive addition to the taxpayer's well-being. Taxpayers who must pay to maintain the same basic health that others enjoy without cost are not better off in comparison. Obviously, the AGI-based threshold does not square with this rationale. Any threshold burdens the very loss of good health that the medical expense deduction should eliminate. A threshold that rises with income would be justified only if a substantial part of medical care was a form of consumption, the purchase of *un*necessary treatment. Before 1986, the medical expense deduction was *not* subject to the AGI-based threshold, and the Tax Reform Act of 1986 apparently created the threshold, not for reasons of principle, but simply to pay for tax cuts elsewhere.

Section 213 does not say that only necessary medical care is deductible, but the courts appear to use a necessity test of sorts in deciding whether expenses for incidental or collateral health-care costs are deductible. In *Ochs v. Commissioner*, the Second Circuit disallowed the deduction of boarding school fees for the taxpayers' children, incurred after the wife had a throat operation and could not deal with the young children's demands.[4] The court's reasoning echoed that of *Smith v. Commissioner*,[5] in which childcare was treated as so indelibly a "family" expense that the court refused to acknowledge its necessity as a business expense for both parents to work outside the home. Despite the courts' vagaries, medical necessity is not the issue.

The inclusion of "transportation" expenses as a deductible medical expense seemed to the Supreme Court to mean that "travel" in the sense of section 162 is *not* deductible under section 213, because travel and transportation are nonoverlapping concepts for purposes of both sections.[6] In *Commissioner v. Bilder*,[7] a specialist advised the taxpayer, a survivor of four heart attacks, to spend the winter in a warm climate. The taxpayer followed that advice, moving his family to Florida for several winter months in the two next years. The Court classified the stays in Florida as travel rather than transportation and disallowed the deduction.

C. Casualty Losses

The subtraction of losses is essential in measuring net income, but Code section 165(c) restricts the deductibility of personal losses to those arising from theft or casualty that exceed 10 percent of AGI in the aggregate, with the first $100 of each loss being barred from the calculation.

---

[4]195 F.2d 692 (2d Cir. 1952).
[5]See Chapter 12.D(2)(a).
[6]See Chapter 12.D(3)(d).
[7]369 U.S. 499 (1962).

Example 13.4: Thieves break into James's apartment ten times in the course of a year, stealing small electronic devices such as radios and toasters, none of which cost more than $100. The same thieves break into Richard's apartment only once during the year, stealing a sound system that cost $1,000. James and Richard are both students, each with an AGI of only $5,000. James cannot deduct any of his theft losses, because each is worth less than $100. Richard, however, can deduct a loss of $400 (= $1,000 loss − $100 per casualty exclusion − $500 AGI-based exclusion).

Sidebar

PERSONAL LOSSES AND THE DEFINITION OF INCOME

Although the deduction may at first glance seem minor from a policy perspective, the subtraction of *all* losses from gross enrichment, personal and profit oriented alike, is a fundamental feature of the income tax. Henry Simons argued that utility theory, used in the "ability to pay" view of income, is only camouflage for political or "aesthetic" judgments about tax rates. To prevent utility analysis from playing any part in his own definition of income, he insisted on limiting income to the increase in an individual's economic power, that is, the individual's ability to control market-traded resources over a given period of time.[9] Since losses reduce economic power, just as additions to wealth increase it, losses should in principle be subtracted from income. Despite the popularity of the SHS definition of income in scholarly commentary and its occasional influence on concrete proposals for refining the income tax, Congress takes a different view.

---

[9]See Chapter 2.D.

The restriction of personal losses to theft or casualty losses lessens the taxpayer's control over the classification of losses. One can still claim to "lose" discarded items but it is fraud to do so. Theft and casualty losses must be both sudden and traceable to events beyond the taxpayer's control. This distinguishes them from the normal consumption of consumer durables — refrigerators, TVs, furniture, education — whose value is gradually exhausted. Yet suddenness does not give the most plausible verdict as to the genuineness of a loss in all situations. The destruction of a house by termites is gradual, yet the loss is akin to that caused by storms and earthquakes. The IRS, however, holds firm to suddenness as the ultimate criterion.[8]

It stands to reason that a deductible loss *cannot exceed the taxpayer's basis* in the loss property. No disposition of property can produce a tax loss greater than the property's basis. In this and every other sense, basis is the limit of the owner's tax investment in the property. Thus, if a taxpayer holds property with a basis of $100 and the property is stolen, $100 is the taxpayer's loss for tax purposes, even if the property had a higher market value when lost.

D. Home Mortgage and Equity Loan Interest

Although interest on borrowing for business and investment purposes is deductible (with an exception for interest on loans to produce tax-exempt income), the same is no longer true for personal interest. Before 1986, the Code allowed the deduction of all personal interest: interest on credit card balances, time purchase of home

---

[8]Rev. Rul. 79-174, 1979-1 C.B. 99 (loss of ornamental trees to insect damage was not sudden and therefore not deductible as a casualty loss).

appliances, and so forth. Since then, only certain home mortgage interest has been deductible.

Today, section 163(h) allows interest on qualified residences' mortgages to be deducted within certain limits. The interest deduction is in two parts. The more generous part allows only interest incurred to buy or improve one or two residences to be deducted, and the maximum amount on which this interest is deductible cannot exceed $1 million. One of the residences must be the taxpayer's (or taxpayers') principal residence, and the other a residence as defined in section 280A(d)(1), dealing with home offices and short-term letting of taxpayers' residences. To ensure that the money is actually spent on acquiring or improving the residence, only interest on an amount equal to the taxpayer's purchase money mortgage plus the cost of an improvements is deductible if the owner refinances. The other part of the deduction is for private equity loans of up to $100,000, which need not be used to acquire or improve the residence that secures the borrowing. The regulations provide an elaborate tracing rule for determining how much of the outstanding mortgage principal belongs to each of these categories, when both exist.

Example 13.5: Kane borrows $1 million with a mortgage to purchase his home. He then borrows $100,000 with a second mortgage — a home equity loan — and uses the proceeds to purchase a boat for recreation. The interest on both loans is deductible, even though the second loan is not used for the purchase or improvement of Kane's home. If Kane had owned the home outright and borrowed $1.1 million for the boat purchase, only the interest on $100,000 of the loan would have been deductible.

SHOULD INTEREST BE DEDUCTIBLE?

It is perhaps natural to consider interest on loans to be an additional cost of whatever the borrowed funds pay for. Hence, a taxpayer who borrows to pay an ordinary and necessary business or investment expense should be able to deduct the interest, and a taxpayer who borrows to pay for consumption should not. Yet arguments about tax neutrality (going back to John Stuart Mill) have persuaded some income tax experts that the interest earned by savings should not be taxed, because this might influence the taxpayer's decision whether to consume now or to save for later consumption. If this line of thought is taken seriously, consumption financed by borrowing should not be burdened by tax either. The only way to accomplish that is to allow consumer interest to be deducted. As one economist has put it, interest is "negative income" and so should be subtracted, just as increments of gross income are added, to a person's real income.[10] Under our income tax, consumer interest was fully deductible until 1986, when Congress restricted the deduction to home mortgage interest for the first time.

[10]Melvin I. White, *Proper Income Tax Treatment of Deductions for Personal Expense*, House Comm. on Ways and Means, 86th Cong., 1st Sess., 1 Tax Revision Compendium 365-366 (Comm. Print 1959); see Stanley A. Koppelman, *Personal Deductions Under an Ideal Income Tax*, 43 Tax L. Rev. 679 (1987-1988).

E. State Taxes

By tradition more than constitutional necessity, Congress chooses not to tax income used to pay certain state taxes. Code section 164(a) implements this policy by allowing income taxes and real and personal property taxes imposed at the state or local level as an itemized deduction. Foreign income and real property taxes are also deductible. The scope of the deduction, however, is not sacrosanct. In 1986, Congress repealed the long-standing deductibility of state sales taxes, leaving only property and state income tax on the list of deductible state taxes. Later, section 164(h) reinstated the deduction for the sales taxes of states that do not impose an income tax, so that residents of all states can now deduct either income or sales taxes. This achieves a rough parity of treatment for residents of states without their own income taxes.

Example 13.6: A sales tax of 6 percent applies to all retail consumer purchases in the State of Horizonia, which has no income tax. Horizonia residents are permitted to deduct their actual sales taxes paid, or an estimated amount based on guidelines provided with their federal income tax materials. New York residents, however, are not allowed to deduct their sales taxes, which reach 12 percent in parts of the state, because they pay the New York income tax, which is allowed as an itemized deduction for federal income tax purposes.

F. Charitable Contributions

Section 170(b) permits the deduction for gifts to certain types of charitable organizations. These include **public charities**, certain governmental organizations and organizations with government support, certain veterans' organizations and fraternal societies, and cemetery companies operated for the benefit of their members. The term "public charity" is shorthand used by tax professionals for charitable organizations described in section 501(c)(3) of the Code. Typical organizations of this type are churches, hospitals, universities, and other institutions that provide public benefit without limitation to a narrowly defined class of beneficiaries. Their statutory description requires them to be organized and operated exclusively for "religious, charitable, scientific, testing for public safety, literary, or educational purposes, or to foster national or international amateur sports competition . . . , or for the prevention of cruelty to children or animals." No part of the net earnings of a section 501(c)(3) organization can "inure" to the benefit of any private shareholder or individual, and no substantial part of its activities can consist in promoting specific legislation or supporting campaigns for political office.

F   A   Q

Q: Are contributions to any section 501(c)(3) organizations *not* deductible, even within the percentage limits applicable to the donor?

A: With only one exception, the language used to describe eligible recipients of deductible contributions exactly matches that used in section 501(c)(3). Section 170(c) allows the deduction of contributions to organizations otherwise described in section 501(c)(3) only if the contribution is to be *used* in the United States or one of its possessions for one of the organization's exempt purposes. A contribution to an exempt organization might therefore not be deductible if the organization uses it abroad. In practice, however, the IRS recognizes the exemption of many section 501(c)(3) organizations that make contributions or grants to support activities of other organizations abroad (not in U.S. possessions). There is no indication that the IRS would disallow the deduction of a contribution to such organizations.

The charitable contribution deduction is limited to 50 percent of the donor's AGI for the year in most cases, with a carryover of the unused gift amount as a deduction to be used in one or more of the next five years (§170(d)). (The AGI limitation is lower for gifts to certain donees, as will be explained further below.) The range of eligible donees is limited to organizations only. Gifts to individuals do not qualify, even if funneled through an eligible donee subject to restriction for the benefit of a specific individual. Eligible donees usually know better than to go along with such a scheme.[11]

What should count as a contribution has occasionally spawned litigation. In *Ottawa Silica Co. v. United States*,[12] what clearly amounted to a gift for state law purposes was held not to be a charitable contribution for federal tax purposes. The would-be charitable contributor was a mining company that gave land for a high school to a school district, knowing that to build the high school, the school district would have to build roads that would benefit the mining company. The court agreed with the government in denying a charitable contribution deduction.

The most peculiar feature of the charitable deduction is that gifts of capital gain property can qualify for deduction at full value if that exceeds the contributor's basis in the property. This generous treatment, delineated in section 170(e), is not available for some capital asset contributions—patents and other intellectual property, as well as any tangible property the recipient charity does not use in its primary activities or disposes of within two years. Also excluded is property that would yield ordinary income at disposition, and the ordinary-income portion of any gain on property that yields both ordinary and capital gain (again, some business property may qualify for favorable capital gain treatment on only part of its appreciation at disposition). However, capital gain property otherwise includes property that would yield long-term capital gain and property used in a trade or business if part of the gain would be taxed as long-term capital gain under section 1231.[13] To complete the picture, it must be added that the charitable contributions are not treated as realization events, so that a contributor does have income in the amount of the appreciation portion of the value of donated capital gain property.

Sidebar

CONTRIBUTIONS AND PRIVATE INUREMENT

Section 170(b) makes deductions to many section 501(c)(3) organizations deductible. If a contribution would be deductible only if the recipient is described in section 501(c)(3), it is important that the description includes the provision that "no part of [the organization's] net earnings . . . inures to the private benefit of any shareholder or individual." The IRS interprets the so-called private inurement restriction broadly, so broadly that it could apply to a nongovernmental entity whose activities indirectly benefited the contributor, such as how the building of a road benefited the contributor in *Ottawa Silica*.

---

[11]There is an exception for gifts in the form of maintaining in the taxpayer's household a primary or secondary school student who is not a dependent, if an agreement with an exempt organization that sponsors students in private homes; the deduction is limited to $50 times the number of months the student is there. §170(g).

[12]699 F.2d 1124 (Fed. Cir. 1983).

[13]See Chapter 14 on section 1231 and on capital assets generally.

F   A   Q

Q: Given that the full value of some appreciated assets is deductible as a charitable contribution, why is the same not true for all assets without restriction?

A: The holders of capital assets typically choose how and when to dispose of them by considering what the after-tax economic yield will be. Holders of property used in business or held for consumption usually have non-tax reasons for making these decisions. The tax preference for capital asset contributions to charity is therefore likely to be more effective as an incentive.

The deductibility of the unrealized gain portion of capital assets obviously conflicts with the principle alluded to in Section C on casualty loss deductions. Normally, for realization purposes, the taxpayer's basis is his or her tax investment in the property, and a greater amount cannot be deducted in the case of loss disposition or casualty. We might expect that something like this should also apply to charitable contributions, namely, that contributors should reap no greater deduction benefit than they might have been entitled to if the property were simply taken from them by a thief or hurricane. The charitable contribution rule, however, is evidently designed to tempt owners of capital gain property to give it to charity by attaching an exceptional tax benefit. In some instances, it certainly is more likely that a potential donor will voluntarily part with property (say, a vastly appreciated work of art) by giving it to charity (a museum) if the alternative is to sell the property for a smaller after-tax benefit.

Example 13.7: A taxpayer who would pay 35 percent of any additional income in income tax may be tempted to gift a $1 million parcel of land to a conservancy trust for a $350,000 tax saving than for a $100,000 saving. If the taxpayer has a basis of only $100,000 in the land, the special treatment of capital gain contributions creates exactly this incentive.

Donors with higher incomes are more likely to own capital gain property and are therefore more likely to benefit from the special tax subsidy. The less wealthy more often make contributions in cash and so are not eligible for it. Donors who do not itemize, of course, get *no* tax benefit for their contributions. This apparently top-down program of incentives has come in for frequent criticism. Charities and their advisors have often mounted campaigns to preserve it against threatened extinction. Since there would be no personal deductions under a pure income tax, the policy issue here is whether the tax system should be used to create an incentive that has nothing to do with the operation of the tax as such. The charitable contribution deduction, however, is more clearly an example of an intended government subsidy implemented through the tax laws than are many other tax expenditures.

One of the most important limits on this deduction is the prohibition against "private inurement." The definition of just one kind of eligible charitable donee carries this prohibition. It is the traditional public charity, referred to in almost identical language in sections 170(c)(2)(C) and 501(c)(3), one of whose essential traits is that no part of its income can inure "to the benefit of any private shareholder or individual." *United Cancer Council, Inc. v. Commissioner*[14] arose when the IRS revoked the Cancer Council's recognition as a section 501(c)(3) organization. The IRS action was based on the relationship between the Cancer Council and its professional fundraiser, Watson & Hughey Co., which succeeded in raising gross contributions of $28.8 million in exchange for fees of $26.5 million. The government regarded this as the tail wagging the dog, sufficiently to count as private inurement, even though the boards and employees of the charity and the fundraiser were not overlapping. The Tax Court agreed, but the Seventh Circuit, with Judge Posner writing the opinion, reversed on the grounds that there was no "siphoning of receipts to insiders of the charity," which the court considered the essential element in private inurement.

G. Miscellaneous Itemized Expenses

Business, investment, and tax-related expenses of employees are disallowed to the same extent as some personal expenses. The disfavored employee business expenses include travel, home office, business meals, and similar expenses that would be fully deductible for a self-employed taxpayer. Investment expenses such as safe deposit box rent, the price of tax software, a tax accountant's or lawyer's fee, even the cost of obtaining a tax ruling from the IRS, all of which are deductible under section 212, are also subject to partial disallowance. Like the threshold for the deductibility of casualty and theft losses, an AGI-based threshold makes a portion of employee business and investment expenses nondeductible, even if together with other personal deductions they exceed the standard deduction threshold.

Note that sections 62(a)(15) and 217 make moving expenses for employment or other business purposes deductible above the line. This category of expense escapes the less favorable treatment of other employee business expenses. The difference can be explained in part by the fact that moving expenses are relatively unusual in most taxpayers' lives and can also be quite large in relation to the modest incomes of many employees. Their disproportionate amount sets them apart from recurring work-related expenses. They pose less of an administrative problem and may also be worthy of special treatment as a tax expenditure, for labor mobility.

F A Q

Q: Are the expenses of moving to a new location for a first job deductible?

A: Yes. The Tax Court rejected an initial IRS interpretation that one must already be employed to claim qualifying moving expense deductions under section 217. The court reasoned that the purpose of the deduction is to remove the tax burden from moving expenses for the sake of employment, and prior employment is irrelevant to this legislative purpose.

The policy behind the threshold disallowance for miscellaneous itemized deductions may be that there are too many small expenses here to justify the administrative expense of auditing them. To avoid unfairness to the honest, low levels of these deductions are simply denied.

---

[14]165 F.3d 1173 (7th Cir. 1999).

The requirements for deductibility under sections 162 and 212 are otherwise the same for employee expenses as for those of the self-employed.[15] We should note that the threshold for employee business deductions dovetails with section 132(a)(3) to cause inequity. If an employer provides tools to an employee who could have deducted the cost if she had bought them for herself, this "working condition fringe benefit" is excluded from the employee's gross income. An employee who must buy the tools for herself benefits from deducting the cost only if, when added to other miscellaneous deductions, they exceed 2 percent of the taxpayer's AGI.

H. Personal (Non-Itemized) Exemptions

Another purely personal deduction escapes the second-class status of the itemized deductions. Taxpayers are allowed deductions called personal exemptions, measured in most instances by the number of members of the taxpayer's or jointly filing taxpayers' household and other dependents. These are discussed more fully in Chapter 11.B(2).

Personal exemptions or their equivalent exist in most income tax systems to protect the necessities of life from any tax burden. Historically, the purpose of the income tax was to prevent duplicative taxes on people's basic subsistence needs and to prevent the poor from complaining of their disenfranchisement. By contrast, other personal deductions are usually regarded as tax expenditures rather than as adjustments whose purpose is intrinsic to the structure of the income tax. This difference between personal exemptions and the other personal deductions may explain why the former are above-the-line reductions of gross income not subject to the restrictions and partial disallowance to which itemized deductions are subject.

I. Alimony, Certain Retirement Savings Investments

Certain other personal expenses also escape the disfavored treatment of itemized deductions, though for different reasons. Alimony is income shifted from one taxpayer to another with the state's approval.[16] Sections 62(a)(10) and 215 allow the payor of alimony to deduct it to from gross income above the line, and section 61(a)(8) requires the recipient to add it to gross income. Considered together, it is as if the money had been earned by the payee rather than by the payor. The result does no harm to the purposes of the income tax, given society's decision that the income should be regarded as that of one ex-spouse rather than the other.

Under complex rules contained in sections 401 et seq., contributions by taxpayers to their own retirement investment vehicles are deductible if these satisfy requirements intended to avoid abuse and ensure comparability with employer-funded investment trusts. The rationale is the same as that of permitting employers to deduct their contributions to employees' investment trusts, while excluding the economic benefit of these contributions from the employees' gross income—the

---

[15]See Chapter 12.A and B.
[16]See Chapter 11.D(2).

specially ordained tax treatment of employer-sponsored retirement plans that meet a host of requirements ensures income for retirees and postpones tax on that income until the golden years.

SUMMARY

- Deductions for a limited number of personal consumption items are subject to various thresholds and ceilings. Because the standard deduction is available in the absence of itemized deductions, only personal deductions that exceed the standard deduction yield a tax benefit.

- Medical expenses must exceed 7.5 percent of AGI to be deductible; casualty losses, with a $100 per incident exclusion, must exceed 10 percent of AGI; employee business expense and miscellaneous deductions must collectively exceed 2 percent of AGI.

- Home mortgage interest on a maximum of $1 million in purchase or improvement loans for one or two residences and interest on $100,000 more in equity loans that need not be used for purchase or improvement of the residences are deductible.

- State, local, and foreign income and real property taxes are deductible, as are state and local personal property taxes, and state sales taxes are deductible if the state has no income tax.

- Charitable contributions of up to 50 percent of AGI are deductible, with a ten-year carryover of any excess amount.

CONNECTIONS

Working Condition Fringe Exclusion and Employee Business Expense Deduction

To qualify for exclusion under section 132(a)(3), a working condition fringe must be a benefit to an employee who could have deducted the benefit if she had paid for it. The exclusion, however, gives the employee the benefit of untaxed value even if the employee would *not* have had a tax benefit on deducting the paid-for equivalent, by virtue of the standard deduction and the percentage limitation on employee business expenses. See Chapter 3.F.

Casualty Loss Deduction Versus Exclusion of Insurance Payments and Recoveries

Gross income does not include payments a taxpayer receives under an insurance contract to cover a loss, whether it is a casualty loss or not. Insurance benefits and recoveries from third parties for personal physical injuries or as workers' compensation are also excluded. The taxpayer who suffers an uninsured loss or injury unrelated to a profit-seeking activity and who does not recover from a third party can only deduct the loss in the case of theft or casualty. See Chapter 4.D.

Medical Expense Deduction Versus Damages for Injuries

A taxpayer who pays her own medical expenses out of pocket gets tax relief only if the amount exceeds 7.5 percent of her AGI. The litigant who received damages for physical injury, including medical costs, and the employee who obtains a workers' compensation award are allowed to exclude the amounts received under section 104(a). The exclusion is equivalent to a deduction.

Capital Assets and the Charitable Contribution Deduction

Capital assets are primarily assets held for investment, that is, neither for consumption nor for business use. Section 1221 contains the precise definition that identifies assets, the fair market value of which can be deducted without recognition of inherent gain. See Chapter 14.A.

Capital Gains and Losses

14

Income from most property held for more than one year and neither used nor sold in the ordinary course of a trade or business is taxed at lower

OVERVIEW

rates than ordinary income. Capital gain, as we call this income, merits special treatment for two reasons. First, gains and losses from the other kinds of property are taxed in special ways related to their role in continuing business activity. Property not held for sale but *used in* business is insulated from a tax burden that might otherwise change managerial decisions. Gain from selling inventory is income of the most ordinary variety, flowing as it does from ongoing human effort — think of the mom-and-pop grocery. Two factors are often cited as grounds for the lower rates for gains from capital assets held long-term: the possible distortion of the amount of these gains by inflation, and the bunching of slowly accrued gain into amounts that would otherwise be taxable at higher marginal rates than equal gains incrementally realized in smaller amounts. The qualifying holding period for such "long-term" treatment, now one year, has been as short as 6 months and as long as 18. In this chapter, we examine the definition of "capital asset," rules that ensure the netting of gains and losses from capital assets held for different periods of time, and other safeguards against abuse of the capital gain preference. There are in fact different tax rates for various kinds of capital gains, and we briefly consider this complex set of rates at the end of the chapter.

A. WHAT A CAPITAL ASSET IS NOT

1. Property Held Primarily for Sale to Customers in the Ordinary Course of Business
2. Depreciable Property and Land Used in a Trade or Business

3. Literary Compositions, Letters, Etc.
4. Notes and Accounts Receivable
5. Government Publications
6. Commodities Derivatives in the Hands of a Dealer
7. Hedging Operation Instruments
8. Supplies

B. PROBLEMS IN CLASSIFYING CAPITAL ASSETS

C. APPLYING THE CAPITAL GAINS TAX RATES TO MULTIPLE CAPITAL ASSET TRANSACTIONS

D. MULTIPLE TAX RATES FOR DIFFERENT KINDS OF LONG-TERM CAPITAL GAINS

E. CAPITAL LOSS CARRYOVER

F. SECTION 1231 AND "QUASI-CAPITAL" ASSETS

A. What a Capital Asset Is Not

Section 1221(a) defines "capital asset" negatively as property not belonging to any of several categories. "Property" is construed broadly, though courts do from time to time give it a less sweeping meaning, arguably for implicit reasons of policy regarding which transactions in the judges' view deserve favorable capital gain treatment. What distinguishes the types of property that are excluded from capital asset classification is usually the manner in which, or purpose for which, the property is held: for example, held for sale, held as part of a hedging operation, or held for day-to-day use in carrying on a business. The types of property excluded from capital asset classification are:

- stock in trade, inventory, and other *property "held primarily for sale in the ordinary course of business"*
- *property used in a trade or business* that is either land or depreciable property
- *copyrights; literary; musical, or artistic compositions; letters and memoranda; and similar property*, if held by the person who created them, one for whom they were created, or one whose basis in them is related to that of either of the former
- accounts and notes receivable acquired in the ordinary course of business *for services rendered or for property held primarily for sale in the ordinary course of business*
- *publications of the U.S. government*
- certain *derivatives*
- *hedging transactions* clearly and timely identified as such
- *supplies* used in a trade or business

As mentioned in the overview, these fall into functionally distinctive groups. Several are types of property held for sale or use in a business or that generate or reduce business income — inventory, notes and accounts receivable, depreciable property, and land (some income of the last two groups get special treatment under section 1231, which is discussed in Section F). Others are types of property sold in specialized business transactions — derivatives and hedges. These are like inventory rather than investment property.

(1) Property Held Primarily for Sale to Customers in the Ordinary Course of Business

What is "stock in trade and other property held for sale in the course of business"? The regular offering of goods for sale is a distinctive characteristic of a major type of trade or business, and we call these goods **inventory**. Cans of beans on the shelves of a grocery are inventory. Land in the hands of a developer is also often inventory, though land is not inventory to an owner who holds on to it with no definite plan for selling it, and so *whether* something is inventory presents an issue of fact as to the owner's intentions. Someone who inherits inventory from a developer may sell it off without intending to continue the decedent's enterprise — such a sales strategy would justify not treating the land as inventory to the inheritor.

What is the "stock in trade" that section 1221 mentions as the broader category to which inventory belongs? It has sometimes been characterized as property held for sale in a business, though not necessarily on a continuous basis. For example, if the contract that establishes a baseball league requires owners of clubs to sell players' contracts if ordered to do so by league management, the players' contracts may be stock in trade, sold from time to time, but not, as it were, on the shelf for sale as a daily matter.[1]

The qualification "to customers" in section 1221(a)(1) keeps the losses of stock investors speculating for their own account from being ordinary rather than capital. In other words, the investor whose purchases and sales are so frequent that they resemble those of a person who trades in stocks in both rising and falling markets is blocked by this language from gaining a tax advantage that is available to mere investors. The distinction is sometimes referred to as that between a **trader** and a **dealer**. In *Bielfeldt v. Commissioner*,[2] the Seventh Circuit found that a taxpayer who invested in Treasury securities on a regular but selective basis was a speculator rather than a dealer. The taxpayer's strategy was to buy the securities when he believed a temporary oversupply had lowered their price; he would sell them, often to the dealers from whom he had bought them, after a short time when the market price had recovered. In *United States v. Winthrop*,[3] a taxpayer who inherited and subdivided various parcels of land over several decades made no consistent effort to sell the lots. The Fifth Circuit found that the taxpayer's "unorthodox" sales methods were nonetheless effective, yielding more than half the taxpayer's substantial total income for the years in question. Given this pattern of successful though eccentric sales, the Court concluded that the taxpayer had held the property primarily for sale to customers in the ordinary course of business.

F   A   Q

Q: Are "day traders" dealers or traders?

A: By the sheer quantity and frequency of the typical day trader's transactions, this activity resembles that of a dealer. Many day traders also engage in short selling, a strategy used by dealers as well. Day traders, however, are often amateurs who have no realistic plan of investment or dealing. The leniency of the tax law toward poor business planning,

---

[1] *Hollywood Baseball Ass'n v. Comm'r*, 423 F.2d 494 (9th Cir. 1970).
[2] 231 F.2d 1035 (7th Cir. 2000) (Posner, J.).
[3] 417 F.2d 905 (5th Cir. 1969).

> where business deductions are concerned, suggests that day trading may qualify as a trade or business in some instances. The courts have not "declared" the law in this regard.

(2) Depreciable Property and Land Used in a Trade or Business

Capital assets do not include depreciable property or land that is used in a trade or business. Land that is *not* used in a trade or business may either be inventory of a business or investment property.[4] If the latter, it is almost always a capital asset. The exclusion for business-related property does not apply to amortizable property as well, although it should. The failure to include amortizable property is just a holdover of the second-class treatment of intangible property under the Code.

Depreciable property gets special treatment elsewhere, primarily in section 1231, and since that treatment differs from the treatment of capital assets, section 1221 must exclude it from the category of capital assets. Capital gain is taxed at a lower rate than ordinary income, and so section 1231 gains are treated more leniently than other business gains, most of which are ordinary. But ordinary losses yield a greater tax benefit than capital losses, as we shall see in Section C. Thus section 1231 gives dispositions of business property better treatment on both the upside and the downside. The existence of this special regime for business property explains why it is not included in the class of capital assets, which are taxed in a different special way. We need not pause here to consider the policy behind section 1231, apart from noting that it deals separately with the property to which section 1221(a)(2) denies capital asset status.

(3) Literary Compositions, Letters, Etc.

The next category of property from which capital assets are distinguished includes, among other things, letters written by or for the person who now owns them. Property law generally treats letters received by the addressee as the property of the addressee. Richard Nixon came to own many of the letters he had written while president. Congress apparently adopted this limitation on the class of capital assets to deny him a charitable contribution deduction for the full market value of the letters when he contributed them to his presidential library. Recall that the amount of a charitable contribution deduction is the donor's basis unless the gift is a capital asset of the donor. As a consequence of section 1221(a)(3), Nixon's charitable contribution deduction for giving noncapital assets to his library was limited to their tax basis, and that was presumably very small.

F   A   Q

Q: Are literary compositions, if owned by their authors, also excluded from the class of capital assets as business property or inventory?

A: Literary compositions and other works of art can fall into the excluded categories of property in section 1221(a)(1) or (2), but their owners can exploit them in other ways.

---

[4]Treas. Reg. §1.1221-1(b).

An author may sell the copyright to the various literary works she writes, treating them as inventory to be disposed of in final sales, but she may also retain the copyright and license publication for limited issuance of the works. A regular practice of holding copyright material in the latter fashion would probably make the works business property described in section 1221(a)(2), but this might be contested. Section 1221(a)(3) resolves all doubts in this regard.

(4) Notes and Accounts Receivable

Next, returning to the pattern set by sections 1221(a)(1) and (2), section 1221(a)(4) excludes from capital assets accounts receivable and other rights to receive payment for services rendered or from the sale of stock in trade and inventory. There are two reasons to single out these bookkeeping items. First, they are a form of property, albeit intangible, and so must carefully be distinguished from the services and property transactions that give rise to them. Second, receivables for services performed might otherwise have an ambiguous relationship to the negative definition of capital assets in terms of property types. Elsewhere in the Code, service receivables are sometimes treated as property, but the Code contains no general rule about the status of receivables.

(5) Government Publications

Government publications obtained from the government for less than the usual retail price are not capital assets, if held either by whoever got them on the cheap or by someone whose basis depends on this lucky person's. Obviously, the government doesn't want a fire sale of its own inventory turned into tax-preferred gain for the clever entrepreneur.

(6) Commodities Derivatives in the Hands of a Dealer

Although securities are typically capital assets, commodities derivatives held by a dealer are not, unless the dealer can show they have no relationship with the activity of being a dealer and are so disclosed on the books of the dealer before the end of the day they are acquired, originated, or entered into. Dealers in financial instruments hold them as inventory, of course, and the same is true for a dealer in corn futures. Capital assets do not include inventory of any kind, but commodities derivatives dealers may sometimes purchase them on their own account, and when properly accounted for, they qualify as capital assets. This exception requires dealers to identify on their books at purchase those commodities derivatives that are not inventory.

(7) Hedging Operation Instruments

To hedge is to hold two or more kinds property whose market values are likely to move in opposite directions when the market fluctuates. Gains on one kind of property offset losses on the other, protecting the holder from the risk of loss on either. For example, a U.S. firm that deals in property on European markets may acquire equal amounts of euros and yen if at the time market forces will lead one to appreciate if the other declines in value. Like commodities derivatives, hedging investments that are clearly identified as such by the taxpayer at purchase escape capital asset status. This avoids the pitfall for the taxpayer that assets purchased for risk avoidance will be treated as speculative investments. The identification requirement protects the government against the risk that the taxpayer will claim that only loss properties are part of a hedging operation and report gains on assets that were really acquired for risk protection as capital gains.

(8) Supplies

Supplies of a type regularly used or consumed by the taxpayer in the ordinary course of business are not capital assets. If supplies bought for use in a business are instead disposed of at a gain or loss, neither the capital assets rules nor section 1231 applies — the gains are ordinary, as are losses.

B. Problems in Classifying Capital Assets

Given that section 1221 defines "capital asset" so narrowly, one would think that borderline cases would be limited to those that are factually close to the excluded classes of property discussed in (1) through (8) above. That is not the case. *Hort v. Commissioner*,[5] which held that a payment from a lessee to get out of the lease was ordinary income to the landlord, relied on the doctrine that any amount received as a substitute for ordinary income was itself ordinary income. In other words, even though the property surrendered would have been a capital asset on literal application of section 1221 and its exclusions, the similarity of gain from selling the asset with gain from exploiting it justified similar treatment. *P.G. Lake v. Commissioner*,[6] in applying *Hort* to the sale of a working oil interest, appeared to apply the same rule to any substitute for an income treatment of future payments that would individually have been ordinary. This analysis has more recently led the Ninth and then the Third Circuit to classify as ordinary income the proceeds received on the sale of the right to receive lottery winnings installments.[7] Obviously, the "substitute for ordinary income" doctrine is too broad on its face to provide a workable rule. Any property can be regarded as a proxy for ordinary income, as valuation by reference to anticipated income from such property attests. The Ninth Circuit in *Maginnis* tried to make the doctrine more intelligible by limiting it to cases in which the taxpayer had not made an investment in the property sold or in which its appreciation had not been gradual. This attempt to achieve a clear division of sales of ordinary income streams into two classes fails for vagueness. What investment, and how gradual must the appreciation be? We must simply bear in mind that section 1221, though not ambiguous, will be interpreted against the taxpayer, expansively in some situations.

---

[5]313 U.S. 28 (1941).
[6]356 U.S. 260 (1958).
[7]*Maginnis v. U.S.*, 356 F.3d 1179 (9th Cir. 2004); *Lattera v. Comm'r*, 437 F.3d 399 (3d Cir. 2006), *cert. denied*, 549 U.S. 1212 (2007).

F	A	Q

Q: Is the holding in *P.G. Lake* an interpretation of section 1221?

A: None of the exclusions from capital asset status enumerated in section 1221 appears to provide a basis for the holding. Remember, however, that judicial decisions have modified or supplemented other parts of the Code with such doctrines as constructive receipt, economic benefit, claim of right, and the tax benefit rule.

C. Applying the Capital Gains Tax Rates to Multiple Capital Asset Transactions

One of the reasons for taxing capital gains favorably is that they may partly be illusory, reflecting inflation rather than real appreciation. Inflation matters because the capital assets are generally investment property that a taxpayer may buy and keep with no sale date in mind. The policy behind the capital gains preference, in other words, assumes an open-ended investment plan.

Over time the investor can sometimes distinguish promising from unpromising investments. Selling the latter before the former is good strategy even without considering tax consequences, and the natural consequence would normally be to give the taxpaying investor deductible losses sooner than taxable gains. The time value of money would therefore favor such investors if capital losses were deducted before capital gains.

A taxpayer who invests in many capital assets may have losses before gains. She may also have gains and losses from many different capital assets in a single year. Some of the assets may be held for more and others for less than the one-year holding period on which special treatment of capital gains is conditioned.

Sidebar

VALUATION METHODS AND CAPITAL ASSETS

We can value virtually any asset by different techniques. A publicly traded share of stock has a market price at any given moment, but stock traders often have other ideas of the value of shares — why else do they sell some shares short, effectively betting against the reliability of the market price? Price/earnings ratios offer a point of reference that some stock analysts take seriously at times in their effort to second-guess the market. Other capital assets are subject to a similar variety of valuation approaches. Many of them (comparison of sale prices versus rental value projections for real estate) consider both market values and the anticipated ordinary income associated with the property in question. The mere possibility of valuing an asset by reference to the income it may produce cannot be a decisive factor in determining whether the proceeds of a sale of the asset should be classified as capital gain or ordinary income.

Sections 1211 and 1222 bottle up capital gains and losses together, so that the losses reduce income only in the same proportion as the relief granted to the gains. Section 1211 allows individual taxpayers to use only $3,000 per year of capital losses in excess of gains to reduce other income. The consequence of this limitation is to reduce the value of capital losses as an offset to ordinary income. For corporations, the limitation is more severe; their capital losses cannot be used at all to offset ordinary income. Section E explains how disallowed capital losses may offset capital gain in other years.

Example 14.1: Buffett sold stock at a capital loss of $100,000 in year one, and had no other capital gains or losses that year. In year two, he had a capital gain of $50,000.

The previous year's capital loss offsets the entire capital gain, and Buffett can deduct a further $3,000 of the previous year's capital loss against non-capital income. In year three, $47,000 of the year one capital loss will remain available to offset further capital gains, but Buffett will be able to deduct $3,000 against noncapital income, even if he has no new capital gains or losses in year three.

Section 1222 provides that capital gains and losses, both long- and short-term, must be netted against each other. To maintain the distinction between short-term gain and long-term gain, because only the latter is taxed at lower rates, the netting takes place in two stages. Stage one nets short-term gains and losses against each other and also nets long-term gains and losses against each other. There are obviously several possible outcomes: gains in both categories, losses in both categories, and gain in one with loss in the other. When there is gain in one and loss in the other, and the net amount is a gain, it is taxed as short-term if it derived from a short-term gain that exceeded a long-term loss or as a long-term gain if it derived from a long-term gain that exceeded a short-term loss. On reflection, it will be obvious that this cross-netting procedure denies some advantages and grants others to the taxpayer with a mix of capital asset transactions.

D. Multiple Tax Rates for Different Kinds of Long-Term Capital Gains

The tax rates applicable to capital gains now depend on the kind of capital asset that generates the gain as well as on the taxpayer's marginal tax rate. The longish computation prescribed in Section 1(h) need not concern us here, because no introductory tax course is likely to focus on it. Instead, it is enough to know that three important categories of long-term capital gain are singled out for different treatment from that accorded run-of-the-mill capital gains, all of which are taxed at a maximum rate of 15 percent, with lower rates for taxpayers whose ordinary income is taxed at lower rates. The three kinds of capital gains that come in for special treatment are gains from "collectibles," unrecaptured section 1250 gains, and gains on sales of certain small business corporate stock.

Collectibles are works of art, rugs, antiques, metal, gems, stamps, coins, and alcoholic beverages.[8] Not all collectibles are held as capital assets, of course, since dealers in them hold them as inventory. Others often do hold collectibles as capital assets, and when they dispose of them at a gain, the top tax rate is 28 percent, a rate that is lower than the current highest rate for ordinary income but almost twice as high as the 15 percent rate that applies to most capital gains.

---

[8]Under section 408(m)(2)(F), the government can add items of tangible personalty to the list of collectibles, but has not done so thus far.

Section 1202 allows the exclusion of 50 percent of the gain on the sale or exchange of stock in small businesses that were incorporated after August 10, 1993, have capitalization not over $50 million, and are engaged in active trade or business. Section 1(h) now takes away some of the benefit of this exclusion by subjecting nonexcluded small business stock gains to a tax rate of 28 percent, like that applicable to collectibles. The net effect is that the top tax rate applicable to these gains is 14 percent (50 percent of 28 percent).

A top rate of 25 percent applies to gain on the sale or exchange of depreciable real property. Some such gain, equaling accelerated depreciation taken, is "recaptured" by section 1250 and taxed at ordinary rates. Before 1997, other gain from the sale of this category of property was taxed at the normal capital gain rate. It is only since 1997 that the higher top rate of 25 percent, referred to above, has applied to these gains.

For taxpayers whose capital gains, when added to their ordinary income, would have been taxed at marginal rates less than 25 percent, special lower rates apply: 5 percent for capital gains other than those singled out in the last few paragraphs, and the rate paid by the taxpayer on his or her ordinary income for collectibles, small business corporation, and unrecaptured depreciation asset gain.

Example 14.2: In the same year, Kravis sold ten shares of stock, which he held with a basis of $200, for $1,000, and a work of art that he held with a basis of $2,000, also for $1,000. The $1,000 loss on the work of art reduces Kravis's capital gain to zero for the year, and he is allowed to deduct the remaining $200 loss against ordinary income under section 1231. The higher capital gain tax rate for collectibles does not disturb the rules applicable to capital losses.

E. Capital Loss Carryover

The Code limits taxpayers' ability to use capital losses to offset other income, but also permits them to be used in earlier or later taxable years when their use is curtailed. Section 1212 allows corporations to carry capital losses back for up to three years and forward for five (longer in some cases) if they exceed the year's capital gains. Individuals can carry forward capital losses that exceed capital gains for a given year to the extent that they exceed the year's capital gains by more than $3,000, the amount of excess capital loss an individual can deduct against non capital income. In the case of a corporation, this means that the loss in excess of the current year's capital gains is treated as a loss suffered in the third year before the actual year, and if not "absorbed" by capital gains in that year, then the remaining loss is carried to the second year before the year in which the loss was originally suffered, and so forth. For individuals, the carryover goes first to the year after the excess loss was suffered, then to the year after, and so forth, with no time limit. Corporate loss carrybacks can result in tax refunds for earlier years, but individual loss carryovers can only reduce tax liability for later years.

F. Section 1231 and "Quasi-Capital" Assets

Property *excluded* from the category of capital assets by section 1221(a)(2), that is, depreciable property and land used in business, receives favorable tax treatment that mimics that of capital assets, on the upside at least. If for a given year there is a net gain from dispositions of this kind of business property, the gain is taxed at long-term capital gain rates; if a loss, the loss is ordinary.

Example 14.3: A trucking company sells three vehicles in the same year. The company had gains of $3,000 and $5,000 on two of the vehicles and a loss of $1,000 on the third. (There was no recapture income on the two gain sales (see Chapter 15.H).) The company has a net section 1231 gain for the year of $3,000 + 5,000 − 1,000 = $7,000, which is taxable at a 15 percent rate, the rate that applies to most capital gains.

Why the bifurcated treatment? Congress passed a predecessor of section 1231 during World War II, as a sweetener for forced sales of ships and other assets to the government. Since 1954, however, current section 1231 has applied to both voluntary and involuntary sales of business assets. Property of this kind differs from inventory and investment assets in important ways. Unlike inventory, it is not sold in the ordinary course of business but simply used up or disposed of when events mandate its replacement. Unlike investment property, it is not chosen for its potential appreciation and if it does appreciate cannot be sold without inflicting costs on the business in which it is involved. For continuity and efficiency, business operators may be under pressure to keep equipment, workspace, and the like on hand. Like depreciation, losses on the forced or business-motivated sale of business assets should offset profits, which are ordinary. In sum, capital treatment for gains and ordinary treatment for losses makes sense for assets that are integral to business activity.

Casualty losses with respect to the same classes of business property are given similar treatment, but if there is a net loss from casualties and involuntary conversions, the net loss is not put through the ordinary section 1231 netting calculation but is allowed to be recognized separately as a loss.

SUMMARY

■ Long-term capital gain is taxed at a lower rate than ordinary income, currently 15 percent for most types of capital assets and most taxpayers.

■ We distinguish capital gain from ordinary income by first dividing all property into capital and other assets.

■ The Code definition of "capital asset" classifies all property *except* property of seven broad types as capital assets.

■ Excluded are inventory and the like, depreciable property or land used in business, a range of expressive property, accounts and notes receivable arising from business sales of inventory, government publications, certain derivatives, hedging transactions, and business supplies.

■ The courts, however, occasionally refuse to classify gain on the sale of an ordinary-income-generating asset as capital gain, reasoning that the asset was merely a proxy for ordinary income.

■ Capital losses in excess of capital gains are not allowed to corporations as a deduction for the year when they arise, and only $3,000 per year of such excess capital losses is allowed as a deduction to individuals.

■ Gains and losses on capital asset dispositions are netted to preserve their long- or short-term character.

■ Individuals are allowed to carry excess capital losses, with their long- or short-term character preserved, forward indefinitely; corporations carry them back three years and forward five in mose cases.

■ Net gain for a taxable year on depreciable property and land used in business is taxed at capital gain rates.

CONNECTIONS

Difference in the Taxation of Business and Investment Activities

The Code broadly differentiates between business activities and investment activities, although it does not keep them distinct for all purposes. Instead, the taxation of gains and losses from specific types of transactions *within* a business can be the same as those from purely investment activities. What triggers the difference in treatment is whether the gains and losses arise from capital assets or not, because all other assets are either sources of invariably ordinary income or qualify for distinctive tax treatment in view of their role in business activities. See Chapters 2.G, 7.C, and 12.A on the difference between business and investment activities.

Comparison Between the Treatment of Capital Assets and Business Assets

As explained in Chapters 6.B and 7.B, early recovery of property's basis benefits the taxpayer/owner in the same way that early deduction of the costs of a profit-making activity reduces the effective tax rate on the profits from the activity. Delay in the recovery of basis, however, is characteristic of how we tax capital assets, because they are usually property held for investment. The lower tax rate applicable to capital gain, however, tends to equalize the tax burden on business and investment activities.

Use of Section 1221 Categories in Other Code Contexts

Section 1221 defines the class of capital assets, and sections 1201 through 1260 state the basic rules for calculating gain and loss on capital assets. Section 1(h) prescribes the tax rates applicable to various types of capital gain. Other Code sections refer to section 1221 in providing special rules for the excluded categories; for example, section 1231(b) defines property used in a trade or business by invoking section 1221 in various ways. Further derivative uses of the capital asset and capital gain definitions are beyond the scope of this course.

Capitalization and Cost Recovery

15

The income tax assigns a basis to virtually every piece of property, tangible or intangible, that anyone owns. Basis can signal advantages or disad-

O V E R V I E W

vantages for the owner. The cost of property that is used up within a year in a for-profit activity is deducted as an expense right away. The owner's basis in the property is briefly equal to this cost but usually has no significance. With the immediate deduction, there is no need for rules governing the recovery of the basis. In contrast, the cost of property that will be used for more than a year is not deductible. Instead, it must be capitalized. This means that the cost or basis of the property cannot be deducted as an expense but remains significant at least through the end of the year of the property's first use. Most capitalized costs can be gradually recovered, that is, they can be deducted over a number of years. Elaborate rules govern this process, which is called depreciation for tangible property and amortization for intangible property. Some few types of property do not qualify for depreciation or amortization. This chapter broadly surveys the rules of capitalization, depreciation, and amortization, emphasizing how they relate to what we have already learned about business and investment taxation.

A. **CAPITALIZATION**

B. **DEPRECIATION METHODS**

C. **PROPERTY-SPECIFIC LIMITATIONS ON COST RECOVERY DEDUCTIONS**

A. Capitalization

The cost of property that lasts substantially longer than the year in which it is put into service cannot be deducted as a section 162 or a section 212 expense, no matter how ordinary and necessary its use in business or investment activity may be. Section 263 instead requires that the cost be **capitalized** or added to the basis either of the property itself or of some other property with which it is used. Tax experts often refer to items that must be capitalized as **expenditures** and to items that can be deducted immediately as **expenses**. *Idaho Power Co. v. Commissioner*[1] offers a straightforward illustration of capitalization of the cost of one asset to the basis of another. An electrical utility used many separate pieces of construction equipment in constructing transmission and distribution assets. The utility tried to depreciate the equipment separately from these, the useful lives of which would have been much longer. The government successfully argued that because the construction equipment was completely used up in building the longer lasting assets, the costs of the equipment should be capitalized to the their basis for depreciation over their longer useful lives. As this suggests, an overview of a taxpayer's broader activities is necessary for determining which costs should be capitalized to separate assets. Normally, however, the costs of property used directly in an ongoing business or investment are capitalized separately, and each is depreciable on its own.

F A Q

Q: If an asset is worn out or becomes obsolete before expected, is the remaining basis recovered at that point?

A: In general, the adjusted basis of business property is deductible for the year in which it is no longer used in the business and cannot be sold. If depreciable property is lost through casualty, theft, or condemnation, section 1231 applies to the resulting gain, which must be aggregated with other gains and losses on business assets that belong to the same year; section 1231 does not apply to casualty, theft, and condemnation losses if these exceed casualty, theft, and condemnation gains for the year. See Chapter 14.F.

---

[1]418 U.S. 1 (1974).

INDOPCO v. Comm'r[2] dealt with a subtler, politically sensitive puzzle about capitalization. The issue was whether the bankers' and lawyers' fees for a friendly merger of the taxpayer into another publicly traded company could be deducted or must be capitalized. The taxpayer argued for deduction of the fees, on the grounds that the merger created no new asset and that the expenses for the merger benefited the disappearing corporation's business in substantial and specific ways. The Supreme Court disagreed, reasoning that the restructuring would benefit the surviving corporation sufficiently to require capitalization of the fees to the entity's "charter."

Capitalization is often an issue when the taxpayer spends money to alter an existing asset, as the corporation in *INDOPCO* did to alter itself. If the outlay improves or changes the asset's identity, it is deemed to be an expenditure that must be capitalized. If it merely restores the asset to its original condition or preserves its erstwhile identity, the resulting "repair" is deemed to be an ephemeral cost of owning (preserving, maintaining, conserving) the asset, which need not be capitalized but can instead be immediately deducted. If damaged or destroyed property is restored and kept in service, the owner cannot deduct the transitory loss but must capitalize the costs of restoration to the property's adjusted basis.[3]

Capitalization issues also arise with respect to ongoing costs incurred with respect to business property. Permanent improvements, along the lines indicated in *Idaho Power* and *INDOPCO*, must be capitalized; maintenance and repair outlays are immediately deductible. The line can be hard to draw, especially when the maintenance or repairs have both immediate and long-term consequences. Regulatory or court-ordered modification of equipment for environmental reasons or to abate a nuisance affecting neighboring property poses one such problem. From the standpoint of the business owner, these costs add nothing to the value of the business product and are therefore not "improvements" in the ordinary sense. Yet they are often classified as improvements because they bring the property up to a standard that all competitors in the industry must meet.

After *INDOPCO*, the IRS promulgated detailed regulations on some of the tax-accounting issues the case dealt with.[4] The *INDOPCO* regulations deal with a great number of narrowly described situations, such as the deductibility of wages and salaries for employees who create intangibles of various sorts. The details are beyond the scope of this discussion, but they strike a different balance between the abstract principle of capitalizing expenditures and the compliance and administrative costs that absolute fidelity to those principles would occasion. *INDOPCO* is no longer the guiding light.

> ### Sidebar
>
> **CAPITALIZATION AND INFLATION**
>
> When a firm must capitalize the annual costs of fungible equipment that it purchases year after year, inflation will cause an imbalance between the firm's straight-line depreciation deductions for recently purchased equipment and earlier purchased equipment. The more recently purchased equipment has a higher nominal cost because of inflation. A firm that is growing more quickly than a competitor may therefore enjoy a tax-based competitive advantage, because it pays progressively less tax on the use of its growing stock of depreciable property. This violation of tax neutrality seems to be an inevitable feature of income taxation, at least if depreciation is based on actual costs of business property.

---

[2]503 U.S. 79 (1992).
[3]Rev. Rul. 71-161, 1971-1C.B. 76; Prop. Treas. Reg. §1.263(a)-3(f)(iv).
[4]Treas. Reg. §§1.263(a)-4 and (a)-5.

Outsourcing was once a source of inconsistent capitalization of assets. In *Encyclopaedia Britannica v. Commissioner*,[5] Judge Posner reinvented the wheel to some extent in discussing the pre-*INDOPCO* treatment of what a publisher spent for a book manuscript. Although the publisher's staff wrote many books in house, it had outsourced the research and writing of a dictionary with a specialized subject matter and paid a separate firm a total contract price in several installments, which it treated as currently deductible expenses. The taxpayer's claim was that the outside work was that of a consultant, no different from the consultants' services the publisher paid for in connection with books it produced in house. Judge Posner rejected the Tax Court's suggestion that the issue turned on whether the taxpayer or the consultant was the "dominant force" in the book's creation. Instead, he emphasized that "[t]his was a turnkey project" that resulted in "producing or acquiring a specific capital asset."[6] Yet in-house production of the same book would not have had to be capitalized. Although *Encyclopaedia Britannica* suggests reasons for the difference in capitalization treatment, it reinforced an inconsistency of approach that at first prompted the holding in *INDOPCO* and then the *INDOPCO* regulations.

B. Depreciation Methods

The rationale of cost recovery for business assets is the matching of an appropriate fraction of the cost of each asset with each period of time during which the asset is used in a profit-oriented activity. In theory, deducting the decline in the value of an asset used to produce income is proper when the asset loses value gradually through "exhaustion" or "wear and tear." In practice, this means that we ignore any possible loss in value due to market forces.

F   A   Q

Q: Is land depreciable?

A: Section 1221(a)(2) distinguishes land from depreciable property, implying that the two categories do not overlap. That is indeed the standard judicial and administrative position. To determine separate cost bases for land and structures purchased for a single price, we allocate the price between these components in proportion to their separate appraisal values as of the date of purchase. The structures are depreciable by reference to their allocated cost basis, whereas the basis of the unimproved land can be recovered only on disposition.

If an asset is not in service during some period of the otherwise ongoing activity, no part of its cost should be deducted from the profits of that period. When it is not practically possible to foresee how long an asset will serve an activity or how much of its value will remain at the activity's conclusion, traditional depreciation deductions were not allowed. **Service or useful life**, the period for which the asset will

---

[5]685 F.2d 212 (7th Cir. 1982).
[6]*Id.* at 218.

probably be used in the activity, is still a basic characteristic of an asset for a cost recovery method, unless other information or other methods of approximation supersede this.

Cost recovery for business assets has changed a lot over the years. For the first decades after the income tax was adopted, taxpayers were permitted to use any of several methods, but the variables that determined the amount of depreciation deductions were largely under taxpayers' control, and administrative audit of the results was often mired in expensive factual disputes between government and taxpayer. In order to see why, we need only notice that deductions were based, at least in the first instance, on the taxpayer's representations as to the useful life of an asset and its salvage value (residual value after the useful life ended). Consistent "mistakes" about the length of the useful life of very similar assets could lead to higher annual depreciation deductions than was justified. But catching such misrepresentations was not easy. In the 1930s, the Bureau of Internal Revenue stepped up its auditing of depreciation claims. In 1942, the agency, now called the Internal Revenue Service, prescribed depreciation lives for each of thousands of asset types in Bulletin F, depreciation's new bible. Twenty years later, the IRS replaced Bulletin F with so-called Guideline Lives. The new system established 75 broad industrial and general asset categories, and permitted service lives shorter than those in Bulletin F. The trend was obvious: Taxpayers were allowed to determine fewer of the vital statistics of depreciable property. Even this scheme permitted the taxpayer to be in control of too great a share of the depreciation computation. Then, in 1971, the IRS switched to the Asset Depreciation Ranges (ADR) scheme, a revision of the Guidelines with an additional element of permissiveness: Taxpayers could add or subtract up to 20 percent from the service lives previously prescribed for similar assets. The effect was to allow higher depreciation deductions across the board for tangible assets. And so, the innovation amounted to an accelerated depreciation system. The common element in all this administrative tweaking of depreciation was to confine the discretion of business operators to choose useful lives, salvage values, and indirectly the amount of the annual depreciation deduction.

In the midst of an economic downturn, Congress in 1981 further simplified depreciation with the Accelerated Cost Recovery System (ACRS). New section 168 gave taxpayers the option of choosing faster depreciation methods — yielding higher deductions in the early years of an asset's use in business activity — with only five classes of assets, for which depreciation periods, which replaced ADRs, were far shorter than likely useful lives. Alternative depreciation, permitting slower cost recovery, could be elected. In either case, ACRS ignored salvage value, the portion of the value of an asset that remains when the asset is taken out of business use. The new approach permits the entire basis of business property to be recovered at accelerated rates over the short periods prescribed. At the same time, Congress introduced expensing (immediate deduction of the entire cost basis) for the first several thousand dollars worth of depreciable property placed in service by a business taxpayer in a given year. In 1986, Congress renamed the accelerated version of depreciation Modified Accelerated Cost Recovery System (MACRS), and it is often called by this acronym to this day.

Economic stimulation was one of the purposes behind ACRS. Congress quickly moved to lengthen depreciation periods and restore something like the original, nonstimulative purpose of cost recovery. But salvage value was kept out of the process, and accelerated methods that drastically overstated the actual loss in value of business assets remained. Since 1981, Congress has often revisited the issue, more often choosing to use cost recovery as a means of stimulating business activity than to establish a realistic means of tracking the economic cost of using tangible property in productive activities.

Through the 1980s, the lenient pattern of accelerated cost recovery favored "Rust Belt" industries over those whose durable inputs were intangible, because section 168 applied only to tangible personal property and structures on land. More recently, section 174 handed industries that use intellectual and other intangible property an equalizing tax break in the form of the "expensing" or immediate deduction of research and experimental outlays. What this means is that money spent for *future* lines of business and types of products became deductible years before the corresponding income arrived. As we saw in Chapter 6.B, early recovery of expenses reduces the effective tax rate on a stream of income; that is, the nominal rate no longer states the actual tax burden on income from the activity because the post-ponement of taxes from preactivity periods saves the taxpayer part of the cost of the tax burden faced in later years. Section 197 now allows purchased goodwill and other intangibles to be amortized over 15 years.

Expensing or immediate deduction of a limited amount spent on property that would otherwise be depreciable under section 168 is also available as an election under section 179. Section E discusses this option.

C. Property-Specific Limitations on Cost Recovery Deductions

Sections 167 and 168 contain the basic rules on depreciation, also called cost recovery in section 168. These sections authorize various methods for the incremental deduction of the cost of tangible property used in a trade or business or in the production of income, that is, in activities for which section 162 and section 212 deductions are permitted. Section 167 contains the pre-1986 statutory depreciation regime, and section 168 the post-1986 regime. Both are still in force, because section 168 allows taxpayers to elect the older depreciation methods of section 167. Section 197 amortization of intangible property is similar to straight-line depreciation under section 168. Thus, even the basic depreciation and related cost recovery rules accord different treatment to tangible and intangible assets.

Two kinds of property with strong appeal to the entrepreneur's or employee's inner consumer are not as rapidly deductible as other tangible business property. Enacted in 1984, section 280F imposes two kinds of limit on their depreciation deductions. Cars in particular are subject to a low annual dollar amount, even if used exclusively for business purposes. Certain other types of property ("listed property"), including computers, cell phones, and other transportation property, can be depreciated under section 168 only if more than half their use is for business purposes. They are otherwise limited to the less advantageous depreciation methods set forth in section 167(g).

Employees cannot depreciate listed property at all unless it is used for the convenience of the employer and as a condition of employment.

F	A	Q

Q: When does an employee's use of property qualify as serving the convenience of the employer and as a condition of employment?

A: We are familiar with these two tests from sections 119 and 280A, but in those sections, "convenience of the employer" and "condition of employment" seem to tell us only that the exclusions of section 119 and deductions allowed by section 280A are not more expansive than earlier judicial and administrative rulings allowed. The regulations do not clarify those rulings. The inevitable conclusion is that Congress used the two tests here as an invitation to the courts to fashion more specific standards.

D. The Mechanics of Straight-Line Depreciation

(1) The Basic Method

From the brief history of tax depreciation in Section B, some aspects of how depreciation deductions are calculated will be familiar. Today the salvage value of depreciable property is ignored. The entire basis of the property can be deducted in increments or "recovered" over a period of years set by section 168 rather than based on the taxpayer's best guess about how long she will use the property in business. One need only know the basis of the property, the prescribed depreciation period, and the formula for dividing the basis of the property into annually deductible amounts.

The simplest such formula is the straight-line method. For buildings, the annual depreciation deduction on this method is the initial basis of the property divided by the number of years in the depreciation period.

Example 15.1: An office with remaining basis of $50,000, depreciable over ten years, would give the taxpayer a deduction of $5,000 each year. It is true for all depreciation methods that the property's basis is adjusted downward each year by the depreciation deduction. In our example, the property's basis would go down to $450,000 at the end of the first year, because $5,000 would be deductible in depreciation of the asset for that year.

Section 1016(a)(2)(A) is understood to mean this when it says, "Proper adjustment in respect of the property shall in all cases be made . . . for exhaustion, wear and tear, obsolescence, amortization, and depletion, to the extent of the amount . . . allowed as deductions in computing taxable income." Section 1016(a) also makes it clear that the basis of depreciable property goes down by the amount that is allowed as depreciation, *whether the taxpayer claims that amount as a deduction or not.* Thus, we sometimes encounter situations in which an asset's basis has been reduced for depreciation even though its owner failed to claim the deduction.

Example 15.2: Amalgamated Manufacturing made an error in its tax return ten years ago, failing to claim any deduction for the first year in which it used a new widget-extruding machine. The basis of the machine was initially $10,000, and a depreciation deduction of $250 would have been proper for that year. Five years ago, the statute of limitations for amending the tax return ran for that first year of use. Amalgamated's basis in the machine is treated as reduced by $250 for depreciation in the closed tax year, even though the taxpayer cannot now claim the deduction. Note that the tax benefit rule does not permit restoration of the basis or current deduction of the amount that should have been deducted.

(2) "Conventions" About When the Property Begins to Be Used for Business Purposes

The straight-line method simply divided the available basis into a number of equal amounts determined by the number of years the Code prescribes as the depreciation period. However, to prevent taxpayers from gaming this or any other depreciation method, section 168(d) requires the taxpayer to follow a "convention" concerning when the property is placed in service. The most common convention is the "half-year convention." Property to which this convention applies is deemed to be placed in service and to become eligible for depreciation at the midpoint of the year in which it is actually placed in service. The straight-line depreciation deduction for a truck put into service in a plumber's business on the first day of the taxable year is one-half the deduction that will be available for each of the succeeding years except the last, for which again only half the normal deduction is allowed.

The half-year convention applies only if the property is put to use for the first time during the first three quarters of the year. If it is put to use first in the last quarter of the year, the "midquarter" convention applies—the property is deemed to start serving the business on the midpoint of the final quarter of the year. Accordingly, only one-eighth of the usual straight-line depreciation deduction based on the initial basis of the asset and its prescribed depreciation period can be taken for the first year, and in the last year seven-eighths of that deduction is taken.

Residential rental property and nonresidential property, as section 168(d)(2) provides, are subject to a midmonth convention—the first year's depreciation deduction is calculated as if the property were put to use at the midpoint of the month in which it is actually put into use.

Example 15.3: An apartment building bought with sitting tenants on March 1 is depreciated as if it were bought on March 15, so that for the first year it is depreciated as if used for 10.5 months of the year. For the first year, then, 10.5 divided by 12 or .875 of the normal full-year straight-line depreciation deduction can be taken, and for the final year of the prescribed depreciation period, if the taxpayer continues to use it that long, only .125 of that amount is deductible for depreciation.

E. Methods of Faster Depreciation

Since the early 1980s, depreciation methods that depart from straight-line symmetry, permitting *more* of an asset's basis to be deducted in earlier years than in later years, have become the norm for most tangible personal property. We say that a method of depreciation is accelerated if the first few years' deductions exceed those set by the straight-line method. The accelerated methods currently made available are **declin-ing balance methods**. All of them make the depreciation deduction for the first year a multiple of the straight-line annual depreciation amount.

Example 15.4: If the basis of an asset with a ten-year depreciation range is $15,000, the straight-line deduction (ignoring conventions about when the property is put into service) would be $1,500. A declining balance method multiplies $1,500 by a number greater than one, such as 1.5 or two. The **double declining balance method** multiplies the straight-line deduction by two (sometimes expressed as 200 percent), so that for the asset in our example, the first year's deduction would be $3,000. The second year's deduction is twice the straight-line amount that would be deductible if the asset were first being put into use with a basis of $15,000, the actual initial basis, *minus* $3,000, the first year's accelerated depreciation amount.

The declining balance of the basis is used in this way in each subsequent year to compute a special depreciation deduction until the resulting amount is less than the straight-line amount, calculated using the asset's then-remaining basis, that is, as if this were the initial basis of an asset with a depreciation period limited to that of this asset's recovery period. In the words of section 168(b)(1)(B), we "[switch] to the straight line method for the 1st taxable year for which using the straight line method with respect to the adjusted basis as of the beginning of such year will yield a larger allowance." For the year in which this "crossover" occurs, and all subsequent years, the same straight-line deduction is taken. Inevitably, the deduction for these final years is smaller than those for the earlier years in which the accelerated method was used *and* smaller than if the straight-line method had been used at the outset.

The applicable convention for the first year of the recovery period postpones the benefit of double declining balance depreciation somewhat. Table 15.1 illustrates how the half-year convention changes DDB depreciation of a seven-year asset.

TABLE 15.1	DDB Depreciation of a Seven-Year Asset with Initial Basis of $5,000			
	Without Convention			
Book Value at Beginning of Year	**Depreciation Rate**	**Depreciation Deduction**	**Accumulated Depreciation**	**Book Value at End of Year**
5,000	.2857 = 2/7	1,429	1,429	3,571
3,571	.2857	1,020	2,449	2,551
2,551	.2857	729	3,178	1,822
1,822	.2857	521	3,699	1,301
1,301	.3333 (.2857)	434 (371)	4,133	867
867	.3333 (of 1301)	434	4,567	433

Continued

TABLE 15.1	Continued			

	With Half-Year Convention			
Book Value at Beginning of Year	Depreciation Rate	Depreciation Deduction	Accumulated Depreciation	Book Value at End of Year
433	.3333 (of 1301)	433	5,000	0
5,000	1/2 of .2857	714	714	4,286
4,286	.2857	1,225	1,939	3,061
3,061	.2857	875	2,814	2,186
2,186	.2857	625	3,439	1,511
1,511	.3333 (.2857)	504 (432)	3,943	1,007
1,007	.3333 (of 1,511)	504	4,474	503
503	.3333 (of 1,511)	503	5,000	0

F. Expensing Under Section 179

Expensing is the immediate deduction of an investment in a profit-oriented activity and usually stands in contrast with gradual cost recovery such as depreciation or amortization of intangibles. Since 1981, however, Congress has allowed a limited part of the cost of depreciable property to be expensed, while the property's basis net of the amount expensed remains eligible for depreciation. A taxpayer can elect to deduct all or part of the cost of new qualifying tangible property and computer software instead of recovering this amount using conventional or accelerated depreciation. The expensed portion of the cost is subtracted from the property's basis. For 2007 through 2010, the total amount that a taxpayer can elect to expense in a given year has been $125,000, with a dollar-for-dollar reduction for the cost of property above $200,000. The ceiling was lifted for 2011 and is scheduled to fall again thereafter.

Since the expensing option is one of Congress's most visible tools for stimulating the economy, an even more aggressive boost to business capital expenditures than accelerated depreciation, we can expect the levels of the section 179 election to vary in the future as the economy fluctuates between boom and bust.

G. Depletion and Intangible Drilling Costs

Methods of cost recovery like accelerated depreciation and expensing are available for oil and gas production, mining, and similar "extractive" operations. Originally, the basis of the property being extracted from the earth was simply allocated over the estimated recoverable units of the product and deducted as the units were sold. Such **cost depletion** is obviously a close parallel to depreciation, although it allocates basis recovery deductions over units produced rather than over an estimated or prescribed depreciation period. **Percentage depletion**, which is now permitted as an alternative to cost depletion, is an open-ended substitute for cost recovery. Section 613 simply allows the taxpayer to deduct a certain percentage of the gross income arising from the extractive activity: 22 percent for minerals like sulfur and uranium, 5 percent for clay used in manufacturing roofing and drainage tiles, and 15 percent currently for small independent oil producers and royalty owners. All percentage depletion faces a 50 percent ceiling on all *taxable* income from a given property. Thus, costs apart from the percentage depletion of a property reduce the overall benefit of percentage depletion.

Example 15.5: If the actual costs for labor and management services in producing oil from a taxpayer's reserves is 65 percent of the gross profits of the production activity, only 35 percent is taxable income, and the 22 percent depletion deduction cannot exceed 50 percent of this portion, or 17.25 percent of the gross profits from the activity.

Section 263 permits the current deduction (equivalent to expensing) of **intangible drilling and development costs**, which include such things as labor, managerial expenses, and even certain materials that are used in the extractive activity. Sections 616 and 617 permit similar expensing for exploration and development costs of non-oil-and-gas extraction. Remember how early recovery of basis gave an advantage to the taxpayer in *Inaja Land*.[8] This is a statutory version of that approach.

H. Recapture

Unlike capital losses, depreciation deductions can always offset ordinary income. But section 1231 provides that the net gain, if any, on sales during a given year of property used in a trade or business is treated as capital. Accelerated depreciation, moreover, can be expected to create artificial gains, because it pushes down the basis of business assets below market value. To prevent artificial ordinary losses from turning into capital gain, Code sections 1245 and 1250 are said to "recapture" the excessive depreciation. Section 1245, which applies only to personal property, provides that any gain on the disposition of such property is ordinary income to the extent of depreciation deductions taken. This makes sense because all such property is eligible for accelerated depreciation methods over artificially short depreciation periods. Section 1250 makes a similar provision for real estate, but only to the extent of the accelerated portion of total depreciation deductions. Since 1986, most depreciable real estate has been eligible only for straight-line depreciation, and so recapture does not apply to it. Low-income housing and certain other types of real property improvements qualify for accelerated depreciation and are therefore subject to recapture under section 1250.

---

[8]9 T.C. 727 (1947), *acq.* 1948-1 C.B.2; see Chapter 6.B.

SUMMARY

■ The cost of business or investment property whose useful life is substantially longer than a year must be capitalized, that is, becomes the basis of the property or of some other property in conjunction with which the first property is used.

■ Depreciation is the gradual recovery of the basis of tangible property used in a trade or business or income-seeking activity over its useful life or over a period prescribed in the statute or regulations.

■ Amortization is the gradual recovery of the basis of intangible property, usually over a Code-prescribed period of years.

■ Depreciation and amortization are closely comparable in overall design, but amortization usually allows the taxpayer only straight-line recovery of expenditures on intangibles.

■ Tangible assets to whose bases expenditures are capitalized are depreciable using either accelerated depreciation methods, which are currently the default rules of the area, or slower straight-line or proportional depreciation.

■ Expensing is more advantageous than depreciation or amortization because it permits all or part of an asset's basis to be deducted for the year in which an asset is put into service. Statutory limits on expensing, however, sometimes allow only part of an asset's basis to be expensed, while the rest must be depreciated.

■ Cost depletion for properties used in extractive industries is like depreciation or amortization, except that depletion allocates a property's basis over the estimated number of units of the extractive product, allowing that much of the gross proceeds of each unit's sale to be deducted from gross income, instead of making such an allocation over the number of years the extractive process is expected to take.

■ Percentage depletion permits a statutory percentage of the gross income of small independent oil and gas producers' product to be deducted, up to an overall 50 percent limit of the activity's taxable income apart from depletion.

■ Intangible drilling and development costs of oil and gas extraction can be expensed, as can the exploration and development costs of most kinds of non-oil-and-gas extraction.

CONNECTIONS

Recovery of Basis on Disposition of Property Compared with Depreciation and Amortization

The *exclusion* from gross income of a portion of the taxpayer's amount realized on a disposition of property is directly comparable to the *deduction* over time of incremental parts of the taxpayer's basis through depreciation or amortization. Both mechanisms prevent the taxpayer's actual or deemed investment from being treated as income. See Chapter 7.A and 7.B.

Early Cost Recovery Methods Versus Recovery of Basis on Disposition

Early recovery of basis, as illustrated by *Inaja Land v. Commissioner*[9] and *Burnet v. Logan*,[10] is a significant advantage to the taxpayer, tending to reduce the effective rate of tax on the activity in which an asset is used. See Chapters 6.B and 7.A. Expensing is the formal equivalent of recovering basis first and treating only later revenue as gross income.

Different Methods of Depreciation for Competing Taxpayers May Violate Tax Neutrality

Tax neutrality requires that similarly situated taxpayers' economic decisions should not be affected by the tax law. Depreciation methods that give one taxpayer a competitive advantage over another by placing their profits under different tax burdens may violate tax neutrality. See Chapter 1.F.

Depreciation and Amortization Should Promote the "Clear Reflection of Income" Standard of Tax Accounting

Permissible accounting methods such as the cash and accrual methods have as their main purpose the "clear reflection of income," as section 446 provides. This is shorthand for the goal of allocating revenue and costs to appropriate subperiods of the longer duration of a taxpayer's profit-seeking activity. See Chapter 10.A.

Capitalization of Environmental and Other Regulatory Costs

Tax neutrality requires that a taxpayer be required to capitalize a cost that benefits society at large if other taxpayers face the same cost over the same period of profit-seeking activity. Expensing of such costs serves neutrality only if the costs are proportional to the gross income of the activity. See Chapter 1.F.

---

[9]9 T.C. 727 (1947).
[10]283 U.S. 404 (1931).

Assignment of Income

16

Tax law must sometimes force round pegs into square holes. Dividing complex business transactions into episodes that fall neatly into separate

OVERVIEW

tax years, parsing economic relations within the family, drawing a line between compensation and fringe benefits — each, despite its useful purpose, is somewhat arbitrary. A further problem of this kind now requires our attention. Early on, the Supreme Court announced that it would sometimes disregard contractual and even more basic legal distinctions to prevent pretax income from being shifted from one person to another. "Correct" attribution of income generally preserves the progressive tax rate structure by preventing higher-bracket individuals from passing pretax income to lower-bracket family members or other related people. Vigilance against income shifting can also foil some tax shelters that make use of participants exempt from U.S. income tax. The case law invalidating "anticipatory assignment of income" deals with a variety of suspect transactions and shifty strategies.

A. The Basic Judicial Rule

Arrangements intended to shift income away from the person who would otherwise be treated as earning it are ineffective for tax purposes. (Note that they may be perfectly valid and continue to bind the parties for other than tax purposes.) Creating this doctrine, *Lucas v. Earl*[1] denied tax effect to a contract between spouses that on its face required all property acquired by either to be "treated and considered" as belonging to both, as soon as earned by either, in joint tenancy with right of survivorship. Automatic co-ownership of the income would have reduced the tax on the husband's earnings from a lucrative law practice, and the spouses would have shared the tax benefit, as they shared the income itself. Without the arrangement, only the husband would have filed a tax return, and the total income he reported would have made him liable for a tax more than twice that on half his income (which is what each would have reported if their contract had been controlling for tax purposes). The spouses, however, entered into their income-sharing contract long before there was an income tax, and lived in a community property state. Theirs was not a case of clever tax planning.

The difference between default treatment of the income and the treatment to which the spouses might have been entitled was a consequence of the progressive rate structure. Higher net incomes are taxed at higher effective rates than lower incomes. For example, 50 percent of $100,000 is $50,000, whereas 25 percent of $50,000 is only $12,500, and twice that amount is still only 25 percent of $100,000 or $25,000. In his brief but imprecise opinion, Justice Oliver Wendell Holmes Jr. disallowed the intended tax consequences of the contract, calling the arrangement one "by which the fruits are attributed to a different tree from that on which they grew."

<table>
<tr><td>F</td><td>A</td><td>Q</td></tr>
</table>

Q: Does the progressive rate structure still cause this problem for married taxpayers?

A: During the first decades of the U.S. income tax, the same graduated tax rates applied to all individuals, whether married or not. Different rate schedules for single and married taxpayers filing jointly were enacted in 1948. The rates for joint filers were lower than those for single filers, for reasons discussed in Chapter 11.C.

The class of transactions subject to this common law doctrine could be enormous. Should employees be taxed on the income they earn for their employer? Should every contractual promise between them for the payment of future income, or transfer in trust of income not yet received, be suspect under the broad fruit-and-tree analogy? If so, even a gift of income-producing property might be disregarded, and the co-owners of a business might not be able to share the fruit of their efforts. The Court's conspicuously terse decision left this in doubt. Later case law, as we will

---

[1]281 U.S. 111 (1930).

see, has narrowed the doctrine somewhat, but as *Lucas* declared, the issue it addressed "was not to be decided by attenuated subtleties."[2]

In *Poe v. Seaborn*,[3] the Court held that because the earnings of either spouse were community property under the law of the State of Washington (as would have been the case under the community property laws of other states), the taxpayer spouses who lived there each properly reported half of the compensation income of the only one of them who was employed. The government argued that the husband's right to manage the income he brought into the community and the wife's inability to sue to alter his decisions except for fraud meant that the income was actually only his. But the Court reasoned that the husband's "broad powers . . . by no means [negate] the wife's

present interest as a co-owner" of their community income. What the taxpayers in *Earl* claimed was their right turned out to be the normal result in community property states, where the income of spouses automatically belongs to them equally.

Commissioner v. First Security Bank of Utah[4] further illustrates the point that legal incapacity is a bar to assignment-of-income analysis. The government argued that income should be attributed to a bank as agent for the sale of credit life insurance, because another affiliate of the corporate group to which the bank belonged received income as reinsurer of the original policies. The Court held that the assignment-of-income doctrine had no application where federal law denied the taxpayer the right to receive the income in question. For individuals, the joint return now creates an even playing field between spouses in community and common law property states. But the Court's early willingness to countenance a sharp discrepancy in the tax treatment of spouses subject to these different regimes indicated that the assignment-of-income doctrine could override both state contract law and federal tax law.

Example 16.1: Jack and Jill lived in a state with common law marital property rules for two years. On January 1 of last year, they moved to a community-property state and lived there for the entire year. If only one of them had positive gross income in each of the three years, the move from a common law state to a community-property state should nonetheless have had no effect on their federal tax liability as joint filers. This is because the joint return includes the couple's income, without regard to income attribution rules.

The broad language of *Earl* has prompted the government to test the application of the assignment-of-income analysis to cases that also fall under other, more specific Code provisions and case law. *Armantrout v. Commissioner*[5] dealt with an employer-funded benefit plan that provided college financial help to the children of key employees. Although the benefits depended on each employee's tuition needs

---

[2]Id. at 115.
[3]282 U.S. 101 (1930).
[4]405 U.S. 394 (1972).
[5]67 T.C. 996 (1977), *aff'd per curiam*, 570 F.2d 210 (7th Cir. 1978).

and number of children who attended college or university, and the employees did not receive the money themselves, the Tax Court classified the benefits as compensation to the parents, to be taxed to them in accordance with the principles set forth in *Earl*. The court pointed out that Code section 83, dealing with transfers of property "in connection with the performance of services," also supported its decision.

In *Schneer v. Commissioner*,[6] the Tax Court was sharply divided over whether *Earl* applies to the contribution by a new law firm partner of as yet unearned receivables for legal work. Code section 721 extends unqualified nonrecognition treatment to contributions of receivables to partnerships. The Court's grudging decision that the potential income from receivables could be shifted to the partnership on these facts left open the possibility that transfer of already earned receivables would not pass muster on assignment-of-income grounds, despite a specific Code grant of unrestricted nonrecognition to partners' contributions of property to a partnership, including receivables.

Sidebar

CONGRESS AND ASSIGNMENT OF INCOME

Given that relatively few judicial rules deal effectively with most assignment-of-income problems, Congress could easily write its own rules. The courts have no greater expertise in analyzing complete economic transactions than the administrative and legislative experts.

B. Transfers of Income from Property

Transfers of gross income not derived from labor are also subject to the assignment-of-income doctrine. The chief of these are transfers of income from property. (*Earl* and *Armantrout* dealt with attempts to assign income earned by the taxpayers as compensation for services.) Broadly, a transfer of property outright, whether by gift, sale, or exchange, includes the income to which the property gives rise. If a taxpayer keeps no interest in the property transferred, income arising from the property afterward will have been validly transferred as well — in more familiar terms, there is no assignment of income as such, and the transfer of both the property and its income is effective for tax purposes. But property, as we all know, is a bundle of rights, and it is possible to transfer some sticks out of the bundle while retaining others.

F   A   Q

Q: Is there a single definition of "property" for the entire Code?

A: No, and the term often has to be interpreted differently within a single subchapter; for example, property includes money for parts of the corporate and partnership provisions but not for others. Generally, however, section 1221, which defines "capital asset," sets the tone for the entire Code by using "property" in its broadest sense, certainly as including intangibles, but as including even such exotic intangibles as literary compositions and rights to payment.

---

[6]97 T.C. 643 (1991).

In a pair of leading cases, the Supreme Court sharply distinguished two types of property-related transfers. *Blair v. Commissioner*[7] held that the beneficiary of a testamentary trust could validly shift parts of an income interest to his children without running afoul of *Earl* if the children became owners of beneficial interests in the trust itself, with the attendant right "to enforce the trust [according to its terms], obtain a remedy for any breach of the trust, and for redress in the case of breach." In brief, if the children stood in the shoes of the donor, their father, and took over all rights connected with the parts of the income interest he had transferred, there was no problem. In contrast, *Helvering v. Horst*[8] held that a donor's gift to his son of interest coupons detached from bonds during the year in which the coupons matured and the interest was payable was ineffective for tax purposes. The gift did not succeed in shifting the income away from the donor: The gross income was first his, and taxable to him, before it became a gift to the son, who took it tax free. The Court surveyed a wide variety of tax and non-tax principles in reaching this conclusion, and it reasoned that the person "who owns or controls the source of the income, also controls the disposition of that which he could have received himself,"[9] so that the income from the source should be treated as the donor's, even if it is given away in advance, because ownership of the source was not given along with the income interest.

Although "coupon clipping" is still a cliché for passive collection of income, bonds now rarely come with such detachable chits. The generalizable core of *Horst* is that equitable or beneficial ownership of property that throws off an income stream, but which includes rights other than the right to the income, determines the correct attribution of the income. For example, an enforceable gift of a sum of money, payable only when the donor realizes an expected gain on the sale of land, would not shift that income to the donee. This, of course, does not even look like a complete gift of an income interest in the land. But such a gift is economically equivalent to an enforceable gift of a share of the proceeds from the land sale, contingent on the sale taking place, where the donee has no right to insist that the sale take place or enforce a contract for the sale against the buyer. If after giving his son the interest coupons, the taxpayer in *Horst* had agreed to the early redemption of the bond by the issuer, the son would have had no claim against either his father or the issuer. On that assumption, the Court's analysis of whose income the interest coupons represented was sound.

Whether the right to an income stream should be treated as property apart from the income stream itself has puzzled the Supreme Court in other cases, such as *Commissioner v. P.G. Lake, Inc.*, see Chapter 14.B (where Justice

Sidebar

CHARITABLE CONTRIBUTIONS OF INCOME

Given the court's sensitivity to dubious schemes for assigning income, the question arises whether a charitable contributor of services must report the value of those services as income and separately claim a deduction under section 170 for the contribution. Treas. Reg. section 1.61-2(c), interpreting section 61, so provides if a taxpayer, on an agreement or understanding with a third party, directs the third party to pay a charitable organization the agreed price of the services; the same regulation, however, says that the value of the service is not income to one who renders service directly to a charity.

[7]300 U.S. 5 (1937).
[8]311 U.S. 112 (1940).
[9]*Id.* at 116-117.

Douglas refuses to distinguish the right to a stream of ordinary royalty payments from the payments themselves), and *Welch v. Helvering*, see Chapter 12.B (where Justice Cardozo is beguiled by the thought that advertising might be capitalized to goodwill to link it to the conversion of goodwill into an income stream).

Recall that section 102(b) denies to gifts of income interest the otherwise broad exclusion of gifts from gross income. At best, the gift of an income stream diverts the income in question to the donee and away from the donor. But the assignment-of-income doctrine may also render ineffective the transfer of an income interest in property retained by the donor.

Example 16.2: John, who is elderly, attempts to give his daughter Doris the right to one-half of his future investment earnings because he depends on her to look after him and because she is in a lower marginal tax bracket. Were it not for *Earl* and its progeny, this arrangement would give John the equivalent of a full deduction for health care payments that would not exceed 7.5 percent of his AGI, thwarting the threshold limitation of section 213. See Chapter 12.B.

C. Are Property Rights to Future Income from Services Different?

The distinction drawn in *Blair* and *Horst* seems straightforward. If the owner of income-producing property transfers all rights in the property to someone else, any income proceeding from the property belongs to the transferee, not the transferor. *Blair* makes it clear that this rule also applies when a part of some income-producing property is transferred, as long as the part incomes *both* income *and* the part of the property from which the income proceeds. If the entire property is a layer cake consisting of an income layer and something that produces the income, the recipient must receive a slice that includes proportionate parts of both layers to pass muster under assignment-of-income analysis. But what if the property is only the intangible right to an uncertain future income stream, the right to be paid for someone's past performance of services?

Long ago, when the study of economics was young, it was sometimes said that capital is simply stored-up labor, because all things of value come from someone's labor, and capital consists of value not yet consumed or otherwise put to use. If we think of all property in this way, the holdings in *Blair* and *Horst* should apply with equal vigor to transfers of intangible rights to payment for past services. That, however, is not how the Supreme Court saw it.

In *Helvering v. Eubank*,[10] a companion case to *Holst*, the Court considered the assignment by a retired insurance agent of commissions he was to receive without further effort on his part when the owners of insurance policies he had sold renewed them. The commissions were income of the taxpayer, the Court held, "for the reasons stated at length" in *Horst*, although most commentators are not sure how those reasons apply here. Three justices dissented, arguing that once personal services were rendered and the right for payment had become the "absolute property" of the person who rendered the services, the property could be assigned, effectively shifting the income to the assignee. It is tempting to interpret the *Eubank* holding as

---

[10]311 U.S. 122 (1940).

abrogating the layer cake approach to assignment of income, whenever the property that produces the income is a bare intangible right earned by past services. Income streams that flow from past services are like interest coupons with no corresponding bond. In *Eubank*, the Court may have thought at some level that the right to a stream of payments is not property at all. See the FAQ above on how broadly property should be understood in the Code and income tax case law.

Later decisions by lower courts cast doubt on this simple understanding of *Eubank*. In *Heim v. Fitzpatrick*,[11] the Second Circuit decided that an inventor could effectively shift most of the income from his inventions to others by transferring patents for the inventions to a corporation and then gifting some of the stock of the corporation to his wife and children. The transfer of the patents to the corporation was conditional: The taxpayer retained the right to take back the patents if the royalties the corporation received from them fell below stated amounts. Despite the strings attached to the transfer, the court concluded that "the rights . . . assigned to his wife and children were sufficiently substantial to justify the view that they were given income-producing property."[12] The moral seems to be that statutorily recognized intangibles, like patents and copyrights, that embody work done by their creators *are* to be treated as the dissenters in *Eubank* argued *all* intangibles embodying work of their creators should.

There is a further wrinkle. If a cash-method partner contributes to a partnership the right to receive payment for work previously performed, Code section 721 has been interpreted as saying that neither the partner nor the partnership recognizes gain or loss. This leaves open the possibility that when the partnership receives the payment, the income is to be treated as that of the contributing partner and not as that of the partnership. The Tax Court in *Schneer v. Commissioner*,[13] more briefly glossed in Section A, held that only receivables for services that had not fully been performed when a partner contributed them to a partnership were able to carry income away from the contributor; with little explanation, the court held that the income later received with respect to receivables that had been fully earned when contributed belonged to the contributor rather than the partnership. The interesting possibility is that even when a service-related property right can validly be transferred as property under a nonrecognition rule that *only* applies to property and not to services, the transfer is still ineffective to shift the income away from the transferor. *Earl* is more potent than the statute.

D. Use of Trusts to Shift Income and Statutory "Grantor Trust" Rules

The use of trusts in tax planning is beyond the scope of most introductory tax courses. A gift in trust, however, can be as effective as an outright gift in shifting income from the trust's creator to others. For this reason, trusts must figure in our exploration of assignment of income.

A trust is an arrangement that separates legal and beneficial or equitable ownership of property. The person who creates the trust is called the grantor, settlor, or

---

[11]262 F.2d 887 (2d Cir. 1959).
[12]*Id.* at 890.
[13]97 T.C. 643 (1991).

trustor. The grantor brings the trust into existence simply by declaring it to exist, although there is usually a written trust instrument. Legal title goes to the trustee, who may also be the grantor, but the trustee holds the property for the benefit of others. In equity, the ownership rights of beneficiaries are fully and unambiguously recognized, and the trustee is bound by an array of duties to the beneficiaries to hold, manage, and distribute the trust property only for their benefit.

If, by the terms of a trust, the grantor surrenders all control over the trust property, the transfer is as effective for assignment-of-income purposes as a simple gift of the property to the beneficiaries, even though the beneficiaries may not immediately receive shares of the property. If the original property or income from that property is not distributed, sections 661 through 668 provide that the retained income is taxed while still in the trustee's hands. This is an *income* tax on trust income, not to be confused with the *estate* tax on property that goes into a testamentary trust. If a will places property in trust, the value of this property is taken into account in measuring the taxable estate, and so is subject to the federal estate tax if it applies.

On the other hand, if a trust pays all its income to beneficiaries in the year in which the income is earned, the trust pays no income tax, but the beneficiaries are taxed on the income as if they earned it directly. If a trust retains any current income, it pays income tax on this itself.

Example 16.3: Grandpa's will placed $100,000 in trust for his grandchildren, leaving the trustee broad discretion whether to distribute any of the income to the children while they are minors. The trustee chooses to distribute all of a child's share of the trust income to the child for each year the child is enrolled in a university. This plan can save tax for the trust and the children collectively, because the children's marginal tax rates can be much lower than those of the trust.

Some trusts are disregarded for income tax purposes because the grantor retains too much control over the trust property and income. These are called "grantor trusts" and are subject to the grantor-trust rules of sections 671-678, which primarily tell us when a trust is to be classified as a grantor trust. The main consequence of this classification is that the ostensible separation of the trust from the grantor is ignored or, as we say, the trust is disregarded, and all of the trust's property and income continue to be treated as belonging to the grantor rather than to the beneficiaries. Tax planners sometimes deliberately give a trust characteristics that will cause it to be disregarded for tax purposes, because they want the trust property to be treated as belonging directly to the grantor. This would be useful if the trust is treated as a separate entity for accounting purposes—so that its liabilities are treated as its own and not those of the grantor, while the deductions and losses of the trust are treated as those of the grantor. This is one of the strategies that Enron made famous when that corporation allegedly used "off balance sheet" financing to make some of the liabilities of the corporation disappear. The idea, however, had been around for many years.

SUMMARY

■ Arrangements that purport to shift income from the person who earns it to another are disregarded; instead, the income is first attributed to the earner, who must pay tax on it and deemed to be given to the other.

■ Similarly, arrangements that purport to shift income from property away from the property's owner may be disregarded, but in some cases they are recognized as effectively shifting the income.

■ The transfer of all ownership of the property from which income arises to another effectively shifts the income as well.

■ The transfer of an income interest alone, with the residual property rights still belonging to the transferor, does *not* shift the income.

■ A transfer of less than the owner's entire bundle of rights in property *may* shift some of the income from the property to another, but only if ownership of that part of the property from which the income arises is transferred with the income interest.

■ Gifts of partial interests in certain types of property, especially statutorily recognized intangibles such as patents and copyrights, do effectively shift the income from these intangibles.

CONNECTIONS

Gifts and Income Shifting

Anticipatory assignments of income that are ineffective in shifting the tax liability for the income to another person are analyzed as if the income were acquired first by the transferor and then given to the transferee, which brings into play some of the rules concerning gifts discussed in Chapter 5.

Income Successfully Shifted Is Treated as That of the Transferee

Contractual transfers of income interests that are recognized for tax purposes as shifting income to someone other than the one who otherwise earned or would have been entitled to the income through property ownership result in the income being included in the donee's income under section 102(b). See Chapter 5.E.

Family Units and Progressive Tax Rates

Income taxation faces difficulties in taxing relatives and others who live together or share resources without the usual arm's-length selfishness of strangers. The assignment of income rules, as they originally developed, tended to keep family units and similar households from treating shared incomes as if they had earned these incomes in equal parts. The joint return pushes back against this result of assignment of income principles. See Chapter 11.A and B.

Exclusion of Corpus Gifts

Section 102(b) provides that gifts of income interests are not excluded from the income of the donee, but a gift of corpus is excluded and protected from later taxation by a carryover or stepped-up basis. See Chapter 5.E.

No Basis Adjustment for Income Interest Gifts

Section 1014 does not provide a stepped-up basis (in years in which the estate tax is in force) to income interest gifts; the opposite result would exempt the income from being taxed either in the hands of the donor or of the donee. See Chapter 5.E. Section 691 accomplishes a similar result for "income in respect of a decedent," that is, income interests acquired through testate or intestate succession.

Table of Cases

Index